GLOBETROTTING OR GLOBAL CITIZENSHIP?

Perils and Potential of International Experiential Learning

Edited by Rebecca Tiessen and Robert Huish

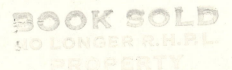

Globetrotting or Global Citizenship? explores the broad range of international experiential learning options available to Canadian students, as well as the opportunities and the ethical dilemmas that come with them. Combining practical advice with critical examinations of international experiential learning, this collection of essays is designed to encourage students and educators to think beyond photo-ops and exotic destinations and to instead consider such programs as a means to develop a deeper global citizenship.

Globetrotting or Global Citizenship? is a valuable guide for students considering going abroad for experiential learning, as well as for instructors and administrators facilitating pre-departure and return orientation sessions. The contributors to the volume discuss a wide variety of programs, from three-month sojourns for high school students to major international health initiatives involving medical graduates, while covering a number of important topics, from post-colonial theory to the practical challenges of working in post-conflict societies. Anyone taking part in international study or volunteering will find the reflections and analysis provided here an excellent starting point for understanding the potential impact of their time abroad.

REBECCA TIESSEN is an associate professor in the School of International Development and Global Studies at the University of Ottawa.

ROBERT HUISH is an assistant professor in the Department of International Development Studies at Dalhousie University.

Globetrotting or Global Citizenship?

Perils and Potential of International Experiential Learning

EDITED BY REBECCA TIESSEN
AND ROBERT HUISH

UNIVERSITY OF TORONTO PRESS
Toronto Buffalo London

© University of Toronto Press 2013
Toronto Buffalo London
www.utppublishing.com
Printed in the U.S.A.
Reprinted 2014

ISBN 978-1-4426-4834-0 (cloth)
ISBN 978-1-4426-2611-9 (paper)

Printed on acid-free, 100% post-consumer recycled paper.

Library and Archives Canada Cataloguing in Publication

Globetrotting or global citizenship? : perils and potential of international
experiential learning/edited by Rebecca Tiessen and Robert Huish.

Includes bibliographical references and index.
ISBN 978-1-4426-4834-0 (bound). – ISBN 978-1-4426-2611-9 (pbk.)

1. International education.   2. Experiential learning.   3. World
citizenship.   I. Tiessen, Rebecca, 1970–, editor of compilation
II. Huish, Robert, 1978–, editor of compilation

LC1090.G56 2014   370.116   C2013-908303-0

This book has been published with the help of a grant from the Canadian
Federation for the Humanities and Social Sciences, through the Awards to
Scholarly Publications Program, using funds provided by the Social Sciences
and Humanities Research Council of Canada.

University of Toronto Press acknowledges the financial assistance to its
publishing program of the Canada Council for the Arts and the Ontario
Arts Council.

Canada Council   Conseil des Arts
for the Arts   du Canada

ONTARIO ARTS COUNCIL
CONSEIL DES ARTS DE L'ONTARIO
50 YEARS OF ONTARIO GOVERNMENT SUPPORT OF THE ARTS
50 ANS DE SOUTIEN DU GOUVERNEMENT DE L'ONTARIO AUX ARTS

University of Toronto Press acknowledges the financial support of the
Government of Canada through the Canada Book Fund for its publishing
activities.

Contents

Contributors

Coleman Agyeyomah is the director of Venceremos Development Consult, a development and organizational change consulting firm in Northern Ghana. For the last fifteen years he has been teaching "The Local Dynamics of Change" course in Ghana as part of the year-away program sponsored by Trent University in Ontario. He has established placement opportunities for both the Trent program as well as St Francis Xavier University's Canada's Development Studies Internship Program. He has two published book chapters that were inspired by collaborations between student interns and a local bonesetter, "Building Bridges from Broken Bones: Traditional Bonesetters and Health Choices in Northern Ghana" (2009, with Jonathan Langdon) and "To Die Is Honey and to Live Is Salt: Indigenous Epistemologies of Wellness on Northern Ghana and the Threat of Institutionalized Containment" (2010, with Jonathan Langdon and Rebecca Butler).

John D. Cameron is Associate Professor and Chair of the Department of International Development Studies at Dalhousie University and an associate researcher with Fundación Tierra in Bolivia. His research focuses on struggles over indigenous self-governance in Bolivia as well as the ways in which development and poverty are represented in the global North in the mass media and NGO advertising campaigns. In his role as Chair of the IDS Department he is very engaged in the management of study abroad and experiential learning programs and also teaches courses on global citizenship.

Uppala Chandrasekera, MSW, RSW, is a social worker with expertise in anti-oppression, anti-racism, and social justice work, focusing on the areas of health inequities and the social determinants of health. Her research and published works examine the impact of the lived experience of discrimination on the health and well-being of marginalized individuals and communities. Uppala brings a wide perspective on health care from her previous experiences working in health promotion and health and social policy, and her advocacy efforts are focused on reducing health disparities and promoting human rights.

Ellyn Clost has worked on research and development projects ranging from media and social impact to Aboriginal land claims in Canada to long-term sustainable development in Northern Ghana. Her brief three-and-a-half month experience as an intern with a public policy firm in Ghana led her to master's research on the intersections of visual representation, colonial histories, and international development through the Cultural Studies Program at Queen's University. She is currently a researcher for a non-profit education organization in Kingston, Ontario.

Marie-Eve Desrosiers is Assistant Professor at the School of International Development and Global Studies, University of Ottawa. She has organized experiential learning-based courses in Rwanda on conflict and conflict resolution in the African Great Lakes region, as well as supervised or mentored graduate research in authoritarian and/or post-conflict settings. Her research centres on governance structures and state–society relations, with a particular focus on the African Great Lakes region.

Julie Drolet is Associate Professor at the University of Calgary. She has facilitated over 550 provincial, national, and international experiential learning placements in Canada and in numerous countries. She is currently engaged in research in the field of international social work, climate change and disasters, and social work field education programs in Canada and internationally, which is financially supported by the Social Sciences and Humanities Research Council of Canada. She has published several articles on experiential learning programs in peer-reviewed journals. Her edited book (with Natalie Clark and Helen Allen) titled *Shifting Sites of Practice: Field Education in Canada* was published by Pearson in 2012.

Marc Epprecht was a co-operant high school teacher in Zimbabwe and Lesotho before going on to do his PhD in history at Dalhousie

University in Halifax, Nova Scotia. He joined Queen's University in 2000 and since then has launched the inaugural Canada and the "3rd world" course in the Development Studies Program. He is currently a Professor and Chair of the Department of Global Development Studies. He has published extensively on the history of gender and sexuality in Africa, including *Hungochani: The History of a Dissident Sexuality in Southern Africa* (McGill-Queen's University Press) and *Heterosexual Africa? The History of an Idea from the Age of Exploration to the Age of AIDS* (Ohio University Press). He has a research "minor" in the ethics of work/study abroad programs and other pedagogical issues in Africa and Development Studies.

Kathryn Fizzell currently works as a secondary school teacher in the York Region District School Board. She has led extra-curricular experiential learning programs for secondary school students in Central America. While pursuing her MA in the Global Development Studies Department at Queen's University, Kathryn conducted a research project on the role that secondary school teachers were playing as facilitators of international experiential learning programs. She also worked as a research assistant on a learn/volunteer abroad research project. Kathryn continues to work for Queen's University as an instructor for online certificate courses offered by the Department of Global Development Studies.

Robert Huish (co-editor) is Assistant Professor in International Development Studies at Dalhousie University, Halifax. He is author of *Where No Doctor Has Gone Before: Cuba's Place in the Global Health Landscape* (Wilfrid Laurier University Press). He has published widely on Cuba's foreign policy strategy in health, soft power, human security, and sport and development, and has published several articles on the ethics of medical education and global health. He is working on a three-year collaborative research project on the dynamics of Cuban internationalism through sport in Central America and sub-Saharan Africa. He teaches courses related to poverty and human rights, global health, activism in social movements, and critical explorations of experiential learning.

Jonathan Langdon is an Assistant Professor in the Development Studies Program and Adult Education Department at St Francis Xavier University. At STFX, he supervises the growing Development Studies Internship Program; previously, he coordinated the Trent-in-Ghana program. He has recently undertaken research looking at the impact of multiple experiential learning experiences across different geographic/ organizational contexts within an undergraduate Development Studies Program. He has published one book chapter on Development Studies pedagogy that also discussed experiential learning in teaching, as well as a chapter on anti-colonial pedagogy (with Blane Harvey) that advocated experiential learning praxis.

Katie MacDonald is a PhD student in the Sociology Department at the University of Alberta. She received her MA in Interdisciplinary Studies from York University and wrote her thesis about the experiences of volunteers in rural Ecuador and the influence of development discourses on how they narrated their experiences. She received a Master of Education from York University where she designed a full-year course for students who volunteer abroad. Her current research is exploring the encounters between young Canadian volunteers and Nicaraguans in Nicaragua. Katie works with Intercordia Canada to facilitate international development projects with students across Canada.

Manda Ann Roddick is currently a Vanier Canada Graduate Scholar (2010–13) and a doctoral student at the University of Victoria. Over the past decade Manda has worked, studied, or volunteered in countries on three continents. She began her overseas experience on a study tour in Malawi in 1999 and went on to volunteer in Costa Rica and Ecuador before serving as a group leader for a youth NGO in Grenada in 2005. In 2008, Manda went to Zacatecas, Mexico, to participate in the first Critical Development Studies course hosted by the Critical Development Studies Network. Her passion for examining aspects of global poverty and social inequality has been central in her academic and volunteer work over the past decade. Manda has presented several papers on the topic of youth volunteerism abroad and global citizenship since 2007; in 2011 she was selected to be a speaker at the Royal Society of Canada's Annual Symposium on "Literacy and Citizenship in the 21st Century."

Lahoma Thomas, MA, MSW, RSW, is currently pursuing a PhD at the University of Toronto in political science. She is a social worker who specializes in political-, sexual-, and gender-based violence. She has been dedicated to addressing these issues at the systemic, community, and individual level through policy development, advocacy, training, and counselling. Her research and related publications have covered a broad range of topics, including the expression of political and sexual violence in settings of conflict and post-conflict, anti-oppression, anti-racism, and human rights.

Susan Thomson is Assistant Professor of Peace and Conflict Studies at Colgate University in Hamilton, New York. Her research and teaching interests are in state–society relations in contemporary Africa, lived experiences of conflict and violence, and ethnographic research methods, with particular focus on research ethics and doing research in difficult environments. She works with undergraduate students in Canada and the United States to prepare them for overseas study and internships in Rwanda and Kenya, including preparing them for Fulbright Fellowships. Her book *Whispering Truth to Power: Everyday Resistance to Reconciliation in Post-Genocide Rwanda* is forthcoming in 2013 from the University of Wisconsin Press.

Rebecca Tiessen (co-editor) is Canada Research Chair in Global Studies and Associate Professor at the University of Ottawa. She is also Adjunct Professor in the Department of Global Development Studies at Queen's University and a Research Fellow at Dalhousie University's Centre for Foreign Policy Studies. She has facilitated international experiential learning programs in Malawi and Kenya. Her current research examines the impact of learning/volunteer abroad programs for Canadian youth and host communities. She has published several journal articles and book chapters on international experiential learning and was lead editor for a special issue on learning/volunteer abroad for the *Journal of Global Citizenship and Equity Education*.

Stacie Travers is a program manager at the Canadian Bureau for International Education. She holds an MA in Educational Studies with a concentration in Adult Education from Concordia University in Montreal. Her interest in ethics and designs surrounding educational models, as well as non-Western and critical perspectives on education led her to complete thesis research on developing meaningful study abroad programs. Before and after this research, she participated in and helped organize study abroad programs at McGill University and Vanier College in Montreal. Her current research examines opportunities for doctoral research support in developing countries.

GLOBETROTTING OR GLOBAL CITIZENSHIP?

Perils and Potential of International Experiential Learning

1 International Experiential Learning and Global Citizenship

REBECCA TIESSEN AND ROBERT HUISH

Is global competency and cross-cultural understanding facilitated through international experiential learning and why does the quest for global citizenship matter? Does international experiential learning produce globetrotters or global citizens? For those who see the world as a place for learning and discovery, and/or have had opportunities to volunteer abroad and travel as part of the educational journey, this book will provide an opportunity to reflect on these questions and to examine international experiential learning programs in relation to ethics, global citizenship, and cross-cultural connections. For those who aspire to community engagement through some form of experiential learning program, volunteer/study/learn abroad or voluntourism program, this book will guide you in the steps ahead, the ongoing reflection and learning necessary throughout the placement, and prepare you for the much-needed reflection and analysis stage upon completion of the experiential learning program. This introductory chapter provides an overview of the book: its purpose and a summary of the contributing chapters. One of the key ethical considerations central to analyses of international experiential learning is the use of communities in Canada and the Global South as extensions of classroom spaces. While we have much to learn from people and organizations committed to social and/or global justice, we must also be careful not to treat communities in the Global South as laboratories for testing an academic or career choice. We must also be mindful of our personal motivations and potentially harmful impacts. Furthermore, our awareness of the ethical impacts of international experiential learning must also contribute to a transformative learning which is grounded in the struggles for equality and justice (see Langdon and Agyeyomah, chapter 3) and facilitate the creation of "authentic allies" (Thomas and Chandrasekera, chapter 5). International experiential learning programs therefore provide a valuable opportunity for reflecting on how much we need to learn about the world around us and the importance of global competency for good citizenship. Learning/volunteer abroad programs also provide rich opportunities for understanding the causes of inequality and finding ways to work in solidarity with our partners in the Global South to challenge and circumvent structures of inequality.

Students in diverse academic programs at colleges, universities, and secondary schools have a keen desire to learn about the world outside the classroom and this book is an effort to reach the broad range of students, scholars, and practitioners who subscribe to international experiential learning programs in diverse academic studies from engineering to development studies to international social work. Experiential learning programs are increasingly popular options for youth who want to learn about the world and relate it back to their academic programs or to reflect with a group and/or group leader about the experiences they encounter. The growing popularity of international learning opportunities is a demonstration of the desire to expand our classroom beyond the confines of secondary and post-secondary institution walls. International experiential learning programs provide one strategy, among many, for expanding minds and opening up learning opportunities by making our classrooms, and our identities, global in scope. Nonetheless, the enthusiasm for global engagement through international experiential learning and the rapid growth in programs offered to those who wish to learn/volunteer abroad have far outpaced our ability to evaluate and understand the impacts of these programs. An internet search for international experiential learning or volunteer abroad programs, at the time of writing this book, resulted in 19,700,000 "hits." The growth industry of learning/volunteering abroad requires immediate and thoughtful reflection. At the heart of our reflection and evaluation of international experiential learning, as documented in the chapters of this book, is the challenge of doing no harm in our efforts to "do good." Several chapters in this collection grapple with the challenges of doing no harm and what it means to "do good."

Before we proceed with an introduction to the key points worthy of reflection and evaluation, we begin with an introduction to the main terms used throughout this book: specifically the language of experiential learning. We define experiential learning as making meaning out of direct experience. The meaning that comes out of experiential learning can be academic, personal, and/or professional. For international experiential learning programs (the primary focus of this book) the direct experience generally takes place in the Global South,[1] and for many students from diverse disciplines participating in international experiential learning the focus is on an improved understanding of inequality, poverty, and global justice. However, we cannot assume that improved understanding of the causes of poverty, inequality, and injustice are universal goals for all participants in these programs. For others, the desire to participate in international experiential learning may be better understood in relation to personal growth, desire for travel and adventure, and/or perceived or real qualifications for specific forms of employment, or even to test an academic or career choice (Tiessen, 2012).

Experiential learning, as a component of academic studies, was popularized through the work of David Kolb. The experiential learning model (ELM) developed by David Kolb and Ron Fry (1974) focused on experience, observation of – and reflection on – that experience, understanding abstract concepts based on that reflection, the testing of new concepts, followed by repetition of the process. The experiential learning model is central to this book and, in particular, the important cycle of action and reflection that students must engage in before, during, and after their experiential learning placements. The layout of the chapters in this book also reflects this cycle of observation, reflection, and action.

International experiential learning programs build on the early work of Kolb to include an international focus requiring travel and cross-cultural experience. International experiential learning has taken on many titles within academic circles to include international service learning, study abroad programs, and practicum placements. International experiential learning can also take place in non-academic programs through internships, volunteer abroad programs, and other experiences where youth learn about the world often in a structured learning format. We employ the broad range of terms throughout the chapters of this book but focus most specifically on international experiential learning because it is a comprehensive term that encompasses the practical, ethical, and theoretical components of the learning/volunteer abroad experience.

Our fascination with the world around us is not new. Decades of travel, centuries of exploration and missionary ventures, and a history of colonialism all reflect the human desire to learn about the world. Youth have also engaged in a long history of learning abroad through backpacking adventures, particularly in Europe, but increasingly in the Global South. As Marc Epprecht (2004) noted in his influential analysis of international experiential learning, or what he termed work-study programs, the connection between travel and international development grew out of "development-oriented work [through] ... the world-wide expansion of North American Christian missions in the late 19th century" (p. 689). Since the 1800s, religious and secular programs alike have popped up around the world to promote global justice, peace, and poverty reduction. The work abroad phenomenon slowly crept into the educational institutions in Canada from the 1950s onwards and we can now witness a broad range of programs catering to diverse interests in many parts of the world and for varying lengths of time in the secondary school system as well as colleges and universities. The formalization of international experiential learning programs as part of the academic offerings and, at times requirements, of some secondary and post-secondary institutions has taken place largely over the last two decades beginning in the 1990s. At the same time that international experiential learning or work/study abroad programs became popularized in Canadian universities, post-secondary institutions became preoccupied with internationalization. As part of the internationalization process, post-secondary institutions have adopted a goal of global citizenship promotion in an effort to expand the institutions and the students' "understanding of what it means to claim or have citizenship in the twenty-first century" (Jorgenson & Shultz, 2012, p. 1). The notion of global citizenship education "has been suggested as a way in which universities can respond to the demand for opportunities to engage in relevant, meaningful activities that enhance students' global perspectives and help them to contribute to a more peaceful, environmentally secure, and just world" (Jorgenson & Shultz, 2012, p. 2). In their study, Jorgenson and Shultz (2012) find that global citizenship education is not a uniform response to urgent global issues and is in fact a contested term. Yet, there is agreement, from the institutional perspective, that post-secondary institutions "have a role to play in preparing citizens that are informed and able to participate in our complex globalized and globalizing world" (p. 15).

The idea of global citizenship education has been adopted more broadly beyond the post-secondary institutional level. Non-governmental organizations such as Oxfam UK developed an Education for Global Citizenship program for primary school children. The guide produced by Oxfam UK provides curriculum ideas for educating global citizens.

Other guides and documents on global citizenship have been developed by NGOs to educate the public about global connectivity and to promote awareness-raising and action. University-level courses on global citizenship have also become increasingly popular. Several authors in this collection have designed and delivered courses that explore the meaning of – and potential for – global citizenship. In an innovative online course created by Dalene Swanson and Shelley Jones, students from around the world reflect on global issues from multiple perspectives and situated locales. In spite of the growing popularity of the term global citizenship, it remains a largely elusive concept with many definitions. Chapter 2 by John Cameron explores these definitions and the significance of the diverse understandings of global citizenship in greater depth. What is clear from this introductory reflection is that the desire for global citizenship identity is closely linked to the growth in international experiential learning, and we explore this link throughout the book.

Growth in International Experiential Learning

The increasing desire for opportunities for international experiential learning has been evidenced in several ways, not the least of which is a growing demand for opportunities to travel, learn, volunteer, and live abroad (Tiessen, 2012). Over the past two decades, we have witnessed a growth in the number of people going abroad (Tiessen & Heron, 2012). However, there are diverse programs available to youth[2] (and to adults) so it is difficult to quantify these program offerings. There are also diverse time frames and some disagreement as to what constitutes experiential learning relative to internships abroad and work/study placements (see Tiessen, 2012).

While interest in experiential learning is growing within universities and colleges, it is important to also recognize the growth of international volunteer opportunities and experiential learning programs in secondary schools in Canada. Kathryn Fizzell and Marc Epprecht (this volume), provide important contextual information about the growth in volunteer abroad programs in high schools.

For some high school students, the overseas experience may include a very short, one or two week program in a developing country combining tourism with a small development project – a program more appropriately titled voluntourism (see Tiessen, 2012), but it too can have an experiential learning component as many of the high school programs include pre-departure orientation and return debriefing sessions to help the students process their experiences abroad and link them to conceptual ideas. Course credits may also be attached to these experiences abroad. The "Me to We" program is one example of a popular program among high school students. "Me to We" is the brainchild of two Canadians – the Kielburger brothers – and their promotional tours have given the Kielburger brothers rock-star status as they combine their educational message about poverty and inequality in the world with a public celebration involving popular musicians and celebrities at the "We Day" annual events. "We Day" events occur each year in various locations across Canada. These events bring together thousands of students as their website boasts, "within stadiums full of cheering young people." "We Day" events often include motivational speeches by famous people such as former United States Vice President Al Gore and actor Martin Sheen, as well as live musical performances by well-known musicians such as Sarah McLachlan and Justin Bieber. There is even a "We Day" dance routine you can learn online.

Events such as "We Day" are exciting opportunities for young people to reflect on their own contributions to global change. For many young people, the "We Day" campaigns incite a desire to travel to the Global South. According to the "We Day" facts online, over 160,000 people have attended "We Day" events since it began in 2007. Many of these same young people who are exposed to "We Day" campaigns and other programs and initiatives geared to youth in high school will demand opportunities to take part in international experiential learning in their secondary and/or post-secondary programs. In part, the phenomenon of "We Day" and other youth-oriented global change initiatives have shaped the students we see entering universities and colleges. Responding to their interests and experiences is an ever growing priority at the post-secondary level. The explosion of interest in – and demand for – international experiential learning can also be explained, in part, by the celebrity endorsements of development priorities.

The growing popularity for these programs is evidenced in the kinds of programs offered to youth and the way that international experiential learning has become a normalized part of the educational curriculum (Tiessen & Epprecht, 2012). Knowing that youth may already have exposure to international experiential learning at the secondary school level, and understanding the nature of the secondary-level international experiential learning programs, shapes how post-secondary institutions must prepare and guide students; particularly if unethical practices are normalized and/or substantive reflection has not been achieved. We examine some of the ethical issues inherent in international experiential learning throughout this book and particularly in the chapters by Robert Huish (chapter 8) and Marie-Eve Desrosiers and Susan Thomson (chapter 7). The exposure to international experiential learning programs at the high school level also raises questions about the nature of global citizenship exposure and the potential for "un-learning" required when working with post-secondary students who wish to travel abroad. International experiential learning that is carried out without critical reflection and ongoing self-analysis has the potential to entrench stereotypes of "others" rather than promoting enhanced cross-cultural understanding (Tiessen, 2012).

Students with an interest in international experiential learning can come from any department in colleges and universities. Some of the disciplines offering international experiential learning as part of the core curriculum include international development studies, international social work, nursing, medicine, other health professions such as occupational therapy, engineering and language programs such as Spanish and French among others.

International development studies (IDS) departments often have their own experiential learning programs with dedicated faculty members to coordinate and deliver these programs, at times travelling with the students abroad. For international social work students, many programs create placements that allow students to hone their social work skills. Boyle, Nackerud, and Kilpatrick (1999) and Krajewski-Jaime, Brown, Ziefert, and Kaufman (1996) contend that international social work placements offer an effective, if somewhat traumatic, way for American social work students to quickly develop cultural competence. The result of such experiences is the development of an international identity by the youth. Previous research on international learning experiences for health professionals has concluded that short-term (less than three months) study abroad programs have a positive influence on cognitive development (Haloburdo & Thompson, 1998; Walsh, 2003; Zorn, Ponick, & Peck, 1995). More specifically, a study surveying the long-term impact of international education opportunities found that the nurses participating in three-to-four month placements reported higher long-term impact than those participating in three-to-four week programs. The strongest impact that was found was the enhancement of global understanding and personal growth (Zorn, 1996). Robert Huish, in this volume, however, argues that the positive experience gained by health professionals may have far more to do with personal gain through clinical practice than improved cognitive development or global competency.

Many youth find opportunities to participate in international experiential learning in the Global South through volunteer-sending agencies and non-governmental organizations (NGOs). Engineers without Borders (EWB) is a popular organization for engineering and non-engineering students alike. Other NGOs provide a range of opportunities for youth to engage in experiential learning: some for credit, some fully subsidized, and others at the expense of the individual. World University Service of Canada (WUSC), for example, offers a number of opportunities for youth who want to engage in experiential learning with diverse program options from the International Seminar (a six week program) to Students without Borders (generally four months in duration). Many of the programs offered by volunteer sending agencies and non-governmental organizations give students the opportunity to earn an academic credit for course material they produce in relation to their time overseas. Other volunteer sending programs such as Canada World Youth, Canadian Crossroads International, CUSO (formerly known as the Canadian University Service Overseas), among others, provide a range of diverse overseas experiences for youth. The Canadian International Development Agency (CIDA)[3] offers similar opportunities in the form of internships as part of its youth employment strategy, and while these programs are more in line with job training than experiential learning, there is an experiential learning component to many of these internships. The Association for Universities and Colleges in Canada (AUCC) offered the Students for Development (SfD) program between 2005 and 2012. The AUCC program gave senior undergraduate and graduate students the opportunity to take part in internships in international development. The work experience gained through the SfD program was linked to the student's field of study or career goals.

There are many programs we have observed within Canada and that fit the international experiential learning model to some degree. Other opportunities are more difficult to understand and evaluate. For example, a Google search of volunteer abroad reveals more than one million results and within those results, among the first listed programs, one can find a "build your own adventure." As a result, the growth industry of international experiential learning is impossible to examine in entirety. In the chapters that comprise this collection, we reflect on what we know through our work. The diverse experiences that the authors share in this collection provide a rich set of examples and a range of international experiential learning programs.

The growth in interest in international experiential learning and/or learning/volunteering abroad must also be examined in relation to privilege and access to opportunities for participation in these programs. As Thomas and Chandrasekera (chapter 5) argue, white power and privilege in academia must be acknowledged as a key source of inequality. The white power and privilege extends to the largest share of those who take part in learning/volunteer abroad programs. Opportunities for international experiential learning also come with a hefty price tag and many youth have lamented their desire to take part in these programs but their financial inability to do so. Part of the appeal for international experiential learning programs or study abroad options in the Global South no doubt arises from financial concerns. Students may choose to live abroad in a country in Asia, Latin America, or Africa (rather than Europe) because the cost of living enables them to do so at a cost that is comparable to living in Canada. For students who can take courses or engage in a practicum program for academic credit, the term abroad is often a realistic option. Other programs provide stipends or living allowances such as the Canadian International Development Agency (CIDA) funded internships. However, these programs are highly competitive and the opportunities are too few to meet the growing demand for international experiential learning. For those who can afford the more expensive options, they can tailor their programs to their interests. This might involve upgrades to nicer hotels, tourist add-ons, and other upgrades. While the opportunities for international experiential learning are not exclusive to those with the financial means to purchase an experience abroad, there are clear limitations and implications for those who lack the means to volunteer/learn abroad.

The sea change that is taking place among youth in terms of interest in international experiential learning for the pursuit of global justice has important pedagogical implications. On the one hand, the desire to participate in international experiential learning programs fosters a longing for global awareness, understanding, and justice that can produce positive impacts such as increased commitment to solidarity and global equality. On the other hand, the surging interest in international experiential learning has the potential to create new inequalities, exacerbate old ones, and produce unintended negative impact in the host communities. The critiques that have emerged in the literature on international volunteering and study abroad programs highlight a need to approach international experiential learning more cautiously and armed with more knowledge and skills for reflection and analysis. Below we summarize some of the key debates on international experiential learning and learning/volunteer abroad programs.

The Need for a Critical Reflection on International Experiential Learning

The rich learning that takes place abroad is argued to contribute to personal growth and individual development of the youth who take part in these programs, as well as to life-long impacts such as increased commitment to community development and international activities (Kelly, 2006). International experiential education and volunteer abroad programs are expected to have a positive impact. Furthermore, "[a] strong presumption in many international development studies programs appears to be that field or work placements are intrinsically effective and good" (Epprecht, 2004, p. 687). However, these perceived benefits rely on assumptions and expectations based on anecdotal evidence and one-off case studies without empirical research and critical reflection.

Pedagogical studies, international development, international social work, and many other fields have brought a now well-established critique of the experiential learning and volunteer abroad programs (see the works of Barbara Heron, Nancy Cook, Kate Simpson, and others). This body of literature challenges the assumptions that learning/volunteer abroad programs are positive contributions to international development. There is a clear recognition that international learning and volunteer opportunities may contribute to some aspects of personal growth of the participant who travels abroad (Kauffmann, Martin, & Weaver, 1992). Yet, a deeper analysis is needed to question the "helping imperative" (Heron, 2007), potential for neo-colonialism (Cook, 2007), and the one-directional flow of benefits. These are among the questions and issues addressed in this collection. The critiques inform our understanding of international experiential learning and provide important insights into the ethical challenges of learning/volunteer abroad programs. However, the critiques have done little to stem the tide of interest in going abroad to learn and/or volunteer. Thus, we must keep in mind that international experiential learning programs are likely to continue regardless of the critiques that have emerged in scholarly research. Considering the reality of ongoing international experiential learning program offerings combined with the growth in scale and scope in the diverse overseas opportunities available to youth, it is our pedagogical desire to provide a balanced and thoughtful analysis of international experiential learning. Thus, this book builds on many of the critiques of international experiential learning, but offers a third way to examine international experiential learning challenges and opportunities in order to better prepare students for the ethical dilemmas they may encounter while abroad. Chapter 3 by Langdon and Agyeyomah provides valuable insights into the importance of what they call "scaffolding" of learning which can assist in the transformative learning process when it occurs on a regular basis before, during, and after the experiential learning program. The notion of scaffolding demonstrates the importance of layers of learning and resonates with Cameron's (chapter 2) reflections on "thick" global citizenship.

The chapters in this collection provide insights and analyses from a broad array of international experiential learning programs from international development studies offerings to programs for health professionals and international social work students. The lessons learned from these diverse academic programs can be applied to any field of study for which international experiential learning is a component of the education process. The book is geared to third and fourth year undergraduate students in any discipline at college or university level study. Graduate students may also find this book an important resource for research projects or their own preparation for – and reflection on – international experiential learning and field research. Educators and study abroad coordinators will gain valuable insights and tools to enhance international experiential learning offerings, particularly for post-placement reflection and analysis. As such, this book is designed as a course guide to facilitate the learning and reflection of students and program coordinators at all stages of the experiential learning cycle (pre-departure, on-site, and post-placement).

Chapter Overviews

This book examines some of the larger questions and critical reflections necessary for an analysis of international experiential learning. This book begins with a discussion of theoretical frameworks for making sense of ethical issues related to international experiential learning. Chapter 2 situates international experiential learning in relation to thin and thick conceptions of global citizenship. In this chapter, Cameron examines the growing usage of the language of global citizenship and maps out the diverse meanings attached to this concept. This chapter examines university-based efforts to promote diverse forms of global citizenship drawing on a broader literature of cosmopolitanism and civic engagement. Cameron's chapter on thick conceptions of global citizenship is a useful starting point for setting a theoretical foundation to the study of international experiential learning.

The authors of chapter 3 call for a deeper critical reflection and reflexivity for international experiential learning. Langdon and Agyeyomah argue for building relationships in international experiential learning that move away from the legitimation of discourses of employability and/or global citizenship. The authors argue that we need to choose between supporting the status quo or effecting change for a more just and equitable world through hyper-reflective activism. This chapter challenges the reader to move beyond the desire for personal growth of the individual travelling abroad to begin to think about experiential learning as a way to transform lives and relations. The authors of chapter 3 provide a rich context for the process of deep reflection on power relations and personal versus development goals in international experiential learning.

Chapter 4 examines the relationship between international experiential learning and career goals. Building on the critical analysis provided in chapter 3, chapter 4 documents the extent of the desire for employability and using international experiential learning to test an academic or career choice. Many international experiential learning programs are advertised or promoted as an opportunity to test an academic background or career choice. In chapter 4, Tiessen draws on empirical research with Canadian youth who have taken part in learning/volunteer abroad programs in the Global South to demonstrate that there are ethical considerations to bear in mind for those who use these programs as a litmus test for future work in international development. What we have learned about international experiential learning programs, as Tiessen's findings confirm, is that participation in learning/volunteer abroad programs is motivated by perceptions of personal gain, particularly to test an academic or career choice rather than broader interests related to global justice or what Cameron calls "thick conceptions of global citizenship."

Chapter 5 also offers a rich theoretical and analytical contribution to the literature on international experiential learning. In chapter 5,

Thomas and Chandrasekera employ a post-development framework to examine the discourses and experiences of international experiential learning. International social work offers many experiential learning programs and the authors of this chapter reflect on power, privilege, and racialization in international social work. Using self-reflexive narratives and observations of racialization in international social work contexts, the authors offer characterizations of experiential program participants. Their findings point to the need for greater investments in education around anti-oppression and anti-racism for participants in international social work placements. The lessons from this study can be applied to all secondary and post-secondary programs offerings international experiential learning options.

The book then moves to a collection of chapters that address what we have learned about the motivations and broader context of the increased demand for international experiential learning, as well as the manner in which experiential learning programs have been designed. Chapter 6 provides lessons learned from international experiential learning programs in secondary institutions. These lessons are critical for reflection on the deconstruction of knowledge or "unlearning" that may be required in subsequent experiential learning programs in post-secondary institutions. In chapter 6, Fizzell and Epprecht examine the nature of international experiential learning in secondary schools with a focus on how secondary school teachers are prepared for – and prepare their students for – the ethical dimensions of international experiential learning in the Global South. The authors make a case for pre-departure preparation and return orientation that includes information on the historical, political, and socioeconomic context and allows opportunities to engage in critical reflection on the causes of inequality in the world. Secondary school teachers, Fizzell and Epprecht argue, require appropriate training and background to facilitate the critical reflection necessary for the full educational experience. The absence of teacher training in relation to critical and ethical reflection in international experiential learning can translate into a particular (and potentially problematic) education for high school students that they carry with them into post-secondary programs.

Chapter 7 focuses on international experiential learning in what the authors call "challenging settings." In this chapter, Desrosiers and Thomson argue that a historical legacy, political leadership, or other factors can make experiential learning in some contexts more difficult than in others. The authors employ the case study of Rwanda, an authoritarian state with a particular historical legacy that can be unsettling for international experiential learning program participants. Building on their own lessons learned, Desrosiers and Thomson propose a strategy of "do no harm" and nuanced self-reflection to better understand oneself and the host country.

Chapter 8 focuses on the ethical dimensions in international health electives with attention to the absence of rigor of social theory and development. This chapter highlights the issues examined in chapters 1 and 5 regarding the ethical problems of treating the Global South as a laboratory for testing a career choice or academic background. The devaluing of global health through programs that send under-qualified medical students into complex clinical settings is the focus of this chapter. Huish underscores the need for alternative models of international experiential learning for global health placements. The findings presented in Huish's chapter have broader applications to all disciplines and specializations.

Chapters 9, 10, and 11 deal with some of the practical issues and preparation required for those taking part in international experiential learning. Chapter 9 of this book is designed to prepare students better for some of the very practical aspects of international experiential learning. In this chapter, Drolet summarizes the benefits of international experiential learning for students and the potential for these programs to make students more effective learners and more culturally and globally competent individuals. The chapter provides concrete information that will be useful for those preparing to go overseas as well as those involved in preparing students for international experiential learning programs.

In chapter 10, Travers examines some of the challenges and ethical issues inherent to international experiential learning and proposes some possible models and methods for reducing harm and increasing the benefits of these programs. This chapter enables the reader to rethink the relationship between travelling abroad and international experiential learning. The author also reflects on the important contributions that can be made through studying or volunteering abroad by highlighting key "learning moments." This chapter provides insights to help create better educational opportunities for those who take part in learning/volunteer abroad programs.

Chapter 11 begins with a claim that there is cause for worry about international experiential learning programs. MacDonald's argument builds on the idea that experiential learning abroad can constitute a neocolonial project. By decolonizing the pedagogy of international experiential learning, students and program facilitators can open up new sites of knowledge and incorporate different ways of knowing. Learning and knowing, the author argues, hinge on our ability to question what we think we know and to situate our knowledge more carefully and more critically. MacDonald's analysis of the placement stage of the international experiential learning cycle is a vital contribution to our reflections on how we make sense of what we are learning.

Chapters 12 and 13 address how we make sense of, and represent our experiences abroad upon our return to Canada. The preparation – or pre-departure – phase of international experiential learning programs requires careful and thoughtful analysis on the part of the program facilitators and participants. The critical analysis that takes place in the pre-departure phase shapes the nature of the placement abroad and also the messages that are transmitted upon our return to the Global North. All three phases of the international experiential learning cycle (pre-departure preparation, placement and return de-briefing, and information dissemination) are intimately linked to each other. The messages that we share about our international experiential learning placements with others in the Global North will also shape the pre-departure experiences for those planning to go abroad.

The stories we tell and the pictures we show when we return from an international experiential learning program constitute an important development education for the broader Canadian public. Chapter 12 is an examination of the visual representations of development and global citizenship through international experiential learning. These visual representations reflect and reinforce a power imbalance. Clost examines the power of photographs through the notion of a visual economy and exposes the underlying message of inequality that is generated through such photos. Ethical issues such as the helping imperative are reinforced through these images and thus re-create a particular image of people living in the Global South as those in need of help or charity. Exposing these problematic images is an important step in understanding the motivations and expectations for those who take part in international experiential learning and the messages they recreate when they return with problematic images. This chapter is a useful starting point for a reflection on how we make sense of our motivations to travel abroad and also our understanding of what we have learned. The visual material that accompanies program advertisements and our post-placement presentations reflects and contributes to the motivations and desires for participation in international experiential learning. A careful analysis of the visual material facilitates a better understanding of how images may reflect a greater desire for globetrotting than for global citizenship.

The author of chapter 13 explains how youth who participate in international experiential learning become the "public faces of development" and their voices are the ones being heard by audiences in the Global North when they return from abroad. Chapter 13 is an exploration of the kind of messages that are relayed through development education when participants return and the challenges these youth experience in the delivery of their message in the Global North. In this chapter, Roddick provides examples of the ethical imperative for more accurate and complex depictions of the Global South.

The final chapter of this volume summarizes the challenges and opportunities for moving beyond globetrotting and the potential for meaningful global engagement and global citizenship. In this chapter, we raise a number of questions that can guide deeper reflections in international experiential learning and can guide the actions required to work towards change in a world characterized by social injustice and inequality.

NOTES

1 We use the term Global South to demonstrate that poverty and inequality are global phenomena and that the high rates of poverty and inequality in the countries identified as medium and low income in the United Nations Human Development Index are linked to wealth, waste, and injustice throughout the world. The notion of a Global South also makes evident that poverty and inequality exist in high income countries. The term replaces the language of the Third World which was popularized in the 1950s and originally used to describe countries that refused to align with the United States or the Soviet Union at the commencement of the Cold War. The term "Third World" eventually was adopted to refer to low income and largely natural-resource dependent or under-developed countries in Africa, Asia, and Latin America. Other terms have been adopted by scholars to distinguish countries considered to have low incomes including the term less developed countries (LDCs) and the South (denoting that most of the low income countries are in the southern hemisphere).

2 The definition of youth employed in this book is the Canadian International Development Agency definition including young people between the ages of 18 and 30.
3 At the time of writing this book, the Canadian International Development Agency (CIDA) was merged with the Department of Foreign Affairs and International Trade to form a new department titled: Foreign Affairs, International Trade and Development (DFATD). Within this new department, the development branch (at the time of writing this book) continues to provide its regular programs and services.

REFERENCES

Boyle, D.P., Nackerud, L., & Kilpatrick, A. (1999). The road less traveled: Cross-cultural, international experiential learning. *Journal of International Social Work, 42*(2), 201–214. http://dx.doi.org/10.1177/0020872899042000208

Cook, N. (2007). *Gender, identity, and imperialism: Women development workers in Pakistan.* New York: Palgrave MacMillan. http://dx.doi.org/10.1057/9780230610019

Epprecht, M. (2004). Work-study abroad courses in international development studies: Some ethical and pedagogical issues. *Canadian Journal of Development Studies, 25*(4), 687–706. http://dx.doi.org/10.1080/02255189.2004.9669009

Haloburdo, E.P., & Thompson, M.A. (1998, Jan). A comparison of international learning experiences for baccalaureate nursing students: Developed and developing countries. *Journal of Nursing Education, 37*(1), 13–21. Medline:9476730

Heron, B.A. (2007). *Desire for development: The education of white women as development workers.* Waterloo, ON: Wilfrid Laurier University Press.

Jorgenson, S., & L. Shultz (2012). Global Citizenship Education (GCE) in post-secondary institutions: What is protected and what is hidden under the umbrella of GCE? *Journal of Global Citizenship and Equity Education, 2*(1), 1–22.

Kauffmann, N.L., Martin, J.N., & Weaver, H.D. (1992). *Students abroad, strangers at home: Education for a global society.* Yarmouth, ME: Intercultural Press.

Kelly, S. (2006). *The overseas experience: A passport to improved volunteerism.* Ottawa: CUSO.

Kolb, D.A., & Fry, R. (1974). *Toward an Applied Theory of Experiential Learning.* Boston: M.I.T. Alfred Sloan School of Management.

Krajewski-Jaime, E.R., Brown, K.S., Ziefert, M., & Kaufman, E. (1996). Utilizing international clinical practice to build cultural sensitivity in social work students. *Journal of Multicultural Social Work, 4*(2), 15–29. http://dx.doi.org/10.1300/J285v04n02_02

Tiessen, R. (2012). Motivations for learning/volunteer abroad programs: Research with Canadian youth. *Journal of Global Citizenship and Equity Education, 2*(1), 1–21.

Tiessen, R., & Heron, B. (2012). Volunteering in the developing world: Perceived impacts of Canadian youth. *Development in Practice, 22*(1), 44–56. http://dx.doi.org/10.1080/09614524.2012.630982

Tiessen, R. & Epprecht, M. (2012). Introduction: Global citizenship dducation for learning/volunteering abroad. *Journal of Global Citizenship and Equity Education, 2*(1), 1–12.

Walsh, L.V. (2003, Nov-Dec). International service learning in midwifery and nursing education. *Journal of Midwifery & Women's Health, 48*(6), 449–454. Medline:14660951

Zorn, C.R. (1996, Mar-Apr). The long-term impact on nursing students of participating in international education. *Journal of Professional Nursing, 12*(2), 106–110. http://dx.doi.org/10.1016/S8755-7223(96)80056-1 Medline:8632096

Zorn, C.R., Ponick, D.A., & Peck, S.D. (1995, Feb). An analysis of the impact of participation in an international study program on the cognitive development of senior baccalaureate nursing students. *Journal of Nursing Education, 34*(2), 67–70. Medline:7707139

2 Grounding Experiential Learning in "Thick" Conceptions of Global Citizenship

Introduction

One of the frequently stated goals of experiential learning programs in Canadian and American universities is to foster the values, aptitudes, and abilities of global citizenship among student participants (Che, Spearman, & Manizade, 2009; Schattle, 2008; Shultz, 2007; Jorgenson & Shultz, 2012). However, before university educators can promote global citizenship and students can practice it, both groups need to understand what the concept means, the principles behind it, and the goals that it seeks to encourage. Unfortunately, as various scholars have noted, the term "global citizenship" is used in many university programs with almost no grounding in the political and ethical debates that might give it any real meaning (Jorgenson & Shultz, 2012; Lewin, 2009; Shultz, 2007; Tiessen & Epprecht, 2012). Indeed, any serious grappling with the range of possible meanings for global citizenship suggests that the current popularity of the term relies heavily on its conceptual vagueness as it is used to represent many different and often contradictory ideas (see Lewin 2009, p. xviii). The goal of this chapter is to anchor analysis of university-based efforts to promote global citizenship in the broader literature on cosmopolitanism, which does grapple seriously with the ethical obligations that both require and follow from the idea of global citizenship. Evaluation of the extent to which experiential learning programs do or do not promote global citizenship is only possible in the context of more rigorous understandings of what the term global citizenship actually means, and this requires engaging with writing on cosmopolitanism.

This chapter begins by further developing the argument for more serious grappling with meaning of global citizenship and grounding it much more carefully in cosmopolitan thinking. It then examines the concept of cosmopolitanism and the central questions which this body of thought addresses. By only scratching the surface of the debates in the literature on cosmopolitanism, this short review will inevitably fail to satisfy serious scholars of cosmopolitanism, but that is not its purpose; the goal is simply to (re)connect thinking about global citizenship with the basic principles of cosmopolitanism. Following this initial exploration the chapter makes the case for grounding global citizenship education in "thick" conceptions of cosmopolitanism that emphasize both positive and negative duties rather than just voluntaristic compassion. The chapter then considers some of the practical challenges involved in incorporating thick cosmopolitanism into experiential learning courses and reflects on what experiential learning courses focused on thick global citizenship might actually look like.

Why International Experiential Learning Needs Cosmopolitan Theory

The idea of "global citizenship" is rooted in and shares much in common with "cosmopolitanism" (from the Greek *kosmopolitês* – "world citizen"),[1] the term that is much more widely used in theoretical debates about moral obligations to the rest of humanity. The term "global citizenship" is undoubtedly much more user-friendly than "cosmopolitanism," which tends to conjure up images of either pink martinis or women's fashion magazines. The literature on global citizenship also tends to focus much more pragmatically on concrete actions and attributes, while cosmopolitan writing is generally much more abstract and theoretically dense – thus failing to lend itself to anyone who feels intimidated by serious theoretical writing. However, in attempting to serve the interests of user-friendliness, writing about global citizenship tends to evade, perhaps conveniently, the challenging ethical and political questions addressed in the literature on cosmopolitanism, in particular questions about moral obligations based on principles of justice (see Brown & Held, 2010; Delantey, 2012; Cabrera, 2010; Rovisco, 2011). As Ross Lewin notes, "everyone seems to be in such a rush to create global citizens out of their students that we seem to have forgotten even to determine what we are even trying to create. Perhaps we avoid definitions not because of our rush to action, *but out of fear of what we may find*" (2009, p. xviii, cited in Jorgenson & Shultz, 2012, p. 2, emphasis added).

Indeed, research on the ways in which universities use the term global citizenship reveals both its contested nature and the different and contradictory agendas attached to it. Despite the use of idealistic language, the motivations for the promotion of global citizenship programs and international experiential learning courses from the perspective of senior university administrators appear to be related primarily to the marketing goals of positioning their universities as key players in the training of a globally-competitive workforce. As Jorgenson and Shultz (2012, p. 6) explain:

> The surge in global citizenship education programs can be seen as a marketing tool to attract students looking for attributes to make them competitive in the global workforce. Research ... has been conducted to validate these claims, citing global citizenship as an institutional response to the demand for globally competent workers for which the lack of cross-culturally trained employees "costs American companies about $2 billion dollars in losses annually." (Brustein, 2007, p. 384)

The motivations that attract students to international experiential learning and global citizenship programs are also diverse and frequently contradictory. Research by Rebecca Tiessen found that students' primary motives for volunteering in developing countries related to career development and to personal learning and growth (2012, p. 14). Not only was "a desire to help others" far down the list of students' primary motivations, but concerns about "social justice or solidarity" were not identified by any of the sixty-eight participants in her study as a motivation for participation in international development volunteer programs (2012, p. 14). In sum, it appears that as a group, neither university administrators nor students associate global citizenship and international experiential learning programs with global justice, a concern also raised by Langdon and Agyeyomah (chapter 3 in this volume). This lack of interest or awareness should be a clear indication of the need to return to the origins of the idea of global citizenship in cosmopolitan thinking, and in particular the rights and especially responsibilities that global citizenship entails. The literature on cosmopolitanism helps to do just that by firmly grounding the idea of global citizenship in the field of justice, and more specifically in the question of the moral obligations which all human beings hold towards one another – regardless of where they may happen to live.

Shifting into the realm of moral obligations removes much of the warm, fuzzy, feel-good appeal which the idea of global citizenship fosters. While cosmopolitanism is increasingly proposed as an urgently necessary – although not necessarily individually appealing – response to the crisis of human suffering embedded in processes of contemporary globalization, the term global citizenship is often used in ways that appear intended to make students and universities feel and look good – but leaves up to them decisions about what such goodness entails. Grounding global citizenship in cosmopolitanism firmly anchors it in the field of both the positive and negative moral obligations associated with being human, that is the duties not just to do good but also to not do harm or benefit from harms that are done to others. Indeed, one of the most useful conceptual benefits of cosmopolitanism for international experiential learning and global citizenship education may be to put negative obligations back onto the agenda. While many students seem well aware of at least vague moral imperatives to "do good," few seem to be aware of the ways in which they may be indirectly implicated in the suffering of others or of any moral obligation to work to end the institutional causes of that suffering. By placing equal attention on positive and negative moral obligations towards the rest of humanity, cosmopolitanism suggests a rethinking of the content of international experiential learning programs and the locations of placements so that they are focused not just on poor communities in the Global South where students can "do good" but also in the centres of political and economic power in the Global North where students might also learn to contribute to the prevention of harm.

Theoretical grappling with the meaning of global citizenship is crucial because understandings of the concept inform the ways in which it is fostered through experiential learning programs. Simply put, theories of global citizenship shape the kinds of experiences that students seek out and the kinds of learning that they (and their professors) hope they will encounter. Of course, the outcomes of experiential learning are inherently uncertain and students may often end up learning things that the instructors of experiential learning programs never imagined and which might even appear to run counter to the "experiences" in which they are engaged. However, if university educators and students do not seriously struggle with the meaning of global citizenship, they confront the very serious risk of inadvertently engaging in forms of experiential learning that may reinforce the paternalistic and neocolonial attitudes that most students of global development criticize in their university studies. As Joanne Benham Rennick argues in a recent volume on global citizenship education in Canadian universities, "unless we establish and embed particular and explicit values in our programming, we are likely to perpetuate neocolonial programming that carries a subtext of 'saving,' 'helping,' and even 'civilizing' partners in the Global South" (see Benham Rennick, 2014, chapter 2). Indeed, April Biccum (2010, 2007) argues that the prevailing narratives of global citizenship that have been fostered in the UK by the Department for International Development (DfID) and the Make Poverty History Campaign already actively generate a form of global citizenship that reinforces neoliberal globalization as well as colonial understandings of the Global North as "developed" and the Global South as needing assistance. Similarly, as Lynette Shultz (2007) found, many university-based global citizenship programs follow neoliberal understandings of globalization, in which the primary goal of global citizenship education is to train globally-competitive employees and entrepreneurs (see also Langdon and Agyeyomah, chapter 3). In a similar vein, Thomas and Chandrasekera (chapter 5) highlight the ways in which non-reflexive approaches to International Social Work – which shares much in common with International Development Studies – can foster "apathetic" rather than "authentic" allies who believe that they challenge injustice while simultaneously reinforcing it. In sum, not all understandings of global citizenship contribute to global justice. It is thus necessary to ask some hard questions about the understandings of global citizenship that are actually fostered in experiential learning programs. As Ulrich Beck argued, "only a devil's advocate who questions well-meaning cosmopolitanism as to its emancipatory function and its misuse can open the debate over the ethics and politics of cosmopolitanism" (2002, p. 47, as cited in Littler, 2009, p. 25).

Moreover, as a growing number of scholars call for more rigorous evaluation of international experiential learning programs (Tiessen & Epprecht, 2012), it is crucial to establish a rigorous definition of global citizenship to serve as the basis for analysis. In the absence of conceptual clarity about what global citizenship means, neither professors nor students can have any understanding of whether international experiential learning programs are contributing to it – or indeed what kinds of ideas, values, and understandings they are contributing to.

To the extent that experiential learning programs deal with ethical issues the focus is typically on behavioural ethics, which examine the appropriate forms of behaviour for individuals when confronted with particular ethically challenging situations in their daily lives. Common topics of discussion in pre-departure orientation sessions for international experiential learning placements include the ethically appropriate responses to begging, to racial and gender inequality in foreign cultures, and to other aspects of "culture shock" (or "cognitive dissonance") as well as the dangers of assuming that North American cultural norms are universal. While behavioural ethics are crucial for international preparation, missing from most experiential learning programs is any serious analysis of normative ethics, that is, consideration of the moral considerations that should guide human behaviour in the first place – prior to encountering specific ethical dilemmas such as a beggar in the street. One of the central debates in the field of normative ethics is that between consequentialist and deontological ethics. While consequentialists assert that morality should be assessed on the basis of an action's outcome or result, proponents of deontological ethics argue that decisions should be based on consideration of the rights of others and the corresponding obligations that such rights impose on the self; that is, action and inaction should be judged on the basis of previously determined moral principles and obligations. The idea of global citizenship implicitly adopts a deontological perspective by asserting, albeit vaguely, that privileged individuals in the Global North "ought" to do something to help individuals suffering from poverty and other abuses of their human rights in other parts of the world. However, writing on global citizenship and experiential learning courses designed to foster it tend to fall short of any full consideration of deontological ethics as they fail to seriously grapple with questions about the ethical obligations that severe poverty and inequality generate; in particular:

• What rights do human beings possess by virtue of their being human?
• What obligations do those rights impose on others?
• How far do those obligations extend?
• What specific actions do those obligations require?

These are precisely the questions that scholars of cosmopolitanism grapple with and any serious initiatives that promote global citizenship need to deal with these questions as well.

While cosmopolitanism has deep historical roots dating back more than two millennia to ancient Greece, contemporary advocates argue that cosmopolitan principles and action are urgently needed *now* because of the multiple human and ecological crises generated by contemporary globalization and the growing mutual interconnectedness that globalization brings about (Brown & Held, 2010, p. 1; Held, 2010, p. 39). The central question raised by contemporary cosmopolitan thinkers concerns the ethical principles that should guide human behaviour and decision-making in the context of contemporary globalization – with an overriding focus on global justice. Initiatives to promote global citizenship need to engage with such an ethical framework before choosing or designing experiences aimed at helping students to better understand and respond to contemporary global problems. Rooting global citizenship in cosmopolitanism can have important implications for the location and other key aspects of international experiential learning programs that may also help to ground them more solidly in struggles for global justice.

From Global Citizenship Back to Cosmopolitanism

Cosmopolitanism is not a unified body of thought but it is characterized by certain core principles. First, at the heart of cosmopolitanism is the conviction that by virtue of simply being human all human beings have certain moral obligations towards all other human beings (see Brown & Held, 2010, p. 1; Lu, 2000). The focus of cosmopolitan thought is thus on the duties of individual humans towards one another regardless of their citizenship in particular nation-states or membership in particular ethnic, religious, or other communities of shared identity. Second, the search to identify such a universal set of duties is based on impartial reasoning – meaning that the principles underlying cosmopolitan obligations must be ones on which all people could agree and act (Barry, 1989, 1995; Held, 2010, p. 46; Nussbaum, 1997, pp. 29–36; Rawls, 1999, pp. 11–12). Testing the universality of moral obligations requires what Seyla Benhabib referred to as "reasoning from the point of view of others" (1992, pp. 9–10) and John Rawls (1971) proposed as the "veil of ignorance" behind which humans would not know their social or economic position in the world before designing moral rules to govern human behaviour.[2] The search for a universal set of principles as the basis for assessing moral obligations does not negate the importance of respecting cultural difference, but it is based on the conviction that there are certain limits to acceptable human behaviour as well as moral requirements to help other human beings in need which in turn indicate certain moral obligations for all human beings.[3] The emphasis on obligations or duties needs to be distinguished from voluntaristic kindness; the fulfillment of cosmopolitan obligations is not optional but rather is a requirement to meet the demands of justice. From this perspective, global citizenship requires not lifestyle choices but the fulfillment of moral duties. Third, those duties are understood to involve both positive and negative moral obligations, that is, positive obligations of beneficence to "do good" as well as negative obligations to not do harm – which also imply obligations to prevent harm to others and to not benefit from the suffering of others (whether consciously or unconsciously). All cosmopolitan thought is engaged in trying to define these obligations more precisely, to whom they apply to, how far they extend, and what specific types of actions and political and institutional changes they require in order to be fulfilled – and it is here that agreement among cosmopolitans generally ends. Nevertheless, there is relatively greater agreement that moral obligations include action to avoid causing (if not also preventing) very serious harm and to alleviate very urgent need – in short to take action to prevent gross violations of human rights (Held, 2010, p. 48).

Critics of the cosmopolitan quest for principles of global justice and the institutional-legal framework to put those principles into practice typically assert that such efforts are simply unrealistic in the prevailing context of state sovereignty (see Nagel, 2005; Dahl, 1999). The cosmopolitan response to those critics typically points first to already-existing and newly emergent examples of cosmopolitan principles in practice – such as the Universal Declaration of Human Rights and the International Criminal Court – and then asserts that "just because something is difficult and improbable under current circumstances does not also mean that it is impossible, or, more importantly that it is not something we ought morally to do" (Brown & Held, 2010, p. 3). However, even among cosmopolitans who agree on the basic ethical principles of global justice, there is much disagreement about the legal and institutional mechanisms for putting cosmopolitanism into practice, on where primary responsibilities for action lie, how far those responsibilities extend, and what particular actions they imply for individual actors.

Cosmopolitanism makes four particularly important contributions to thinking about global citizenship. First, it pushes global citizenship beyond the realm of voluntary choices into the sphere of moral obligations. Second, it emphasizes not just the positive moral obligations that already inform many articulations of global citizenship – if only vaguely and in an under-theorized manner – but also negative obligations to not cause harm or benefit from harm done to others as well as to prevent harm. Since many global citizenship programs and courses already focus significant attention on "doing good" (although not always understood as an obligation), the rest of this chapter will focus attention on the neglected obligation to not do harm. Third, cosmopolitanism is about the universal obligations of all humans towards all other humans; although greater obligations do fall on those with greater resources and capacities to act, global citizenship is not just a responsibility of the privileged, but of all people.[4] Fourth and finally, cosmopolitanism puts heavy emphasis on the personal responsibility of all humans to be aware of the consequences of their actions on other humans. As Held explains, "actors have to be aware of, and accountable for, the consequences of actions, direct or indirect, intended or unintended, which may radically restrict or delimit the choices of others" (2010, p. 71). This emphasis on personal accountability requires lifelong processes of research, analysis, and critical reflection by all individuals so that they are aware of the ways in which their actions affect the lives of others – and so that they can then make informed decisions about their ethical obligations in the light of that knowledge.

One difficulty with cosmopolitan thinking that also has important implications for global citizenship is the problem of motivation; that is, how to get people not just to think like cosmopolitans but to act like them too. Since global citizenship courses and programs are presumably designed not just to encourage students to think about global citizenship but also to act like global citizens, concerns about strategies of motivation are paramount. According to Andrew Dobson, the prevailing understandings of cosmopolitanism seek to motivate cosmopolitan action through an emphasis on shared humanity; that is, we should all act like cosmopolitans "because we are all members of a common humanity" (Dobson, 2006, p. 168). The difficulty with this approach, Dobson argues, is that in practice, appeals to "common humanity" turn out to be a weak motivation for real action. As he puts it, "the cerebral recognition that we are all members of a common humanity seems not to be enough to get us to 'do' cosmopolitanism" (2006, p. 182). In short, we may believe in the principles of cosmopolitanism, and may even think that we are cosmopolitan, but we don't often actually behave that way. As noted above, there is much debate about what specific actions cosmopolitan principles require. The concern raised by Dobson, however, is that even when agreement on cosmopolitan principles does exist, it does not translate into concrete action. Because of the weak motivations provided by articulations of cosmopolitanism that rest on principles of shared humanity as the basis for action, Dobson labels these as thin forms of cosmopolitanism. He then proposes an alternative conceptual framework of thick cosmopolitanism to foster much stronger links between cosmopolitan thinking and action.

Global Citizenship as "Thick" Cosmopolitanism

In the search for a more powerful source of motivation for cosmopolitan action, Dobson works with the assertion that "we are more likely to feel obliged to assist others in their plight if we are responsible for their situation – if there is some identifiable causal relationship between what we do, or what we have done, and how they are" (2006, p. 171). Here he builds on the arguments of Andrew Linklater, who similarly argues that "cosmopolitan emotions are most likely to develop when actors believe that they are causally responsible for harming others and their physical environment" (2006, p. 125). Emphasis on linkages of "causal responsibility," Dobson and Linklater both argue, fosters "thicker connections" between people than attention to shared humanity and also helps to shift beyond "the territory of beneficence and into the realm of justice " (Dobson, 2006, p. 172). As an example of causal responsibility, Dobson points to climate change and the clear evidence that the governments, corporations, and citizens of countries in the Global North are deeply implicated in the causes of changing climate patterns that have serious negative impacts on the lives of people in the Global South. He also builds on the work of human rights scholar Thomas Pogge, who has argued in various works that the contemporary institutions of global trade systematically discriminate in favour of the Global North and against the Global South – and thus also deeply implicate citizens of countries in the Global North in the material poverty and suffering of people in other parts of the world. As Pogge puts it:

> We are familiar, through charity appeals, with the assertion that it lies in our hands to save the lives of many or, by doing nothing, to let these people die. We are less familiar with the assertion examined here of a weightier responsibility: *that most of us not merely let people starve but also participate in starving them.* (2002, p. 214, emphasis added)

Recognition of the chains of causal responsibility that link would-be global citizens in the Global North to strangers in other parts of the world are a much stronger motivation for cosmopolitan or global citizenship action, Dobson asserts, than appeals to common humanity. Moreover, emphasis on linkages of causal responsibility highlights not just positive duties of aid but also negative duties to prevent injustice – here in the form of efforts to end the injustice inflicted on others through climate change, global trade rules, and other institutions such as university pension, endowment, and scholarship funds that may benefit individuals in the Global North while harming people in the Global South (Dobson, 2006; Linklater, 1998; Slim, 2002). Summarizing the distinctions between thick and thin understandings of cosmopolitanism, Dobson concludes that "thin conceptions of cosmopolitan citizenship revolve around compassion for the vulnerable but leave asymmetries of power and wealth intact; thick conceptions of cosmopolitan citizenship attempt to influence the structural conditions faced by vulnerable groups" (2006, p. 169).

Work by scholars of human rights and moral philosophy helps to further specify the kinds of moral obligations and practical actions that thick conceptions of cosmopolitan or global citizenship entail (see Ashford, 2007; Caney, 2007; Gewirth, 2007; Wenar, 2007). In particular, building on Pogge's analysis of the human right to basic necessities and his argument that extreme poverty constitutes a violation of that human right, Elizabeth Ashford (2007) examines the positive and negative duties that emerge for citizens in affluent countries. Extreme poverty, she reasons, generates not only a positive duty of beneficence towards those suffering from hunger and material deprivation (see also Singer, 1999, 2009) but also a negative duty *not* to contribute to their suffering *or* to benefit from it. She then points out the ways in which individuals in the Global North do indirectly benefit from unfair global trade rules through access to cheap food and material goods at the expense of individuals and communities in the Global South.

However, one of the principle difficulties with the negative duty to not benefit from the harm done to others through global trade rules, scholarship and pension funds, climate change, or virtually any other global phenomena, is that the causal linkages between actions in one part of the world and suffering elsewhere are complex, indirect, and often hidden. It is not generally individual actions that directly cause others to suffer, but rather participation in complex global systems that are beyond the capacity of any single individual to control or change. The complexity of the linkages of causal responsibility that bind affluent individuals in the Global North to those suffering from extreme poverty in other parts of the world thus raises difficult questions about responsibility and obligations; in particular, as Pogge asks: *who is morally responsible to do what to end extreme poverty?* One common response, Ashford notes, is that because it is primarily global institutions, such as the World Trade Organization (WTO), that are responsible for the suffering caused by unfair global trade rules, those institutions should also be responsible for ending it. This response could be understood to let individual citizens in the Global North off the hook. However, Ashford argues, because global institutions like the WTO respond to democratically elected governments, individual citizens do in fact bear very significant negative duties to work towards the reform of global institutions that contribute to extreme poverty. As she puts it, "until just institutions have been brought about that specify and enforce both kinds of duty [positive and negative], the onus is on individual agents in affluent countries to take the initiative in accepting responsibility for fulfilling these duties and in deciding how to do so" (2007, p. 218). In short, faced with extreme poverty in the Global South, individuals in the Global North possess negative moral obligations to work towards the reform of institutions that contribute to that suffering and to create other new institutions – such as climate change agreements – that might help to prevent future suffering. From this perspective, the primary moral obligations of privileged individuals in the Global North are to work for the reform of unjust global institutions and the creation of just ones. If these moral obligations are also understood as core components of global citizenship, we need to ask if and to what extent international experiential learning programs are oriented towards these goals of creating just institutions.

The Challenges of Taking "Thick" Conceptions of Global Citizenship Seriously

One of the practical implications of "thick" conceptions of global citizenship is that, by emphasizing complicity in the suffering of others and moral obligations to fulfil negative duties to not contribute to or benefit from that suffering in addition to positive duties, the range of actions that qualify as global citizenship is significantly reduced. From this perspective, global citizens must fulfil both their positive and negative moral obligations. Moreover, placed in the context of positive and negative duties, global citizenship ceases to be a lifestyle choice and becomes a moral obligation to act and not act in certain fairly specific ways. Since the range of global injustices in which we are implicated is so broad – climate change, unfair global trade rules, university scholarship, and pension funds are just the beginning – affluent individuals still face a wide spectrum of options about how they might act to fulfill their positive and negative duties towards the rest of humanity. Nevertheless, even with this broad range of options, it is clear that thick global citizenship calls for informed and sustained political action aimed at ending the suffering of others in which we are implicated. This means that some activities that have been frequently presented as expressions of global citizenship – such as international travel, volunteer work, and ethical consumption – might no longer qualify at all or at best might be better understood as thin forms of global citizenship.[5]

One of the tensions that pervades much of the literature on cosmopolitanism relates to conflict between the relativist imperatives to take other cultures seriously and the universalist imperatives implied by a single set of cosmopolitan principles. These theoretical tensions become particularly strong at the moment of translating ideals of global citizenship into the content of experiential learning programs: should experiential learning emphasize understanding and appreciation of other cultures[6] (at the risk of postmodern cultural relativism) or focus on thick forms of global citizenship oriented towards political action (at the risk of universalism). While these approaches need not necessarily be mutually exclusive, in the far from ideal context of inadequate time and resources, students and their professors need to make decisions about how to operationalize the conceptions of global citizenship that they want to promote and practice. In this context, John Rawls's *The Law of Peoples* (1999) may be particularly helpful as Rawls seeks to identify a set of universally acceptable moral principles that all peoples would agree to if placed behind a veil of ignorance in which they did not know their social or economic position in the world.

Constraining the definition of global citizenship to its thick form can also make the concept much less appealing. I discovered this first hand through a seminar course I taught in 2011 with a group of students in International Development Studies. On reading and discussing the works of Dobson, Pogge, Ashford, and other scholars of cosmopolitanism and human rights cited above, this group of students came to accept *in intellectual terms* the idea that global citizenship entails positive and negative obligations to undertake action oriented towards global justice. However, they resisted the idea *in emotional terms*; that is, they did not like and did not accept the idea that they as specific individuals should be morally obliged to undertake certain kinds of actions –

especially political activism – in order to fulfil their negative obligations
as global citizens. The students were very clear not only that they preferred thin forms of global citizenship that did not impose any obligations on them and believed that they should be able to choose how to
exercise their global citizenship but also that the broader general public
would also reject any attempt to limit global citizenship to its thick forms.

It is also very likely that effort to foster thick cosmopolitanism through
experiential learning programs will make university administrators
and lawyers and perhaps some parents very nervous. As I explore further in the next section, experiential learning programs that seek to foster thick forms of global citizenship will presumably aim *not* to produce
"little developers" (as criticized by Biccum, 2010), but rather to encourage the acquisition of attitudes and skills related to political struggles
for global social and environmental justice. While those skills do not
preclude the ability to work through and for large institutions, they
may also conjure up images of balaclava-wearing, rock-throwing pro-
testers in the minds of liability-focused administrators. Indeed, this
was precisely the mental image offered up by one administrator at my
university to ideas for an experiential learning course focused on thick
cosmopolitanism. The negative responses of both students and senior
administrators to the promotion of thick forms of global citizenship in
experiential learning courses are not sufficient reasons to stick with
the loose definitions of global citizenship in use at most universities in
Canada. However, it is important to recognize that taking thick conceptions of global citizenship seriously is also likely to make the concept of
global citizenship itself more controversial and less popular. Alterna-
tively, decisions to favour thin over thick forms of global citizenship
should be made in the context of an understanding of the alternatives
and the forms of thinking and action that are and are not encouraged
by them.

International Experiential Learning and Global Citizenship as if Global Justice Mattered

Defining global citizenship as thick cosmopolitanism has significant implications for both the content and the physical location of international
experiential learning programs that aim to foster and practice global
citizenship. First, in preparatory courses students need to grapple not
just with the behavioural ethical challenges they are likely to encounter
during the specific period of time while they are overseas but also with

the much broader normative ethical questions related to the ethical obligations that all human beings hold towards one another. As part of this ethical grappling, students also need to think through both the positive and negative moral obligations which cosmopolitan understandings of global citizenship suggest as well as the specific actions which those obligations suggest they should undertake. Finally, in the context of the high level of personal responsibility and accountability that thick global citizenship requires, students must also learn to research and analyse the implications of their everyday actions, both direct and indirect, for the well-being (or suffering) of people in other parts of the world.[7] Following this three-layered process of analysis and reflection, students and their professors might then begin to think together about the types of experiential learning activities that would best help them to fulfil their roles and develop their capacities as global citizens.

Taking thick global citizenship seriously requires particularly careful attention to often neglected negative obligations. Taking those negative obligations seriously requires research and analysis in order to become aware of the ways in which one may be negatively impacting on the well-being of other people through indirect participation in unjust social institutions or in large-scale social-political and economic processes that generate inequality and injustice. Following the arguments of Pogge and Ashford, outlined above, it seems clear that negative obligations in the face of extreme levels of global poverty then require action to reform the institutions that create and reproduce extreme poverty and inequality. For students engaged in international experiential learning programs, this means seeking out placements in which they can both contribute to struggles for institutional reform and develop their capacities to continue such work in the future. Political struggles to reform global institutions can, but do not necessarily involve political protest. Because the causal links between the everyday lives of individuals in the Global North and the injustices that result are so complex and struggles for social and environmental justice cannot be limited to any single set of strategies, there are multiple ways in which experiential learning courses could serve and foster thick global citizenship. Indeed, following Antonio Gramsci's arguments about the need for a "long march through institutions" to bring about radical political change, even experiences that focus on the functioning of mainstream bureaucratic institutions, including professional legal training, could foster skills related to the exercise of thick cosmopolitanism – as political and legal change often requires a deep understanding of technical and legal details. What is important is thus not so much the specific skills that students develop through experiential learning courses, but the broader theoretical, ethical, and political context in which they understand those skills. Put differently, it is important to ask to what extent experiential learning courses help students to understand their own learning process as part of a broader struggle for global social and environmental justice as opposed to the acquisition of skills needed to become a "little developer" (Biccum, 2010, p. 107) or simply a successful professional. In this context, student "experiences" that appear to foster thin or "soft" forms of global citizenship may also provide opportunities to promote something thicker, depending on how students analyse them. As Andreotti argues, such processes of reflection are the key to what she calls "critical global citizenship education":

> It is important to recognise that "soft" global citizenship education is appropriate to certain contexts and can already represent a major step. But it cannot stop there … If educators are not "critically literate" to engage with assumptions and implications/limitations of their approaches, they run the risk of (indirectly and unintentionally) reproducing the systems of belief and practices that harm those they want to support. The question of how far educators working with global citizenship education are prepared to do that in the present context in the North is open to debate. (Andreotti, 2006, pp. 49–50)

The idea of thick cosmopolitanism also has important implications for the choice of locations for international experiential learning programs and placements that aim to promote global citizenship. Such programs already place heavy emphasis on the fulfilment of positive obligations to "do good" by placing students with NGOs that provide services or advocate for socially and economically marginalized people in the Global South. However, international experiential learning programs almost completely ignore negative obligations to not cause suffering or benefit from it – which might suggest action closer to home or closer to the centres of global political and economic power. While fulfillment of the positive obligations associated with thick global citizenship often leads students to the places where the symptoms of poverty are most extreme, fulfilment of negative obligations is more likely to lead to the centres of power where the causes of poverty are concentrated. Thus, a placement with a human rights organization in Ottawa or Washington might contribute much more to the development of students' capacities to fulfil their negative obligations than an internship with an NGO in Africa or South America. Indeed, fulfillment of negative obligations might not even require leaving the university campus. For example, in 2009 students at Dalhousie University undertook research and pressured the university administration to release information on whether its pension and endowment funds held investments in oil companies operating in Sudan (see Canadian Press, 2009). These initiatives arguably helped the students to develop the capacities needed to fulfill their negative obligations much more effectively than if they had actually travelled to Sudan to attempt to provide direct services to people in need. Indeed, the student campaign involved significant experiential learning about media relations, pension fund research, and the lobbying of senior university officials. Given the number of universities that have created special scholarships to support international experiential learning programs, the negative obligations associated with thick global citizenship suggest that the students benefitting from those scholarships might research the sources of the funding that support them as part of their learning experience.

Conclusion

It is widely assumed and asserted that experiential learning, especially in foreign locations, will foster global citizenship. However, these claims and assumptions generally rest on weak conceptions of global citizenship that fail to grapple seriously with the origins of the term in the rich and closely related literature on cosmopolitanism and which almost completely ignore the negative obligations associated with cosmopolitanism. While global citizenship is frequently presented as unquestionably good, there are many different versions of it on offer – ranging from thin to thick and soft to critical. Students engaged in international experiential learning programs need to take these theoretical debates about global citizenship (often under the title of cosmopolitanism) much more seriously so that they operate with clear conceptions of both the forms of global citizenship that they seek to promote and the range of practical actions that could fulfil the obligations associated with global citizenship. If students and professors involved with experiential learning courses do not engage with these debates, they face the very real danger of engaging in and promoting "soft" forms of global citizenship that perpetuate voluntaristic, charity-based, and neocolonial approaches to issues of global social and environmental injustice. In this chapter I have argued that experiential learning courses should be grounded in thick conceptions of global citizenship that recognize the complicity of citizens of countries in the Global North in the perpetuation of injustice around the world and the moral obligations that follow from that complicity. Some readers may disagree with this approach, but at the very least they should understand the origins of the concept of global citizenship in cosmopolitanism and the obligations that it entails. They may choose to reject the idea that they hold obligations towards other human beings – in which case they should also stop using the concept of global citizenship.

NOTES

1 The term "cosmopolitanism" is first attributed to Diogenes the Cynic (c. 412 B.C.), who, when asked where he came from, responded "I am *kosmopolitês* [a citizen of the world]" (Nussbaum, 1997, p. 28).
2 Rawls (1971) proposed the "veil of ignorance" as a mechanism for identifying principles of justice to apply *within* the jurisdictions of nation-states, but cosmopolitans argue for a "veil of ignorance" at the global level to identify moral principles on which all humans could agree. Rawls's (1999) *The Law of Peoples* extends the "veil of ignorance" to the global sphere, but as the basis for negotiation among state-like peoples rather than among individuals.
3 Rawls (1999) argues that, if placed behind a veil of ignorance, all peoples – regardless of cultural differences – would agree to certain universal obligations towards one another, including respect for human rights and a duty to assist other peoples living under unfavorable conditions (1999, 37, pp. 113–120).
4 See for example Appiah's (2006) discussion of cosmopolitan ethics among people from different religious and ethnic backgrounds in West Africa.
5 Indeed, critical analyses of these activities – including some written by students – already raise serious questions about whether and to what extent they reflect the principles of global citizenship. (See for example: Apale and Stam, 2011; Gula, 2006; Moore, 2011; Raymond and Hall, 2008; Richey and Ponte, 2011; Simpson, 2004; Tiessen, 2009, 2012).
6 For example, see Dalhousie University's "Certificate in Cultural Communication," which emphasizes a conception of global citizenship focused on "understanding of cultural differences and a greater ability to communicate effectively and appropriately in intercultural contexts": http://www.dal.ca/dept/interculturalcommunication.html.

7 In addition to issues related to climate change, global trade rules, and university pension and endowment funds, such research might involve the commodity chains that link people in different parts of the world; for example, the connections between the purchase of a cell phone in Canada and the child soldiers involved in conflicts over the control of coltan in the Democratic Republic of Congo or the children and their families who work in Guiyung, China – the world's largest electronic waste site.

REFERENCES

Andreotti, V. (2006). Soft versus critical global citizenship education. *Policy & Practice: A Development Education Review, 3*(3), 40–51.

Apale, A. & Stam, V. (Eds.). (2011). *Generation NGO*. Toronto: Between the Lines.

Appiah, K.A. (2006). *Cosmopolitanism*. New York: Norton.

Ashford, E. (2007). The duties imposed by the human right to basic necessities. In T. Pogge (Ed.), *Freedom from poverty as a human right: Who owes what to the very poor* (pp. 183–218). New York: Oxford University Press.

Barry, B. (1989). *Theories of justice*. London: Harvester Wheatsheaf.

Barry, B. (1995). *Justice as impartiality*. Oxford: Clarendon Press.

Benhabib, S. (1992). *Situating the self*. Cambridge, UK: Polity Press.

Benham Rennick, Joanne. (2014). Canadian values, good global citizenship, and service learning in Canada: A socio-historical analysis. In Joanne Benham Rennick & Michel Desjardins (Eds.), *The world is my classroom: International learning and Canadian higher education.* (Chapter 2). Toronto: University of Toronto Press, Scholarly Publishing Division.

Biccum, A. (2007). Marketing development: Live 8 and the production of the global citizen. *Development and Change, 38*(6), 1111–1126. http://dx.doi.org/10.1111/j.1467-7660.2007.00445.x

Biccum, A. (2010). *Global citizenship and the legacy of empire*. London: Routledge.

Brown, G., & Held, D. (Eds.). (2010). "Editors' introduction." In *The cosmopolitan reader* (pp. 1–13). Cambridge, UK: Polity Press.

Brustein, W. (2007). The global campus: Challenges and opportunities for higher education in North America. *Journal of Studies in International Education, 11*(3–4), 382–391. http://dx.doi.org/10.1177/1028315307303918

Cabrera, L. (2010). *The practice of global citizenship*. Cambridge, UK: Cambridge University Press. http://dx.doi.org/10.1017/CBO9780511762833

Canadian Press. (2009). Dalhousie students ask if Halifax school has investments in Sudan. March 6. Retrieved from http://www.ngnews.ca/Living/2009-03-06/article-318778/Dalhousie-students-ask-if-Halifax-school-has-investments-in-Sudan/1

Caney, S. (2007). Global poverty and human rights: The case for positive duties. In T. Pogge (Ed.), *Freedom from poverty as a human right: Who owes what to the very poor* (pp. 275–302). New York: Oxford University Press.

Che, S.M., Spearman, M., & Manizade, A. (2009). Constructive disequilibrium: Cognitive and emotional development through dissonant experiences in less familiar destinations. In R. Lewin (Ed.), *The handbook of practice and research in study abroad: Higher education and the quest for global citizenship* (pp. 99–116). New York: Routledge.

Dahl, R. (1999). Can international institutions be democratic? A skeptic's view. In I. Shapiro & C. Hacker-Cordón (Eds.), *Democracy's edges* (pp. 19–36). Cambridge, UK: Cambridge University Press. http://dx.doi.org/10.1017/CBO9780511586361.003

Delantey, G. (Ed.). (2012). *The Routledge handbook of cosmopolitan studies.* New York: Routledge.

Dobson, A. (2006). Thick cosmopolitianism. *Political Studies, 54*(1), 165–184. http://dx.doi.org/10.1111/j.1467-9248.2006.00571.x

Gewirth, A. (2007). Duties to fulfill the human rights of the poor. In T. Pogge (Ed.), *Freedom from poverty as a human right: Who owes what to the very poor* (pp. 219–237). New York: Oxford University Press.

Gula, L. (2006). *Backpacking tourism: Morally sound travel or neo-colonial conquest?* (Unpublished honours thesis). Dalhousie University, Halifax, Nova Scotia.

Held, D. (2010). *Cosmopolitanism.* Cambridge, UK: Polity Press.

Jorgenson, S., & Shultz, L. (2012). Global citizenship education (GCE) in post-secondary institutions: What is protected and what is hidden under the umbrella of GCE? [Special Edition]. *Journal of Global Citizenship & Equity Education, 2*(1), 1–21.

Lewin, R. (Ed.). (2009). *Handbook of practice and research in study abroad: Higher education and the quest for global citizenship.* New York: Routledge, Taylor & Francis.

Linklater, A. (1998). Cosmopolitan citizenship. In K. Hutchings & R. Dannreuther (Eds.), *Cosmopolitan citizenship* (pp. 35–56). London: MacMillan Press.

Linklater, A. (2006). Cosmopolitanism. In A. Dobson & R. Eckersley (Eds.), *Political theory and the ecological challenge* (pp. 109–129). Cambridge, UK: Cambridge University Press.

Littler, J. (2009). *Radical consumption: Shopping for change in contemporary culture.* Berkshire, UK: Open University Press.

Lu, C. (2000). The one and many faces of cosmopolitanism. *Journal of Political Philosophy, 8*(2), 244–267. http://dx.doi.org/10.1111/1467-9760.00101

Moore, Emma. (2011). Guilt trips: A personal perspective on the ethical quandaries of travel in the developing world. Winner of the 2011 Irving & Jeanne Glovin [Student] Essay Award at Dalhousie University. http://arts.dal.ca/Files/Emma_Moore_Glovin.pdf

Nagel, T. (2005). The problem of global justice. *Philosophy & Public Affairs*, *33*(2), 113–147. http://dx.doi.org/10.1111/j.1088-4963.2005.00027.x

Nussbaum, M. (1997). "Kant and cosmopolitanism." In James Bohman & Matthias Lutz-Bachman (Eds.), *Perpetual peace: Essays on Kant's cosmopolitan ideal* (pp. 25–51). Cambridge, MA: Massachusetts Institute of Technology Press.

Pogge, T. (2002). *World poverty and human rights*. Cambridge. UK: Polity Press.

Pogge, T. (2007). Severe poverty as a human rights violation. In T. Pogge (Ed.), *Freedom from poverty as a human right: Who owes what to the very poor* (pp. 11–53). New York: Oxford University Press.

Rawls, J. (1971). *A theory of justice*. Cambridge, MA: Harvard University Press.

Rawls, J. (1999). *The law of peoples*. Cambridge, MA: Harvard University Press.

Raymond, E.M., & Hall, C.M. (2008). The development of cross-cultural (mis) understanding through volunteer tourism. *Journal of Sustainable Tourism*, *16*(5), 530–543.

Richey, L.A., & Ponte, S. (2011). *Brand aid: Shopping well to save the world*. Minneapolis: University of Minnesota Press.

Rovisco, M. (2011). *The Ashgate companion to cosmopolitanism*. Burlington, VT: Ashgate.

Schattle, H. (2008). Education for global citizenship: Illustrations of ideological pluralism and adaptation. *Journal of Political Ideologies*, *13*(1), 73–94. http://dx.doi.org/10.1080/13569310701822263

Shultz, L. (2007). Educating for global citizenship: Conflicting agendas and understandings. *Alberta Journal of Educational Research*, *53*(3), 248–258.

Simpson, K. (2004). Doing development: The gap year, volunteer-tourists and a popular practice of development. *Journal of International Development*, *16*(5), 681–692. http://dx.doi.org/10.1002/jid.1120

Singer, P. (1999). The singer solution to world poverty. New York Times (Sept 5, on-line edition). http://www.utilitarianism.net/singer/by/19990905.htm

Singer, P. (2009). *The life you can save: Acting now to end world poverty*. New York: Random House.

Slim, H. (2002). Not philanthropy but rights: The proper politicization of humanitarian Pphilosophy. *International Journal of Human Rights*, *6*(2), 1–22. http://dx.doi.org/10.1080/714003759

Tiessen, R. (2009). Youth ambassadors abroad? Canadian foreign policy and public diplomacy in the developing world. In J.M. Beier & L. Wylie (Eds.),

Canadian foreign policy in critical perspective (pp. 141–155). Toronto: Oxford University Press.

Tiessen, R. (2012). Motivations for learn/volunteer abroad programs: Research with Canadian youth [Special Edition]. *Journal of Global Citizenship & Equity Education*, 2(1), 1–21.

Tiessen, R., & Epprecht, M. (2012). Introduction: Global citizenship education for learning/volunteering abroad [Special Edition]. *Journal of Global Citizenship & Equity Education* 2(1), 1–12.

Wenar, L. (2007). Responsibility and severe poverty. In T. Pogge (Ed.), *Freedom from poverty as a human right: Who wwes what to the very poor* (pp. 255–274). New York: Oxford University Press.

3 Critical Hyper-Reflexivity and Challenging Power: Pushing Past the Dichotomy of Employability and Good Global Citizenship in Development Studies Experiential Learning Contexts

JONATHAN LANGDON
AND COLEMAN AGYEYOMAH

Experiential learning opportunities are crucial components of Development Studies (DS) programs.[1] Seeing and being involved in social change processes directly offers Development Studies students the chance to understand the complexity of change, as well as the multiple layers of power dynamics – including the impact of one's own involvement – at play. In addition, our fifteen years of experience in this area has shown us that experiential learning provides a key platform from which students can deconstruct and begin to question their classroom education as well – an important starting point for developing a critical hyper-reflexive approach to social change engagements. Given the importance of these opportunities, and their potential for scaffolding deep reflective learning that questions global/local power relations and one's own role in these relations, it is important for all of us engaged in building the experiential elements of Development Studies programs to ask critical, reflective questions about them on an ongoing basis. In the discussion that follows, we share our own critical concerns that we have been reflecting on in our ongoing work, and some ways that we have tried to address these concerns. We share these thoughts here as a contribution to a conversation amongst colleagues who, like us, see our programs as potentially challenging, or at least questioning current global inequity. Given the complexity involved in these layered processes, we also wish to acknowledge how we continue to struggle to question power through our pedagogy on an ongoing basis.

The fifteen years of work[2] we base our comments on here are, primarily, experiential learning programs in Ghana, with both Canadian and

Ghanaian participants. This places certain limitations on our contextual comments – made towards the end of the chapter. However, this Ghanaian focus also allows us to advance thoughts on experiential learning not solely based on the impact it has on students from the Global North. This chapter emerges from our having supervised, and having helped to establish, a number of successful and unsuccessful experiential learning internships with students, where success is determined by the depth of engagement of students in their experience; it also emerges from our feeling that, despite a growing sense of what needs to be done to ensure a successful internship, many of our internships failed to introduce students to the potential to challenge status quo power dynamics, in Ghana, or globally. This is, in our minds, a major disconnect, for if these experiences are not opening up the possibility of challenging or at least destabilizing the status quo, they are instead normalizing its operation.

With this experience in mind, we share four thoughts below. First, we ask critical questions of the self-reflexive turn in Development Studies, especially where there have been important reflections on Eurocentrism due to the interdisciplinary nature of the field, but little thinking on how to link this to teaching, on the one hand, and experiential learning programming on the other. Second, we reflect upon concerns we have about recent trends in experiential learning in general, and in DS in particular, especially in their operationalization in countries in the Global South. Our focus here is the fact that clearly anti-status quo experiential learning programs seem to be disappearing as experiential learning programs, such as service learning and co-op programs, have become a major feature of arguments made by university administrations as to the economic worth of a university education. Third, we argue for a deepened approach to self-reflexivity, what we call critical hyper-reflexivity, in Development Studies experiential learning; the key here is a scaffolding rather than framing approach that allows for ongoing dialogue-based learning that can tackle disorienting dilemmas as they happen, rather than in debriefing processes after the fact. Finally, the fourth thought we share is that our placement choices should reflect an ideological commitment to challenging the status quo; we ground this last point in our experience in Ghana, where we have seen the growing impact of a solidarity approach to internships with people's ongoing struggles, rather than a more mainstream approach to placing students with stable, well-established NGOs that are more likely than not facilitating the stability of the global capitalist status quo (cf. Barry-Shaw &

Oja Jay, 2012). At the same time, this last point is rooted in something many of us who teach Development Studies likely feel in contemporary times: the contrast between capitalist globalization's momentum, and its clear failure to reduce the ever-widening gap between rich and poor, as well as its major climate change implications, underscore the importance of challenging its operations, perhaps along the "ethical dimension" lines based on "necessity" that Philip McMichael has outlined (2009, p. 291). We feel experiential learning programs, especially if they are grounded in a critical and hyper-reflexive practice and are based in ideological contexts that challenge the status quo, are an important place to introduce our students to the reality that another world is possible (cf. Cavanagh & Mander, 2004).

Self-Reflexivity Ain't Enough

Barbara Heron (2005) presents a compelling discussion of the way privilege – if only examined from a sense of positionality – does not truly destabilize knowledge-power hierarchies. In fact, she notes, it can actually further entrench them as those who have reflected on their privilege feel a new sense of power in being more ethical than those who have not. As an interdiscipline, DS has certainly been undertaking some serious self-reflexivity over the last decade. This self-reflexivity ranges from the introspective pieces at the heart of special journal issues in the Canadian Journal of Development Studies (e.g., Bowles, 2004; Nef, 2004; Angeles, 2004; Parpart & Veltmeyer, 2004) and World Development (e.g., Kanbur, 2002), to the critical Radical Development Studies collection edited by Uma Kothari (2005) (see also Edwards, 2002; Harriss, 1999). The question is, has this self-reflexivity moved beyond the performative question of positionality to truly question the interdiscipline's relations with Eurocentric power (Langdon, 2009; Dei & Simmons, 2009)?

Sumner (2006) has documented many of the critical realizations that led to this self-reflexivity. He notes three main critiques of development practice on the one hand and development studies on the other. These range from the post-development critique of the Eurocentric logic that dominates ideas of progress (cf. Rist, 1997; Escobar, 1995), to the technocratic tendency within development practice to depoliticize projects (cf. Ferguson, 1990), to the critique that, despite more than a half-century of development work, the gap between the rich and poor is greater than ever (cf. Stiglitz, 2002). In terms of DS, Edwards (1989, 2002) has questioned the relevance of the interdiscipline, if on the one hand it is not engaging more with practitioners, and on the other if it is not contributing to addressing these central critiques of practice. Sylvester (1999) has extended the Eurocentric critique levelled against development as a practice to development studies, noting that DS has much to learn from post-colonial theory as it makes room for subaltern voices – a point further explored by Ilan Kapoor (2004), who argues from a spivakian perspective, that DS must become hyper-reflexive in order to truly connect with and be responsive to subaltern voices. Olukoshi (2004, as cited in Sumner, 2006) reveals the necessity for this when he notes that mainstream development literature has a tendency of placing non-Westerners in the textboxes of reports and textbooks; this is despite the self-reflective contributions such as Loxley's (2004) argument that part of DS's strength and distinctiveness is its southern focus. Sumner (2006, p. 647) concludes his dissection of the future of DS by underscoring the need for the discipline to "open more spaces for alternative 'voices'." In this sense, Sumner speaks to the "subject matter" (2006, p. 647) of DS, and yet like so much of the self-reflective literature of the last decade, there is no mention of the ways this "material" is taught to or learned by students of DS. While Sumner (2006, p. 648) argues, "The assumption of much DS work is that knowledge is not contestable," we would argue that the assumption of much DS teaching is that the pedagogy of DS teaching is not even worth mentioning (Langdon, 2009). The material, it would seem, teaches itself.

One of the rare exceptions to this dearth of self-reflection on the teaching of development studies is Morrison's (2004) "Teaching and Studying Development: Making it Work." In previous work by one of us (Langdon, 2009), Morrison's work was applauded for stepping into territory largely untouched by others, but the work was also critiqued for the way it revealed the Eurocentric framing of the interdiscipline alluded to above. As Chamberlin (2003) notes, the framing of the stories we tell has deep implications on whom the story positions as insiders and outsiders. In her description of the dangers of a single story, Adichie (2009) echoes this, noting if "we begin with the failure of African states and not the colonial history that formed these states" we end up with a flattened image of Africa that "fits easily into stereotypes." This sensitivity to the way in which stories are told and framed echoes Foucault's (1980) analysis of discourse and power, drawing connections between who decides what is and is not legitimate knowledge, and ultimately who the discourse benefits. At the same time, Apple (2004) notes the way in which curricular choices reflect ideological alignments often in unstated and perhaps even unconscious ways. The unstated knowledge hierarchy critiqued above is visible, for instance, in Morrison's (2004) framing of a compulsory DS theory course by Eurocentric voices (e.g., Smith, Weber, Marx) as the roots of development – a framing process that can suggest to students that notions of societal betterment are the purview of Western thinkers alone. Excluded from this framing exercise are voices from outside the West, even as are voices critical of the Western bias in development thinking. These other voices are only added later in Morrison's proposed course contents. Building on Bunch's (1987, p. 140) famous statement, "you cannot just add voices" outside the Western frame and "stir" and hope to dispel Eurocentrism.

Both Heron (2006) and Epprecht (2004) note the importance of framing learning in order to obviate Western biases with reference to experiential learning – discussed further below. From our vantage point, it is not merely the material that matters in delivering DS courses, but the politics inherent in the way in which this material is framed that indicates to students which type of knowledge matters more than others. This is why one of us has argued (Langdon, 2009) for a more complex process of framing DS curricula – one that begins with multiple iterations of social change and places voices from many contexts (indigenous, for instance) on equal footing in suggesting the scope of that most contentious of terms, "development." Both of us work hard to make this a central feature of our pedagogy. Coleman, for instance, works with the bonesetter Gumrana Issahaku to challenge Ghanaian and Canadian student perceptions of health through Northern Ghanaian conceptions of relational wellness (cf. Agyeyomah & Langdon, 2009; Agyeyomah, Langdon, & Butler, 2010). Jon uses First Nations literature as well as the accounts of communities and individuals impacted by mainstream development, and invites First Nations colleagues, along with colleagues visiting the Coady International Institute from contexts around the world to join his class in Canada to recontextualize the foundational assumptions many students have of Canada's history.

Morrison's article is only one example of the dangers of approaches to teaching DS that have not reflected beyond the material to be covered but to the politics of teaching this material. While we have not conducted an extensive study of DS curriculum and course syllabi, we have collected course material from Northern Ghana's University of Development Studies Integrated Development Studies Program, as well as various Canadian DS programs (including McGill, Guelph, Trent,

Queen's, and Humber), as well as having taken twenty-five courses between us in Development Studies programs in the UK and Canada in
the last ten years. Using a discourse analysis method, building on Foucault's (1972) point that the way knowledge is framed signals its legiti-
macy, we found that most introductory courses on development
grounded discussions of social change in a Eurocentric history, before
adding in assertions from other contexts. It is not that these courses did
not acknowledge that social change was not invented in Europe, but
that the politics of the pedagogy undermined this assertion because of
the way courses were framed discursively. As Willinsky (1998) notes, in
discussing challenging Eurocentrism in a number of discipline-specific
classrooms, assertions of knowledge claims from contexts other than
the West need deeper emphasis if they are to challenge the normalized
Eurocentric view North American students have. Dei and Simmons
(2009) have made a similar point in the context of Ghanaian classrooms.
The key point here is that a very conscious and deliberate effort to emphasize non-Western voices and realities at the outset and in framing
what social change means is necessary to challenge the normalized
view that it is European history that will show the way for the rest of
the world. While we acknowledge here the limited basis of our study,
and very much believe that there are large numbers of us Development
Studies instructors that are working daily to challenge this knowledge
hierarchy, we have not seen evidence of this in what we have so far
been able to study, nor are there publications that we are aware of
where people are doing this – with the exception of Ghana's Integrated
Development Studies program at the University for Development
Studies that has a strong emphasis on endogenous knowledge as the
foundation of local change throughout the design of the curricula (cf.
Millar, Haverkort, & Apusigah, 2012).

From this vantage point we feel confident in making the provocative
assertion that Morrison's neglect of the politics of pedagogy is not uncommon. Sumner's (2006) article is indicative of this, as is even the
work of critics such as Sylvester (1999) and Kapoor (2004), who focus
on material content without addressing pedagogic processes and their
deep implications on the way in which students absorb normative
knowledge hierarchies. This lacuna echoes Heron's concern, noted
above, that self-reflexivity that focuses only on the "what" (privilege of
positionality) and not the "how" (the way power circulates) can in fact
deepen knowledge hierarchies. As Brookfield (2001) has noted, the way
in which educators mirror the material they are teaching – especially in

contexts critical of mainstream norms – has ramifications on the way in which students think of the world in new ways. He argues that educators that are not conscious of their own power dynamics in a course intending to question power can undermine the intentions of the course. This is clearly a difficult proposition, and is one that both of us work on continuously. We do not wish to give the impression that this is simple, and we are both sure that there are students out there who would say that we have each failed to walk this talk fully. Nonetheless, the critical hyper-reflexive process we both believe in helps to force us to work on this on an ongoing basis. At the same time, Apple and King (1983) illustrate how the very structure of schooling shapes what students learn – one of the reasons experiential learning is important as it allows not only for a different learning context but also a reflective space where students can deconstruct their previous classroom education and question some of the norms that frame it.[3]

Before turning to discuss the important position of experiential learning in Development Studies, we wish to recapitulate our main point in this section. While the recent reflexivity of Development Studies scholars and programs is to be applauded, there is a danger that much like the student who only reflects on his or her position of privilege, if DS merely reflects on its Eurocentric bias, without a deeper unpacking of the ways in which this bias is reinforced through pedagogic actions, the potential change to DS will only be superficial. We have found it is precisely in the experiential learning components of DS programs where this reflexivity can be deepened the most, and where a conscious pedagogic scaffolding approach can work with students to challenge Eurocentric thinking, and through this open up a space for thinking differently about social change.

Experiential Learning – Beyond Making It Work

Morrison (2004) underscores the importance of experiential learning in terms of DS curriculum. A quick survey of the members of the Consortium of Canadian University Programs in International Development Studies (CCUPIDS) suggests that this importance is reflected by most of these programs (http://www.idsnet.ca/about.html).[4] This importance is also reflected in Northern Ghana's University of Development Studies, where the third year of study is composed of practical learning in various contexts throughout the North, known as the Third Trimester Field Practical Programme (http://www.uds.edu.gh/history.php).

Despite this widespread emphasis, the outcomes of experiential learning in DS programs are in no way guaranteed (Sherraden, Lough, & McBride, 2008). It is largely based on this uncertainty – captured by Heron (2006) above – that the need to frame these experiences through reflective practices is largely accepted (cf. Epprecht, 2004; Heron, 2005; Morrison, 2004). Yet, it is debatable if these framing processes can be successful if there is disagreement over what these programs are intended to do. As Epprecht (2004) notes in his review of experiential overseas programs in DS contexts, there is tension between those focused on employable skills training and those intending to engender critical reflexivity. This variance is not surprising as there is a similar debate at the heart of experiential learning itself. As Weil and McGill (1989, p. 3) illustrate, there are four distinct, yet often overlapping "villages"[5] of experiential learning proponents: village one is focused on the connection between academic recognition of work/life experience and employment/professional body destinations; village two is focused on the ways experiential learning can change the "structure, purpose, and curricula" of educational programs; village three sees experiential learning as a means through which emancipatory social change and community action can be enacted; and, village four focuses on personal growth through the increase of self-awareness and effective group participation.

What we argue below is that, despite Epprecht's (2004) revelation that many of the Canadian DS experiential learning programs began with clear anti-capitalist intentions, contemporary experiential learning programs have largely grounded themselves in village one/ employability logics and village four/self-improvement and group contribution logics, largely silencing the village three/social change stream. These two prominent villages can be simplified to a dichotomy between employability or good (global) citizen outcomes – neither of which directly challenge the global capitalist status quo. We see this being a trend not only in Development Studies but across other areas as well. Ultimately, following Kincheloe (2000), we discuss below how this flattening of debate echoes representations of educational debates over the last century, and is bound up in classist and nationalist agendas. It is based on this analysis that we argue later in the paper for a reinsertion of status quo challenging elements into experiential learning approaches, especially if DS is to contribute to McMichael's call for an ethical form of social change.

Morrison's (2004) title is reflective of this dichotomy in experiential learning programs, as it suggests teaching and studying development can "make it work" – either lead to a job or to the success of the program. Interestingly, this double entendre upon the title is only lightly touched upon throughout the Morrison piece, and the conclusion suggests experiential learning is more important for critical thinking formation than it is for providing students an opportunity to develop skills for working in the agencies DS, according to Sumner (2006), trains students to join. Child and Manion (2004), in a study of Canadian DS graduate and undergraduate students, advance an interesting assertion that it is only when DS students leave DS programs, and not when they enter, that they are far more concerned with the employment potential of this interdiscipline – suggesting DS programs may be conveying that students "make" development "work," inadvertently or not. Certainly in some Canadian DS programs this message is clear from the outset. Saint Mary's International Development Studies Program, for instance, conveys a clear message about the employment potential of DS on its homepage:

> Our program of study will provide you with a solid education for employment in national, international, and civil society organizations for which a thorough understanding of local, regional, national and international development perspectives and policies is required. (http://www.smu.ca/academic/arts/ids/)

Sherraden, Lough, and McBride (2008, p. 414) show in their review of literature on international volunteer programs that "personal advancement" is a key outcome to volunteers, over concientization and its potentially decolonizing effects. In other contexts, the Association of Universities and Colleges of Canada (AUCC) has explicitly added a employable skills focus to its "Students for Development" program – an organization that explicitly funds DS students to undertake experiential learning in a location outside of Canada. While Tiessen (2007, p. 80) has noted the way the genesis of this program was rooted in "global citizenship to promote Canadian values abroad," the current program objectives also note a strong desire to "provide Canadian students with work experience abroad" that "complements their field of study and career goals" (AUCC, 2011, p. 1). This attention to career outcomes is a new facet of AUCC programming, and can be understood as being part of a more general realignment of the Canadian International Development Agency's (CIDA) objectives to the current Canadian Conservative government's globo-capitalist preoccupations.

This shift is indicative of a rising tension in experiential learning programs related to overseas placements in general. Simpson (2005), for instance, documents how in the UK going overseas to do volunteer work – previously identified with anti-establishment pretensions – has been turned into a neoliberal marketplace for professionalization. The "gap year," as it is called, is now a time to go overseas and work in an area with very little training to increase one's prospects back home. The ethics of using the Global South in particular as the receptacle for "experimentations ... free from qualifications" (Simpson, 2005, p. 465) is especially disturbing. One instance of this, promoted on an organization's website, describes a European volunteer (with no background in the health profession) assisting in operations and delivering babies in Ghana as part of her or his learning. Ignoring the fact that the UK has helped to contribute to health staff shortages in Ghana as a result of head hunting of nurses and doctors (Young, 2008), the lack of accountability of this exploding industry to "offer professional and CV advancement" is appalling (Simpson, 2005, p. 465). At the same time, Simpson (2004) has also shown that the other outcome often on offer in these types of learning programs – broadening ones understanding of the world and therefore reducing prejudice – is also problematically pedagogically pursued. She describes how these types of volunteer programs contribute to the reification of cultural senses of superiority – where young people from the Global North feel they have the right to go to locations in the Global South and "help" residents live better. This outcome runs very much counter to the "deepen[ed] understanding of other cultures and their own" that DS students can gain, according to Morrison (2004, p. 199), from experiential learning opportunities. However, the volunteer experiences Simpson documents are not taking place under the auspices of an educational institution. In fact, Simpson argues they are occurring as if "learning automatically occurs through travel" (Simpson, 2005, p. 461). She goes on to note that no reference to experiential learning scholarship is present within these programs, with its long tradition of scaffolding interpretations and critical thinking with experience. As we discuss further on, drawing on this scholarship, looking closely at what critical thinking means, and the ways in which self-reflexivity can dead-end in the simplified narrative of becoming a better person/citizen is necessary if we are to move past this dichotomy into the kinds of actions that can produce a more ethical dimension. Before turning to the discussion of reflection and critical thinking, it is important to note how much of this tension, between skills outcomes for work, and critical thinking for better citizens have been present in educational debates going back at least to the US public school debates of the late nineteenth and early twentieth century.

Kincheloe (2000), a leading figure in critical pedagogy (cf. Kincheloe, 2005) circles, has provided a historical account of what could be understood as the hidden curriculum of experiential/vocational education. In doing so, he documents the famous Snedden/Dewey debates of the 1920s where a popularized account of the dichotomy above draws some of its origins. On the one side of the debate is Snedden, drawing heavily on Taylorism to describe a public education reform where learning was to be linked with economic productivity. On the opposite side was Dewey who, according to popular representations, stood for the evolution of a democratic ethos – a morality of existence based on a learner-centred education that encouraged one and all to believe education could lead to a future of his or her own making. This debate was also taking place within a larger reformist agenda that saw the massive rise of public schools in the US, and a growing association between school and the creation of US national citizenship identity – one that invited the massive waves of immigrants to the US to reimagine themselves within the country's national narrative. The overall result of this reformist time period is the solidification of a two-tier public educational system, not only in the US but also in other Western contexts where academic and vocational outcomes were separated from one another, creating (or perhaps solidifying) a classist system that formed some students into well-educated citizens, and others into well-trained workers (Kincheloe, 1999, 2000). Yet, importantly for our discussion here, Kincheloe (2000) underscores how this popularized view of Dewey ignored how he worked hard to undermine this form of dualism and instead advocated an educational system that would produce students as comfortable with their hands as with their heads. It also ignores how Dewey saw the creation of this duality as a solidification of class formation – something his approach was designed to contest. Kincheloe (2000, 2005) further argues this dualism, so present in current western educational modelling, is predicated on the Cartesian subject, or the false hierarchical dichotomy between mind and body.

What is at stake in the current experiential learning context could appear on the surface as a realignment along the lines of the more complex version of Dewey's argument – the incorporation of hands-on experience in academic contexts. However, instead of a nuanced, class-conscious blurring of the value of both practical and theoretical knowledge, what has instead emerged in many experiential learning programs within universities (not just in Development Studies) is a recapitulation of the simplistic binary of employability versus citizenship – and not the "thick" version of global citizenship Cameron describes in chapter 2 of this volume. In a recent (2010) guide to study abroad experiences in the US, entitled "The Global Classroom," authors Lantis and DuPlaga argue that there are primarily vocational skill development and global citizenship reasons for engaging in learning abroad opportunities. Similarly, the rise of service learning programs on campuses across North America has been accompanied with these two programmatic justifications, largely ignoring contexts that challenge the status quo. In fact, in many cases, as arts programs (including social sciences and humanities) have come under increasing pressure from mainstream media outlets to justify their continued existence (cf. Cohen, 2009), service learning programs have surfaced as a way to "transfer" skills from the social science/humanities classroom to the workforce (Eyler & Giles, 1999). Even in examples such as Myers-Lipton (2008) and Wilson (2008), that do incorporate experiential learning in contexts that challenge the status quo, the logic used to frame this learning is civic engagement, and the outcomes pointed to with pride by Wilson (2008), for instance, are not that a women's shelter didn't get closed, but that students have found their way into employment with such not-for-profits as the Center for Community Solutions. Schratz and Walker (1999) further describe the hidden curriculum of service learning, where many of the assumptions that justify its existence remain unexamined, and therefore unquestioned. One of the unquestioned assumptions of service learning, according to the two authors, is similar to the dichotomy presented by Lantis and DuPlaga (2010), namely that the benefits of service learning are either in making a better-trained student or a more moral, socially engaged citizen-student. In navigating this hidden curriculum, Schratz and Walker (1999) echo the call for reflexivity to make these unstated outcomes apparent to students, community partners, and faculty alike. And yet, as we stated above, the nature of this reflexivity matters. Having noted the dangers of unexamined program intentions/educational outcomes, it is towards a more detailed discussion of reflexivity that we now turn.

Reflecting upon Reflexivity

Heron (2006, p. 7) argues, in the growing age of short-term placements (anything less than one year) – also arguably a response to neoliberal market trends – there is a strong necessity to frame students' experiences prior to departure through preparatory classes on such topics as "colonization, globalization, Third World debt, and identity and diversity and anti-oppressive practices." She also argues (2005, p. 347), drawing on Razack (1998) (also drawn on by Thomas and Chandrasekera in chapter 5 of this volume), that "a pivotal moment [in challenging the solidification of Northern superiority] lies in deconstructing, rather than simply de-briefing, students' understanding of their practical experience following their return." Epprecht (2004) notes that many Canadian Development Studies programs include a pre-departure and post-return debriefing for students engaging in placements overseas. He argues for the importance of these framing processes to include language lessons to encourage students to truly connect with local contexts – especially important in the current shift to shorter-term placements where language acquisition is not as possible. He also argues for the importance of emotional as well as intellectual support for what he calls the "re-entry" phase. This bookending of reflective pedagogical processes is echoed by others as well (cf. Morrison, 2004). Without diminishing the importance of this type of before and after approach to reflexivity, it nonetheless runs counter to much writing on experiential learning, as well as service learning, that notes the importance of ongoing rather than episodic reflective engagement. Fowler (2007), for instance, notes the importance of an ongoing action-reflection cycle for successful experiential learning. Schratz and Walker (1999, p. 50) delve further into this discussion, advocating for an engaged approach to reflective processes, where students "can talk about experience disconnected from the immediate need for action," and yet "do so with immediate implications for changes in action." This cyclical approach echoes Kolb's (1984) original reflective learning cycle. From a transformative learning perspective (cf. Mezirow, 1981, 1998) this ongoing reflective dialogue process makes it more likely that "critical incidents" (Schratz & Walker, 1999, p. 48), or what are called disorienting[6] dilemmas in the transformative learning literature, can be deconstructed in the post-incident period to avoid the cynicism and disconnection that both Epprecht (2004) and Heron (2011) note is a strong possibility in these programs. In addition, important to this approach is the notion that this reflective learning is cumulative, meaning that not only is it important to reflect after a disorienting dilemma occurs but also that to continue to do so helps to unpack its multiple meanings further. While some in the Development Studies field may argue that this dialogue-based reflective approach is possible only in service learning contexts where students are not thousands of kilometers away in their placement, Ash and Clayton (2009; see also Ash, Clayton, & Atkinson, 2005), have provided an important set of reflective tools to work with students regardless of where they are. They advocate for an evolving prompt-based method for deepening student critical questioning of themselves and of their surroundings. This approach to reflection allows for a conversation to emerge between instructor and student that gets at the particularities of the context and experience and is able to encourage students to delve into their own assumptions and biases in a cumulative and situation-based manner.

Both of us have used this cumulative, dialogue-based method with success in being able to draw out deep lines of questioning despite the short nature of the placement (less than a year, as Heron, 2011, defines it). In fact, we would both argue that (within reason) it is less the length of placements that can induce superficial or cynical conclusions in students, than it is the reflective process they are following. In our experience, the before and after model, which treats cross-cultural experiences as a sort of vacuum chamber one must prepare for, and decompress after, does not lead to the deepened action-reflection that experiential learning scholarship advocates (cf. Ash, Clayton, & Atkinson, 2005; Kolb, 1984; Boydell, 1976). Instead, Development Studies would do well to promote ongoing and cumulative reflective practices that do not separate contexts away (you reflect when you are in another culture) from contexts at home (no need to reflect on power and privilege here). The before and after approach not only perpetuates potential othering and exoticisation, but denies students the important realization that "everywhere is local for somebody" (Shiva, 2012). By reflecting on their own context with the same dialogue-based method, what can often appear as normal can be revealed as deeply embedded with power relations and ideological assumptions. Building a cumulative reflective process can then help students connect what they have seen in contexts not their own with those they think of as home, seeing how similar issues impact local change efforts, though in different ways.

This type of scaffolding of cumulative pedagogic dialogue moves distinctly away from notions that experiential learning in and of itself does the teaching, and rather situates this learning in a web of ongoing action-reflection processes that provide students not only an opportunity to continually deepen the reflections on experiences and their connections to change theories but also with an approach to what Kapoor (2004) calls hyper-reflexivity that they can continue to engage in as a lifelong learning strategy. Kapoor's call for hyper-reflexivity, which is drawn from the work of Spivak, is a detailed attempt to make Development Studies continuously more open and responsive to subaltern voices.

At the heart of this discussion, though, is the question of the intended outcome of this critical (hyper) reflection. Is this critical reflection merely a form of critical thinking designed to generate better citizens, better neighbours, better volunteers, or is it designed to generate a deep sense of reflexivity that is connected to action that is constantly engaged in challenging power relations and the status quo? As Brookfield (2000) has noted, not all critical thinking is the same, nor does it produce the same types of educational outcomes. While tracing the various traditions of critical thinking, he argues that a reflective practice that brings personal transformation into dialogue with societal transformation can respond to post-colonial and postmodern critiques of a unitary self, and of universal Eurocentric progress, without eschewing the potential impact of emancipatory ideals and their implications for ongoing struggles with power relations. The key to this form of reflexivity is its ongoing, always-evaluating process, but also its decidedly action-oriented stance. To be hyper-reflexive, in other words, should not mean to refuse to engage for fear of replicating power relations, but it should also not mean a naïve critical thinking that is simply about thinking of others, and being a good neighbour without thinking through why it is easier to enact this in some neighbourhoods than others as power relations are less palpable.

Yet, creating this ongoing critically hyper-reflective process is not the only ingredient necessary for deepened, and mutually beneficial placement processes that help students question themselves and the world without leading to disconnection, simplistic acceptance of privilege, or a desire to act in ways divorced of any analysis of power. Of equal importance is an attention to the placement contexts, especially from an ideological point of view.

It's Not Where You Go, It's the Struggle You Meet

"Why not have a class, say Sociology 306, be about enacting a factory take-over?"

> – Panel respondent at 2011conference of the Canadian Association for the Study of International Development (CASID)[7]

The problem with the two narratives of educational outcomes described above is that neither is interested in questioning the status quo. Whether students emerge from experiential learning as good global citizens – the "thin" type, as John Cameron puts it in chapter 2 of this volume – or good cogs in the market wheel, the ideological underpinning of globalized capitalism remains unchallenged in their minds – even if reflective processes have revealed its inequity. If it matters how we frame these learning processes in order to encourage questioning of the self and of the world, then certainly it matters how the outcomes of programs like these are being framed by the institutions in which they are housed. As a continuation of the kind of cumulative hyper-reflexivity promoted above, the very institution that students are embedded in should be looked at critically. Similarly, the types of placement opportunities that are available to students says much about what kind questions can be critically asked, and which ones are off limits. What if experiential learning processes were founded upon such direct action as the factory takeover proposed above? What if we placed ideological intentionality alongside some of the other values we use in determining our list of placement opportunities, such as organizational integrity, effectiveness, transparency, as well as the degree to which they can accommodate the student?[8] Ignoring social movements, or organizations that question the status quo, not only in their own country but more globally, as potential hosts for Development Studies students because more established, less critical NGOs have better infrastructure to support students is problematic on two fronts. While it may suit the growing risk aversion of universities, in the North and South, it (a) undermines what critical work students may have been exposed to that questions the power dynamics of different development actors (governments, aid agencies, and NGOs), and (b) normalizes these entities as the only organizations legitimately dealing in social change.

Epprecht (2004, p. 695) notes the danger of "bad local partners" that may be "corrupt, ineffective and/or downright harmful to development." He also notes that these traits are not reserved for local partners in the Global South alone, as Northern placement agencies can also display similar failings. At the same time, Heron's (2011) recent research also delves deeply into the question of reciprocity, looking at the kinds of benefits many host organizations in the Global South receive for being involved in these types of learning processes. She focuses especially on the burden placed upon these hosts, even where there are clear benefits for their involvement. Heron argues that Northern institutions, such as the universities that promote experiential learning abroad programs, must bear the ethical responsibility of recognizing this burden. At the same time, with the growing prevalence of these programs, this type of relationship needs to be understood as a form of globalization. While these points are useful to nuance the relationship between students, their sending institutions, and their hosts, for us an equally important point is the failure to include ideology (those who actively challenge capitalist globalization) in this matrix of analysis.

Schratz and Walker (1999) note that a major disconnect for students involved in service learning is between the agendas of their academic institutions and the agendas of their placement organization. This can create dissonance between the expectations of both in the mind of the student. In our experience, paying close attention to the stated and unstated agendas of host organizations/movements is as important as uncovering the hidden curriculum and assumptions of academic programs, like Development Studies. This is especially true in cross-cultural north-south contexts, where the impact of a Eurocentric neo-liberal form of globalization generates a series of funding and power relationships that can lead even the most altruistic of organizations into market-based relations.

There is a wealth of literature that documents the ways in which NGOs betray their stated social justice objectives. Kamat (2002), for instance, has shown how even pro-poor NGOs can replicate capitalist and colonial agendas through their responses to the underlying logic of funding – resulting in what Dip Kapoor (2005) calls the "taming of the grassroots." This is all the more so in NGOs that only try to legitimate their work to donors, and not to those pejoratively referred to as recipients or beneficiaries (Ndegwa, 1996). Ndegwa (1996) has described how important it is to differentiate between NGOs, noting how two organizations that may look very similar in intent reveal their ideological and ultimately on-the-ground alignment though the politics of their interventions. Hearn (2001) connects this nuanced analysis to Ghana, where we both work, and describes the uses and abuses of civil society –

perpetuated through multiple levels of co-optation. Barry-Shaw and Oja Jay (2012) provide a similar exposé on the ongoing co-optation and complicity of Canadian NGOs. We feel that – given these critiques – NGO placements need to be scrutinized as sources of stabilizing capitalist power, rather than challenging the status quo.

It is into this often murky world that development studies students wade – assessing as they go the match between the stated and real NGO agenda and the match between their values and those of the organizations. This murky reality is often very much in contrast to the image of humanitarian agencies such as NGOs that inexperienced students often hold, believing they are always there for the greater good. At the same time, Development Studies students who have been exposed to some of these critiques also sometimes enter their internships with the intention of uncovering the co-opted side of their placement organization. This intention is just as problematic and ultimately neoliberal in purpose as that of a two-faced NGO because it reifies a false objectivity that ignores Canadian student culpability in enacting global power relations.

We have experienced both sides of this double-edged sword, where placement organizations have taken advantage of student interns to present themselves as being well connected, and have used students to help procure community resources – or to legitimate agendas that are detrimental to community life. At the same time, we have also witnessed the hierarchical version of global citizen in action, where Canadian students take it upon themselves to be global watchdogs of their placement organization – not something normally done by their Ghanaian colleagues. Furthermore, we noted how some placement NGOs use the apparent employable skills of both Ghanaian and Canadian interns to undermine their own staff's labour demands, and to solicit funding based on the temporary presence of a student with a particular skill set. In essence, the lesson we have drawn from these various experiences is that nothing can be taken for granted in a cross-cultural experiential learning opportunity such as a work placement in a NGO working on development issues in the Global South (although we would argue that the simplistic analysis that it is better therefore to gain this experience in one's home country is no defence against these problems).

With this realization in mind, we have been working on approaches to building experiential learning relationships that move away from the legitimating discourses of employability on the one side, and global citizenship on the other side, while at the same time squarely contending with the problematics of hidden placement NGO agendas. These approaches are not a cure-all but are rather an outgrowth of our own learning. Along these lines, we have, in recent years, endeavoured to search for placement opportunities that are much more grounded in people's struggles than those with a more mercantile or reformist agenda. We have written about the outcomes of these approaches tangentially (Agyeyomah & Langdon, 2009; Agyeyomah, Langdon, & Butler, 2010) where students have worked closely with a bonesetter in Northern Ghana to challenge allopathic medicine. We have also been placing students with a community radio station in Southern Ghana that is part of a movement to protect an artisanal salt production way of life, in the face of government and corporate plans for expropriation of the salt resource (cf. Langdon, 2011). Both of these examples provide students with an opportunity to witness the very difficult process of negotiating contested terrain of actual struggles, rather than taking part in an externally derived and funded programmatic intervention. The conversations and reflections that come out of this space of real engagement are much more complex than those emerging from enactments of development programming. For instance, students begin to actively unpack how certain ideological stances taken by these organizations/movements have implications on struggles, and see that there is much more grey to pushing an agenda derived from a given marginalized community than there is in the linear simplicity of a development project. Students often also deeply question their own roles in this struggle, as well as the framing process that has led them to this placement. For instance, one student recently wrote a reflection on the aftermath of a demonstration she witnessed, where an official knocked over placards the demonstrators had placed around an exhibition that explained their struggle and demands:

> Over the summer I have felt increasingly annoyed with having to worry about the overarching problems stemming from the "outsider coming in to help" perceptions. I kept wondering when the consequences of development initiatives in our past would stop affecting what we do in the present, when we could stop worrying about the "first world" coming to "save" the "third world" stereotypes and get back to people helping each other no matter what "world." Then I realized it's not about that, it's about everyone having different roles to play and at that moment outwardly standing in the face of opposition wasn't my place but it was the place of the women of Ada. They are the ones directly affected by the Songor [salt] situation and they know how to operate appropriately in the Ghanaian

context, thus they did the same thing I wanted to do but in a more indirect way. Instead of picking the placards back up in a confrontational way, which may have shut the whole exhibition down, they rather stood up and continued the walk through the story of the Songor lagoon depicted on the canvas regardless of who the audience was and what they thought.[9]

Here, the Canadian student[10] involved is clearly working through the difficult balance of a solidarity approach, or what Thomas and Chandrasekera (chapter 5) describe as becoming an authentic ally, where we collectively struggle to change global inequity and challenge the capitalist status quo, but where we have different roles to play in this struggle – an approach that helps mitigate the saviour motif in much thin global citizenship thinking. This questioning is healthy, and allows for a fruitful dialogue on the nature of solidarity rather than a banal rehearsal of global citizenship versus acquiring skills discussion. In the end, the key organizing difference that putting ideology back into these discussions leads to is that these situations introduce students to contexts where people are struggling, but where they are doing so based on their own and not an external agenda; this often makes students feel less sure of the role they can play in this context, but by the end of the experience they begin to see how much they have learned in unstated and undefined ways – precisely because so much of the work in contexts like this is ambiguous and doesn't have easy answers. This learning is also clearly provoked and deepened through ongoing prompt-based reflexive dialogue, which is exemplified by the reflection above. The implications that often come with contesting the status quo are important to experience first hand – and they make for a much more engaged learning environment as a result, where people push beyond skills and instead learn to develop solidarity with those that are struggling. This also helps to unpack the stigma associated with dissent, and sheds light on ongoing neoliberal globalized attempts to criminalize it. We are not alone in advocating for a more overtly activist experiential learning approach, as both Myers-Lipton (2008) and Wilson (2008) illustrate. Robert Huish, one of the editors of this volume, has also been squarely challenging the removal of dissent in his Development Studies course on activism in practice.[11] We are, however, conscious of balancing the exposure of students to dangers they may not understand, which is an important aspect of discussions with host organizations/movements, and a further important layer of the selection process we are constantly engaged in.

Conclusion

These then become the two concluding thoughts we wish to advance for broader debate: (1) DS experiential learning processes need to incorporate pedagogical scaffolding within the placement process – if for no other reason than the growing reality that placements are shorter, and therefore need more provocative dialogue to push past mere remarks on positionality. In addition, key to this is a recognition of the multiple outcomes of reflective processes and the need to support students to not only transform themselves, but to take critically hyper-reflexive actions in our world; and (2) DS placement processes need to choose between supporting the status quo or destabilizing it, and if those designing them truly want a more equal and ethical world, the latter is necessary. This means incorporating the ideological position of organizations – and the practical manifestations of this ideology – into decisions about placement opportunities, even though this may create more risk for all involved. Given the many issues facing the world today, our cumulative experience tells the two of us that we need experiential learning opportunities that demonstrate how people are engaging in active struggles to take charge of their own lives and realities. This experience cannot only foster a critical hyper-reflexive activist spirit but it must also build bridges between struggles founded on solidarity rather than charity.

NOTES

1 Neither one of us believes these experiences have to be in a context other than the one we know, as we have both witnessed how students experience disorienting dilemmas in places they come from/know with just as profound learning impacts than they do in places they have never been to before.

2 We have both been involved in the Trent in Ghana program since its inception in 1997. This program sees Canadian and Ghanaian students spend an academic year engaged in intensive academic classes and then internships focused on social change in Ghana. Contrary to Epprecht's (2004) interpretation, the program is not supervised by an on-the-spot Trent Faculty member – a Canadian non-academic coordinator handles logistics of the program, while Ghanaian coordinators handle the academics (a fine example of partnership in action). Coleman, for instance, has,

since the program's beginnings, been the main organizer of the Northern Ghanaian component of the course, entitled "Local Dynamics of Change"; as well, he continues to play a key role in the establishment of student placements, especially in the North. Jon was first a student in the maiden year of the program, but later took on the role of non-academic coordinator from 2001 to 2003. During this time he also taught one of the courses – something he continued his involvement with until 2005, even after finishing his role as logistics coordinator. In his capacity as Assistant Professor at St. Francis Xavier, Jon now supervises the experiential learning program of the Development Studies program – many of whose placements take place in Ghana.

3 In our experience in the Trent program, both of us heard the constant refrain from students that this learning process taught them more than their entire classroom education. The sense of the way classroom learning was being re-evaluated also surfaced in qualitative interviews conducted with Trent In Ghana (TIG) students at the midpoint and closing days of the 2004 program (Langdon, 2004).

4 I think it is important to note here, and where we draw from Saint Mary's website below, that DS programs may well be responding to institutional pressures to make their programs more "marketable." But, as Foucault (1980) reminds us, it is precisely through these types of institutional utterances that discourse is formed, with its very real effects on people through biopower.

5 Weil and McGill (1989) use the image of villages to capture the various different uses of experiential learning in adult education, as they suggest a relationship between those in each area, but that people can also move back and forth between villages. Saddington (1998) added that the framework of educational practice connects with these villages in different ways, where a progressive framework connects with villages 1 and 2, a humanist framework with 1 and 4, and a radical framework with village 3.

6 We both feel this terminology is much more productive, and less othering than the tired notion of culture shock. Not only does it include an understanding of disorientation through experiences in one's own contexts, it also includes emotional disorientation that can spark the transformation of one's worldview. This approach also builds bridges, in our experience, between Ghanaian and Canadian students that otherwise would not exist in a "culture shock" model.

7 Ironically, Myers-Lipton (2008) actually has a service learning class called Sociology 164 that engages in various acts of radical activism.

8 See Epprecht (2004) for a useful list of placement qualities.
9 Personal communication with anonymous student. Used with permission.
10 There are three Ghanaian young people who are also involved in this process, and who – despite being from the area – have also reflected upon the way information about this struggle was never shared with them, and that it is only with this experiential learning opportunity that they have come to understand this struggle. They are now committed to supporting the movement through radio broadcasts. One of them has even created a radio drama on the community radio station that depicts the struggle to increase popular interest.
11 Huish spoke about this course at the 2012 Youth Activism Conference. His speech is available as a podcast here: http://soundcloud.com/youth-activism-conference/bob-huish-yac-discussion

REFERENCES

Adichie, C.N. (2009). *The danger of the single story*. TED Talks [video file]. Retrieved from http://blog.ted.com/2009/10/07/the_danger_of_a/

Agyeyomah, C., & Langdon, J. (2009). Building bridges from broken bones: Traditional bonesetters and health choices in Northern Ghana. In J. Langdon (Ed.), *Indigenous knowledges, development and education* (pp. 135–147). Rotterdam: Sense Publisher.

Agyeyomah, C., Langdon, J., & Butler, R. (2010). "To die is honey, and to live is salt": Indigenous epistemologies of wellness in Northern Ghana and the threat of institutionalized containment. In D. Kapoor & E. Shizha (Eds.), *Indigenous knowledge and learning in Asia/Pacific and Africa perspectives on development, education, and culture* (pp. 245–264). New York: Palgrave Macmillan.

Angeles, L. (2004). New issues, new perspectives: Implications for international development studies. *Canadian Journal of Development Studies, 25*(1), 61–80. http://dx.doi.org/10.1080/02255189.2004.9668960

Apple, M. (2004). *Ideology and curriculum* (3rd ed.). New York: Routledge.

Apple, M., & King, N. (1983). What schools teach. In H. Giroux & D. Purpel (Eds.), *The hidden curriculum and moral education* (pp. 82–99). Berkeley, CA: McCutchan Publishing Corporation.

Ash, S.L., & Clayton, P.H. (2009). Generating, deepening, and documenting learning: The power of critical reflection in applied learning. *Journal of Applied Learning in Higher Education, 1*(1), 25–48.

Ash, S.L., Clayton, P.H., & Atkinson, M.P. (2005). Integrating reflection and assessment to capture and improve student learning. *Michigan Journal of Community Service Learning*, 11(2), 49–60.

AUCC. (2011). *Students for development program brochure, 2011–2015*. Ottawa: Association of University and Colleges of Canada.

Barry-Shaw, N., & Oja Jay, D. (2012). *Paved with good intentions: Canada's development NGOs from idealism to imperialism*. Halifax: Fernwood.

Bowles, P. (2004). International development studies in Canada. *Canadian Journal of Development Studies*, 25(1), 9–13. http://dx.doi.org/10.1080/02255189.2004.9668956

Boydell, T. (1976). *Experiential learning*. Manchester: Manchester Monographs.

Brookfield, S. (2000). The concept of critically reflective practice. In A. Wilson & E. Hayes (Eds.), *Handbook of adult and continuing education* (pp. 33–49). San Francisco: Jossey-Bass.

Brookfield, S. (2001). Unmasking power: Foucault and adult learning. *Canadian Journal for the Study of Adult Education*, 15(1), 1–23.

Bunch, C. (1987). *Passionate politics: Feminist theory in action*. New York: St. Martin's Press.

Cavanagh, J., & Mander, J. (2004). *Alternatives to economic globalization: A better world is possible* (2nd ed.). San Francisco: Berrett-Koehler Publishers.

Chamberlin, J.E. (2003). *If this is your land where are your stories: Finding common ground*. Toronto: Alfred A. Knopf Canada.

Child, K., & Manion, C. (2004). A survey of upper-year students in international development studies. *Canadian Journal of Development Studies*, 25(1), 167–186. http://dx.doi.org/10.1080/02255189.2004.9668965

Cohen, P. (2009, Feb 24). In tough times, humanities must justify their existence. *New York Times*. Retrieved from http://www.nytimes.com/2009/02/25/books/25human.html?pagewanted=all

Dei, G., & Simmons, M. (2009). The indigenous as a site of decolonizing knowledge for conventional development and the link with education: The African case. In J. Langdon (Ed.), *Indigenous knowledges, development and education* (pp. 15–36). Rotterdam: Sense Publisher.

Edwards, M. (1989). The irrelevance of development studies. *Third World Quarterly* 11(1), 116–135.

Edwards, M. (2002). Is there a "future positive" for development studies? *Journal of International Development*, 14(6), 737–741. http://dx.doi.org/10.1002/jid.920

Epprecht, M. (2004). Work-study abroad courses in International Development Studies: Some ethical and pedagogical issues. *Canadian Journal of*

Development Studies, 25(4), 687–706. http://dx.doi.org/10.1080/ 02255189.2004.9669009

Escobar, A. (1995). *Encountering development: The making and unmaking of the third world*. Princeton: Princeton University Press.

Eyler, J., & Giles, D.E., Jr. (1999). *Where's the learning in service-learning?* San Francisco: Jossey-Bass.

Ferguson, J. (1990). *Anti-politics machine: Development, depoliticization, and bureaucratic power in Lesotho*. Cambridge, UK: Cambridge University Press.

Foucault, M. (1972). *Archeology of knowledge*. New York: Routledge.

Foucault, M. (1980). *Power/knowledge: Selected interviews and other writing*. New York: Pantheon Books.

Fowler, J. (2007, May). Experiential learning and its facilitation. *Nurse Education Today*, 28(4), 427–433. http://dx.doi.org/10.1016/j.nedt.2007.07.007 Medline:17881093

Harriss, J. (1999). The DSA at twenty-one: A critical celebration of development studies. *Journal of International Development*, 11(4), 497–501. http://dx.doi.org/ 10.1002/(SICI)1099-1328(199906)11:4<497::AID-JID604>3.0.CO;2-I

Hearn, J. (2001). The 'uses and abuses' of civil society in Africa. *Review of African Political Economy*, 28(87), 43–53. http://dx.doi. org/10.1080/03056240108704502

Heron, B. (2005). Self-reflection in critical social work practice: Subjectivity and the possibility of resistance. *Reflective Practice*, 6(3), 341–351. http:// dx.doi.org/10.1080/14623940500220095

Heron, B. (2006). Critically considering international social work practica. *Critical Social Work*, 7(2). http://www1.uwindsor.ca/criticalsocialwork/ critically-considering-international-social-work-practica

Heron, B. (2011). Challenging indifference to extreme poverty: Considering southern perspectives on global citizenship and change. *Ethics and Economics*, 8(1), 109–119.

Kamat, S. (2002). *Development and hegemony: NGOs and the state in India*. Oxford: Oxford University Press.

Kanbur, R. (2002). Economics, social science and development. *World Development*, 30(3), 477–486. http://dx.doi.org/10.1016/S0305-750X(01)00117-6

Kapoor, D. (2005). NGO partnerships and the taming of the grassroots in rural India. *Development in Practice*, 15(2), 210–215. http://dx.doi.org/10.1080/ 09614520500041864

Kapoor, I. (2004). Hyper-reflexive development? Spivak on representing the third world 'other'. *Third World Quarterly*, 25(4), 627–647. http://dx.doi.org/ 10.1080/01436590410001678898

Kincheloe, J.L. (1999). *How do we tell the workers? The socio-economic foundations of work and vocational education.* Boulder, CO: Westview.

Kincheloe, J.L. (2000). *Toil and trouble: Good work, smart workers, and the integration of academic and vocational education.* New York: Peter Lang.

Kincheloe, J.L. (2005). *Critical pedagogy.* Rotterdam: Sense.

Kothari, U. (Ed.). (2005). *A radical history of development studies: Individuals, institutions and ideologies.* London: Zed Books.

Kolb, D. (1984). *Experiential learning – Experience as the source of learning and development.* New Jersey: Prentice-Hall.

Langdon, J. (2004). Report on experiential learning and student reflections in Trent-in-Ghana program. Tamale, Ghana: Institute for Policy Alternatives.

Langdon, J. (2009). Reframing development studies: Towards an IDS teaching praxis informed by Indigenous knowledges. In J. Langdon (Ed.), *Indigenous knowledges, development and education* (pp. 37–58). Rotterdam: Sense Publisher.

Langdon, J. (2011). Social movement learning in Ghana: Communal defense of resources. In D. Kapoor (Ed.), *Critical perspectives on neoliberal globalization, development and education in Africa and Asia/Pacific* (pp. 153–170). Rotterdam: Sense. http://dx.doi.org/10.1007/978-94-6091-561-1_10

Lantis, J., & DuPlaga, J. (2010). *The global classroom: An essential guide to study abroad.* Boulder, CO: Paradigm Publishers.

Loxley, J. (2004). What is distinctive about international development studies? *Canadian Journal of Development Studies, 25*(1), 25–38. http://dx.doi.org/10.1080/02255189.2004.9668958

McMichael, P. (2009). *Development and social change* (4th ed.). Thousand Oaks, CA: Pine Forge Press.

Mezirow, J. (1981). A critical theory of adult learning and education. *Adult Education, 32*(1), 3–24. http://dx.doi.org/10.1177/074171368103200101

Mezirow, J. (1998). On critical reflection. *Adult Education Quarterly, 48*(3), 185–198. http://dx.doi.org/10.1177/074171369804800305

Millar, D., Haverkort, B., & Apusigah, A. (2012). *Learning together: Developing inclusive knowledges and sciences towards operational methods for endogenous research, education and development.* Amsterdam: COMPAS Network.

Morrison, D. (2004). Teaching and studying development: Making it work. *Canadian Journal of Development Studies, 25*(1), 187–200. http://dx.doi.org/10.1080/02255189.2004.9668966

Myers-Lipton, S. (2008). Using service learning to change social structure: The Gulf Coast Civic Works Project. In S.C. Tannenbaum (Ed.), *Research, advocacy and political engagement* (pp. 144–157). Virginia: Stylus.

Ndegwa, S.N. (1996). *The two faces of civil society*. Bloomfield, CT: Kumarian Press.

Nef, J. (2004). International development studies and ethical dilemmas in academia. *Canadian Journal of Development Studies, 25*(1), 81–100. http://dx.doi.org/10.1080/02255189.2004.9668961

Olukoshi, Adebayo. (2004). The interactions of the United Nations with the African Research Community. Paper presented at the 40th Anniversary Conference of the United Nations Research Institute for Social Development (UNRISD), Social Knowledge and International Policy Making: Exploring the Linkages, Geneva, 20–21 April. Retrieved from http://www.tni.org/sites/www.tni.org/archives/africa-docs/olukoshi.pdf

Parpart, J., & Veltmeyer, H. (2004). The development project in theory and practice: A review of its shifting dynamics. *Canadian Journal of Development Studies, 25*(1), 39–59. http://dx.doi.org/10.1080/02255189.2004.9668959

Razack, S. (1998). *Looking white people in the eye: Gender, race, and culture in courtrooms and classrooms*. Toronto: University of Toronto Press.

Rist, G. 1997. *The history of development: From Western origin to global faith*. London: Zed Press.

Saddington, J.A. (1998). Exploring the roots and branches of experiential learning. Paper presented at the Sixth International Conference on Experiential Learning, Tampere, Finland, July.

Schratz, M., & Walker, H. (1999). Service learning as education: Learning from the experience of experience. In K. Weigert & R. Crews (Eds.), *Teaching for justice: Concepts and models for service learning in peace studies* (pp. 33–56). Washington, DC: American Association of Higher Education.

Simpson, K. (2005). Dropping Out or Signing Up? The Professionalisation of Youth Travel. *Antipode, 37*(3), 447–469. http://dx.doi.org/10.1111/j.0066-4812.2005.00506.x

Simpson, K. (2004). "Doing development": The gap year, volunteer-tourists and a popular practice of development. *Journal of International Development, 16*(5), 681–692. http://dx.doi.org/10.1002/jid.1120

Sherraden, M.S., Lough, B., & McBride, A.M. (2008). Effects of international volunteering and service: Individual and institutional predictors. *Voluntas, 19*(4), 395–421. http://dx.doi.org/10.1007/s11266-008-9072-x

Shiva, V. (2012). *Just food* [video file]. Retrieved from http://www.youtube.com/watch?v=4WW_XK47DNc

Stiglitz, J. (2002). *Globalization and its discontents*. New York: Norton.

Sumner, A. (2006). What is development studies? *Development in Practice, 16*(6), 644–650. http://dx.doi.org/10.1080/09614520600958363

Sylvester, C. (1999). Development studies and postcolonial studies: Disparate tales of the 'Third World'. *Third World Quarterly, 20*(4), 703–721. http://dx.doi.org/10.1080/01436599913514

Tiessen, R. (2007). Educating global citizens? Canadian foreign policy and youth study/volunteer. *Canadian Foreign Policy, 14*(1), 77–84. http://dx.doi.org/10.1080/11926422.2007.9673453

Weil, S., & McGill, I. (1989). *Making sense of experiential learning: Diversity in theory and practice.* Bukingham, England: SRHE and The Open University Press.

Wilson, N. (2008). The politics of service learning in introduction to Women's Studies. In S.C. Tannenbaum (Ed.), *Research, advocacy and political engagement* (pp. 128–143). Virginia: Stylus.

Young, A. (2008). *Brain drain in Ghana* [blog post article]. Retrieved from http://davostoseattle.wordpress.com/2008/09/21/from-our-own-correspondent-brain-drain-in-ghana/

Willinsky, J. (1998). *Learning to divide the world: Education at empire's end.* Minneapolis, MN: University of Minnesota Press.

4 Career Aspirations and Experiential Learning Abroad: Perspectives from Canadian Youth on Short-Term Placements

REBECCA TIESSEN

Introduction

The significance of experiential learning as an important educational tool for linking theory and practice is well articulated in chapter 2 by Langdon and Agyeyomah. The authors of chapter 2 draw our attention to the "employability logics" posed in relation to "good global citizen outcomes" neither of which, they argue, "challenge the global capitalist status quo." This is a trend the authors have observed in Development Studies programs and other fields. Nonetheless, experiential learning is heralded as an important educational tool for linking theory and practice in both academic institutions and volunteer sending programs. As a result, opportunities to volunteer in international contexts, particularly in the Global South, are widely used to prepare students for their careers by offering skills development and practicum placements. In this chapter, I provide empirical evidence to support some of the arguments made in chapter 1 by Cameron and chapter 2 by Langdon and Agyeyomah in relation to "thick" and "thin" global citizenship and the role that international experiential learning plays in the context of skills training and/or global understanding, solidarity, and community-based action.

A starting point for this research is the argument that we know little about the motivations for – and benefits of – international experiential learning in the context of cross-cultural understanding, solidarity, and/ or the pursuit of career goals, and even less about how these international experiences have influenced career choices and political action, and to what end. In this chapter I examine the relationship between international experiential learning and career aspirations for young

Canadians aged 18–30. To do so, I examine the findings from research I carried out between 2007 and 2011 with 100 youth in Canada who participated in in-depth qualitative interviews as part of a broader international development research-centre funded study on "Creating Global Citizens: The Impact of Learning/Volunteer Abroad Programs." Specifically, in this chapter I examine the ranking of motivations for travelling to the Global South on international experiential learning programs. The two most common motivations identified by the participants in this study for participation in learning/volunteer abroad programs included: (1) cross-cultural understanding, and (2) to test an academic background or career goal.

In total, 34 per cent of the study participants considered cross-cultural understanding to be their main motivation for participating in international experiential learning. The narratives that corresponded with this reflection demonstrate, however, a very strong link between the value of cross-cultural understanding in the context of finding employment. Cross-cultural understanding was described by the study participants as a skill that was learned as a result of international experiential learning and a skill that could be documented on their résumés. The second most common motivation expressed by the youth was the desire to test an academic background or career choice. The study concluded that 32 per cent of the participants considered that testing an academic background or career choice was their main motivation for participation in learning/volunteer abroad programs. To a great extent, this motivation overlapped with the desire for cross-cultural understanding when it is linked to employability as noted above. For the motivation of testing an academic or career choice, the responses included references to key skills needed for finding work in international development or other career fields such as medicine, engineering, etc. As one of the participants noted: "I think testing whether or not this was a career that I wanted and testing how my education background would transfer into a career and into a work situation" were key motivations.

Over the course of the interview, we asked the participants to reflect on whether their learning/volunteer abroad experience did have an impact on their career goals. The majority of participants (roughly three-quarters) said that it did, with most of those participants indicating that the experience had a positive impact on their career goals. The themes that emerge from these discussions include the professional rewards of learning/volunteering abroad, skills learned, desire for additional learning (usually the pursuit of a graduate degree), and a

commitment to work involving helping others. For many of the participants, the learn/volunteer abroad program served as a litmus test for
their career choices, enabling them to decide if they want to continue a
career in international work or pursue different and/or Canadian-
based poverty-related work. Almost all respondents agreed that their
overseas experience has helped or will help them find employment.
The findings presented in this chapter are examined in relation to other
studies documenting the career aspirations of youth who volunteer
abroad (see Lough, McBride, & Sherraden, 2009; Mohajeri Norris &
Gillespie, 2009). The findings resonate with scholarly contributions to
the field of post-colonial studies on travel/volunteer/study abroad
(see Baaz, 2005; Heron, 2007; Simpson, 2005) in which ethical implications, power dynamics, and the general inequitable nature of international learning/volunteer programs are characterized by Northern
sojourners travelling to the Global South to test an academic career
choice or gain skills for the purpose of finding employment.

In Canada we are seeing a growing trend towards international travel
to the Global South as part of, or a continuation of, the educational experience. This growth reflects broader international trends. The expansion of international volunteering and learning abroad programs can
be observed in terms of the numbers of volunteers but also the growth
in organizations providing such opportunities (McBride & Sherraden,
2007; Plewes & Stuart, 2007). Analysing learning/volunteer abroad
programs is fraught with challenges not the least of which is account-
ing for diverse programs each with different preparations, orientations,
support, and debriefing. Add to this challenge the uniqueness of each
individual and their diverse attributes, skills, knowledge, and capabilities, and it is difficult to make sweeping generalizations about volun-
teer/learn abroad programs. However, research that has documented
both qualitative and quantitative findings provides insights into trends
and common themes. The study presented here provides insights into
the career aspirations of youth from across Canada and from diverse
backgrounds.

Career-Driven Motivations and Testing Academic Choices

In a study conducted by Lough, McBride, and Sherraden (2009), the
authors found that participants considered their international volunteering experience to be instrumental in changing their life plans and
helped to define educational and career objectives. The participants in

Lough, McBride, and Sherraden's study noted that the international volunteer experience shaped what they considered to be their "ideal career path." International experiential learning can also serve as a "catalyst to selecting future academic, volunteer, or employment paths" (Pires, 2000, p. 39). The study conducted by Pires demonstrates that American students who participated in study abroad programs in Africa often returned to the United States with a "strong desire to pursue some kind of further involvement with the continent" (Pires, 2000, p. 42). The participants in this study often found work volunteering with organizations such as Peace Corps or other non-governmental organizations that would contribute to their skills building.

Another study involving a survey, conducted by the Institute for the International Education of Students (IES), involved a total of 3,723 participants out of more than 17,000 alumni who participated in the Institute's study abroad program between 1950 and 1999. The goal of the study was to examine the long-term impact of study abroad programs in relation to additional academic pursuits, career choices, language skills, and personal development. The study found that "of those who participated in an internship or field experience while abroad, the majority reported that the international work-related experience assisted them in their careers" and that "48% reported working or volunteering in an international capacity at some point since college" (Mohajeri Norris & Gillespie, 2009, p. 386). The authors conclude:

> Given that study abroad affected the career choices of nearly two thirds of respondents and half of respondents developed careers with global aspects, the longitudinal data from the IES alumni survey clearly indicate the effect of study abroad decisions on future career development. The findings are a useful resource for professionals and faculty advising students on specific program elements to select when shaping their study abroad experience. (Mohajeri Norris & Gillespie, 2009, p. 394)

Overall, the authors of this report found that 77 per cent of respondents said they "acquired skills abroad that influenced their career path, and 62 per cent credited studying abroad with igniting an interest in a career direction they pursued following their IES program" (Mohajeri Norris & Gillespie, 2009, p. 394).

In spite of a growing body of literature on learning/volunteer abroad programs. We know little about the impact of these programs on career development, in part because few studies have been longitudinal in nature, tracking career progression of participants in learning/volunteer abroad programs. However, several authors have documented that students who go overseas do so for the purpose of career development (Hannigan, 2001). Conclusions drawn by Hannigan (2001) suggest that practical work experiences abroad do help students to become more clear about their career goals (Hannigan, 2001).

A study conducted by the American Council on Education involved a survey with 500 high school seniors planning to attend university. "More than 60% reported that they were interested in international education to gain career-related experiences" (Mohajeri Norris & Gillespie, 2009). Sherraden, Lough, and McBride (2008) have argued that international volunteer and learning opportunities provide students with knowledge, skills and experience that can prepare them for living and working in the knowledge-based economy. The development of skills, particularly "higher order" skills is correlated to increased income and is linked to employability (Powell & Bratović, 2007). The opportunities generated through learn/volunteer abroad programs are believed to broaden horizons and offer opportunities to explore potential careers. Previous research suggests international service increases volunteers' skills and ultimately employment and earning potential. The majority of volunteer alumni agreed with this assertion. Findings, however, differed considerably by program (Lough, McBride, & Sherraden, 2009).

In a study by Roschelle, Turpin, and Elias (2000), the authors found that students bring unique skills to their service learning placements. The skills became essential to the function of the organizations. This study highlighted the skills as the ideals of social justice and multiculturalism which they are exposed to through the general education curriculum at the University of San Francisco – a Jesuit school. The students "acquire scholarly tools including critical thinking, the ability to distinguish between various political analyses and the policies they foster, the ability to analyze individual-level to structural problems, knowledge of various social science methodologies to employ in their work, and participatory research and program evaluation techniques" (p. 843; see also Desrosiers & Thomson, chapter 7). It is important to recognize that most people engaged in their studies are concerned with the employment potential and this is true of international development studies students as well (Child & Manion, 2004).

Experiential learning programs may be a way to even further "test" a career choice for youth graduating from academic programs but as Langdon and Agyeyomah (chapter 3 in this volume) have argued, "experiential learning is more important for critical thinking formation, than it is for providing students an opportunity to develop skills for working in the agencies of IDS." As such, development studies programs may be preparing students for some forms of employment but not for broader learning and reflection on international development more generally. Simpson also addresses these concerns in her earlier work in 2005, where she notes that gap year programs are more about increasing one's prospects at home (Simpson, 2005). While Langdon and Agyeyomah (chapter 3) address these issues in greater detail and with more critical engagement in this book, I provide some empirical findings from research with Canadian youth.

Researching the Motivations of Career Aspirations

The research findings presented here are part of a larger five-year study funded by IDRC.[1] The study consists of interviews with young Canadians (aged 18–30) who have recently (within the last 3–12 months) returned to Canada after spending three to six months on an internship, volunteer placement, or practicum placement in a developing country. The interviews were carried out over the phone and took between one to three hours to complete. The sample for this paper consists of 100 interviews with returned volunteers: 80 women and 20 men. The interviews took place between January 2007 and November 2010. Our sample included students who were taking part in practicum placements or volunteering abroad for credit as well as youth who had graduated and were volunteering with CIDA or non-governmental organizations. International service learning is specific to students but it is important to expand this group because the international volunteer placement is frequently seen as an extension of academic studies and often a required step before beginning a career or before starting graduate studies.

Youth Perspectives

When the research participants for this study were asked if their experiences abroad affected their career goals and plans, the majority said that yes, they had. Only a small percentage (twelve individuals) indicated that the experiences abroad did not affect their career goals; in part, because they already had clear goals in mind that their experiences abroad had solidified. The rest of the participants (6 per cent) were undecided.

The responses need to be understood, however, by dividing the responses into those who felt their experiences abroad affected their career goals negatively or positively. In total 70 participants (60 women and 10 men) said that the international experience had a positive impact on their career goals. As one participant noted: "I feel really committed now to using my background and skills that I have to helping people receive and in India especially." However, 28 individuals (21 women and 7 men) said that the experience abroad had a negative impact on their professional and career goals. For example, Alice said: "No … I don't see myself wanting to work abroad anytime soon."

The themes emerging from these responses included those who saw the experience abroad as professionally positive and had confirmed a path participants have already set out on in terms of a development-related career internationally and in Canada, a desire to learn more, and learning new specific tasks/skills (cemented, critical/questioning, refocus, confidence, affirmed, skills, deeper understanding, language, etc.). Irene noted:

Yes … I think for my career it has made me realize what a good job really is and … I don't have to get paid a lot of money because I feel now that I can survive and enjoy and thrive on a lot less money than I probably would have wanted to make at some point in my life … and so that has influenced my career goals. I'm still very much interested in working in the environmental field like I was before, but also I'm trying to make a more, bring in more of a community aspect and, like I said, kind of make … the social justice aspect into that and not just thinking about, you know, saving the ecosystem, but saving people who enjoy the ecosystem, just to be very simplistic and … yeah, it definitely influenced my interests or my career goals.

The participants talked about the skills that are learned while abroad as contributing to human capital. The theory of human capital is premised on the argument that knowledge, skills, education, and learning opportunities can be exchanged for increased opportunities, earnings, power, and status (Salisbury et al., 2009, p. 122). The higher order skills and abilities that may be acquired through international experiential learning can contribute to increased income generation and economic growth or "more lucrative and interesting international positions in private and public sectors" (Sherraden, Lough, & McBride, 2008, p. 15).

Some of the participants mentioned the relationship between their experiences abroad, their career goals, and their academic focus; a total of 20 participants (17 women and 3 men) noted that their experience abroad affected their academic focus. In total, 23 participants expressed an interest in graduate studies or furthering their education as a result of their experience abroad and their career goals. Some indicated an interest in graduate work in international development, while others indicated an interest in learning more practical skills through an MBA or a nursing degree. Erika, for example, said: "Definitely, I'm going to be doing my masters. I don't think I would have done my masters in international social work. I think it has made me passionate about international social work. I feel like especially in developing countries, community work is interesting."

Katrina thought the completion of an undergraduate degree and a CIDA internship would be sufficient to get a job in international development but realized after her internship that she needed more education. The internship was instrumental in helping her understand that she needed more education. Although, she does not specify whether she will do specialized skills training, a master's degree, or some other educational advancement program. Most of the participants who said they would return to school said they were planning to pursue a master's degree. Others decided that additional graduate research (pursuing a PhD) would be postponed or abandoned. Tracey, for example, said she didn't want to pursue a PhD after living abroad to do her MA research. She noted that "academic research can be extremely intrusive and often when we apply it to our theories and when we write it up it really loses all of its meaning and value for the people that we research, and so it kind of put a bad taste in my mouth for academia." For some who decided not to continue with post-graduate education, they favoured a role that involved a more "helping" orientation because of a perceived intrusiveness of graduate research in the Global South.

Many of the participants talked about the desire to build skills and a career path in tandem with the motivation of helping others. Volunteering abroad, particularly among youth, is therefore widely considered to be a way to "help others" as well as to "explore career options and to increase the likelihood that they might be able to pursue the career they want" (Stukas, Clary, & Snyder, 1999, p. 11).

Test Driving a Career Choice or Academic Background

One of the most common findings in this research is the motivation expressed by many of the participants to use the international experiential learning program as a way to test their academic background or career choice. During the interviews, participants were not asked about testing a career choice or academic background but it surfaced often. Of great importance to the participants, then, was the impact their international experiential learning experience had on their ability to test an academic background or career choice. Ingrid said,

> I first went over essentially testing whether I wanted an international career. That was one of the reasons I guess for going and after my experience there I decided that it wasn't appropriate at my level of expertise really to be working overseas yet, in a development capacity. So my aim is to work in development in Canada for the next ten years and then re-evaluate whether I have the, the interest and the capacity to, to work overseas again and so now I've come home and I'm working for the closest thing to a microfinance organization in Calgary.

Isabelle said her experience abroad taught her that she didn't have the right personality to do the work she had dreamed of doing throughout her undergrad: "I used to think I wanted to do very grassroots work with people in developing countries but I realized I'm not as charismatic or outgoing enough to do that."

Other participants noted negative professional experience while abroad. Some said they were no longer interested in NGO work and decided to pursue something either completely different or related (i.e., policy research). Some participants turned to – or returned to – a domestic focus, because of personal values, treatment by hosts (good or bad), a revelation of complexities of international development, or personal capacity (homesickness, being able to rough it, understanding and relating to others), for example. Ernesto said, "I'm probably more reluctant after working in Zambia to ... pursue a career in NGO work. Certainly in local level NGO work: I don't think that's my calling. I think that's something, I'm not precluding anything, but it reaffirmed my interest in pursuing kind of other angles ... so it was quite valuable from a career standpoint."

Other participants noted that they felt they could have a bigger impact working in Canada than internationally. Stephan noted:

> Before, I wanted to work strictly in international development. When I came back to Canada I was working with youth that were new to the country. One of the challenges on the volunteer trip was that I was not very culturally relevant. I did not leave a lasting impression. Had someone locally been given the same opportunities by the Argentina government rather than the Canadian government, they might be better off. So I

learned I was much more culturally relevant in the community where I grew up, which is why I'm working in Toronto now.

Anjali has decided, as a result of her time overseas that she doesn't like the lifestyle she observed other expats living while she was abroad nor did she feel at home. She said:

> I've decided that living abroad forever or having that kind of lifestyle, an expat lifestyle, isn't really for me. That I kind of need a place that I can call home and I'm always going to be interested in travelling and I would never turn down the opportunity to live abroad for a certain period of time, but I can't really foresee myself doing it for, you know, the next forty years of my career, I think. I kind of think it's something I'll do a bit more when I'm younger and maybe once or twice when I'm older but I don't think that, you know, hopping around every three to four years is really, really what I need, personally.

Caitlyn expressed concerns about her ability to have an impact as one of the reasons for not wanting to continue in international development work. She wondered: "I'm not really helping. Foreigners going to other countries, is this really a solution? Can we really help? Is this just a selfish thing?"

For some of the participants, volunteering overseas has made it clear that development work is not right for them. In fact, many of the participants became less globally minded in their career goals as a result of their overseas placements, desiring to focus their efforts in their own home communities or in Canada more generally. Enid, like others, now has more desire to work in Canada or "something that focuses on my back door." Anne very clearly explains that the overseas experience resulted in her not wanting to be an expat and concluded quite strongly that she now knows that development work is not for her. Judy expressed having second thoughts about a career in development. She thought her studies in international development were about a desire to work in the field but is now realizing that she is interested in the subject but not the work.

Others, like Crystal, wish to continue in international development work but to do so from a Canadian foreign policy approach.

> I decided that I didn't want to do micro level work – that I wasn't interested in being an expat, in particular, living in another country. It made me become more interested in sort of the larger global policy around impacts,

the local realities of people in developing countries, so I'd like to work more towards Canadian foreign policy and how we interact with countries like Namibia … in ways that are more ethical.

The most common reference was a desire to work or continue academic studies locally (53/100 participants). Therefore the majority of the youth desire local work/activities. As Shelley said: "Ahh yeah, they [experiences abroad] have made me much more resolved to work in Canada … which, yeah I sort of, I really like it here, we've got a lot of things right; we don't have it all right."

Olivia is one individual who expressed the opposite effect. She noted:

This was my first time living abroad. I'd travelled abroad before but this was my first time living abroad ... and it was changing, it was just so different from what I'm used to and it just takes you so far out of your comfort zone that it, it just opens you up to a lot and for me personally it made me think that it might be something that I'm interested in doing in the future as a career.

The Relationship between International Experiential Learning and Finding a Job

Almost all respondents agreed that their overseas experience has or will help them find employment. Most participants agreed that their experience had affected their career goals and plans, whereas only about half were currently employed in a position related to their overseas experience. What can be learned from this data is that the belief in, rather than the actual outcome of employability, seems to be more important to the participants in the short-term placements. In other words, the fact that the experience is on their résumés is hope for them that they will at some point in the future gain employment as a result, but immediate results were not expected. Overall, the youth consider the international experiential learning an essential component for résumé building.

The majority of participants felt that their international experiential learning opportunity would help them find employment; seventy-two people said so. Natalie said:

Oh yeah, yes I do actually I think … I think yeah, the research I did, I think that was, that looks really good on a CV. I think it sort of impresses people that I went abroad. I don't really know. I hope so but I'm not convinced that it will. So we'll see and I'm sort of in between jobs right now, so … that's something that I think about a lot whether or not I'm employable due to South Africa.

Natalia's was one of several references by the participants to the importance of the experience "looking good on a résumé."

Only nine people said the experience abroad was unlikely to help them find employment. Brad said:

I don't think it'll help me find employment. I mean I had a job just after I got back from Uganda at a summer camp where I worked for many years through university and I haven't been employed since, but part of that is because of the recession and stuff, or the economic crises, because I have been offered jobs and then accepted and then the next day been laid off, you know?

An interesting response from Nadine demonstrates that international experiences can be perceived as a liability for some people: "No, when people see I've travelled so much they think I'm not stable." Nora also reflected on the potential perceived liability of someone who travels a lot: "I've done so much travelling that I think that most employers are afraid I'm going to take off again. Even though I don't have the money to do so. Maybe in the future, but I haven't found an employer that was impressed [by international experiential learning]."

Even the participants who were unsure or undecided expressed optimism that the overseas experience would likely be beneficial. It is important to keep in mind that the participants were interviewed a few months after their return and most of them had not yet found careers in international development or community work which they perceived to be related to their experience abroad. Therefore, the optimism has to be understood as only that and not a reflection of the reality of the situation. For those participants who had been back in Canada for a longer period of time, they expressed frustration as noted above with the limited opportunities for employment in their chosen field and the challenges of a difficult economic climate.

The length of time abroad is believed to have an impact on one's desire and ability to find employment in a career in international development. Longer-term placements abroad of one year or longer are correlated with international career plans compared to shorter-term placements (Dwyer, 2004, p. 159). Furthermore, participants who considered the international experiential learning opportunity important for finding work noted the importance of professional skills learned, the significance of the experience abroad for getting into graduate school, and for leading to more internship opportunities – opportunities for organizational networking, gaining references, and overall, opportunities that look good on a résumé. April said the experience abroad will give her a competitive edge "and take me into different niches that not every doctor wants to go and do." For Carol, who was able to get a reference letter from her supervisor in Egypt, she felt that this experience helped her get into the master's program she wanted to do in a very competitive school. "I do think, I mean, just having that work experience on my resume as well as that reference letter definitely helped me with my application, for sure. Like without that experience ... I would say it'd be borderline, I don't know, but that experience definitely pushed me up there."

Brooke was offered a job as soon as her experiential learning program was over. She attributes her job offer to "having an understanding of the world that people are really attracted to. I think that it contributes to your overall professional development." For Ernesto, the placement in Kenya enabled him to get another placement elsewhere in Africa so he considered the skills he had learned as essential for finding new opportunities. He is now in law school and said: "If the question is about employability there's no doubt that internships are very valuable." Judy noted:

I think actually it [the internship] would [help find a job] because it was a very, very specific skills base. I got a lot of hands-on experience ... and actually the nature of the work was hands-on. And if you're doing research with people you've got to talk to them and have activities with them, so it was automatically very experience-based ... I actually think that it would really help. It almost did. I was short-listed for that job. They didn't mind that it was NGO work in a totally different field, you know? They still considered it [relevant experience].

Several other participants noted the perceived importance among employers of the international experience including how the experience contributes to personal growth or that participation in these programs is a reflection on positive personal attributes. Andrew thinks that his employability is related to a strong résumé, noting his placement in

India. Andrew believes that employers see him as adventurous with a "forward personality type attitude." Hannah commented on how the experience has helped her grow and understand people better and Irene said her experience has forced her to think differently – an attribute that employers appreciate, in her perspective. Lena remarked that when employers see your experience listed in Africa on your CV, they assume the person can handle tough situations, is adventurous, and outgoing. "So I think, to a lot of employers, it looks fancy."

Claudette is hopeful that her experience abroad will help her find work. She reflected candidly, "It hasn't but I would say it will, like if I want to apply for work in a developing country it would help that I've had experience living in a developing country." Preston is less certain about the relationship between the experience abroad and getting a job than many of the other youth and noted: "Since I'm currently unemployed, I don't think it's helped me find anything. But I think it's, it's given me mind shift, it's given me the mental tools and resources to be able to better know what I want, what I want to do, you know?"

Francine's remarks are exceptional, reflecting more critically on the perceived résumé-building nature of the international experience, she said: "I'm not sure. I don't ascribe to the 'power' that comes with having an internship on your résumé. To be honest, I would not even have applied had it not been for the insistence of the coordinator."

Fiona said: "So far it's not doing so good, but I think eventually it will. I think if I add enough of that kind of experience, it's going to help. But stand alone? No. It's not really doing anything." For Stella, who thought the experience abroad would help her find a job, she realizes that the short-term nature of the experiential learning program is insufficient. She said: "I've been looking for a job since last October but I'm still unemployed. So maybe it's because, it's a little bit too little experience to work in head office work, maybe it'll help me when we are ready to go overseas but even so, three months isn't that long."

The youth are reflecting on job prospects in a particularly difficult economy when joblessness is at one of the all-time highest and few jobs are opening up in the Government of Canada. Brad said he hasn't been employed for some time but attributes it to the contemporary economic challenges, noting that funding for jobs is difficult to maintain.

When asked whether their current employment is related in any way to their international experiential learning programs, many said no, they were not related at all. Holly, who works in retail said, "It's a half-upscale boutique and the other side of the store is selling touristy things to cruise ship people. It's not overly fulfilling but it's a paycheque anyway." Holly has found it challenging to find work related to her skills, academic background, and international experience, noting, "There's a lot of people who have the same, the same background as I do around here, but I've applied for a significant amount of things since I got home and haven't had any success with that. So it's, it's been a little frustrating." Molly, who has an academic background in international studies, also noted that she has only a part-time job that is unrelated to her background or experiences abroad "but I'm looking for a job in the NGOs and in international development right now."

Francois currently works at Mr. Sub and said:

> No, there's really no connection [between his current work and academic background]. I tried to find work in my field but I was looking for something short term as well. I'm actually planning another big trip starting in September. I am biking with some friends down to South America ... So I wasn't able to find anything in my field because I'm only here for the summer, right? So I found what I could. I'll be glad when it [the job at Mr. Sub] is over.

Rethinking the Career Path

Some participants now strive to combine volunteering and educational interests in their work. For the volunteers in this study who chose career paths in their home country, many of the research participants noted that they now work with immigrants or refugees, while others continued to do work in the areas of social and global justice.

The most common reference to the relationship between experience abroad and career goals in our research was reflected in a desire to work locally in Canada. A total of thirty of the participants made explicit reference to their desire to turn the skills they learned abroad into doing work in Canadian communities. Adam noted, "I guess what I'm saying is that my career goal isn't just to be working in international development, [or] in foreign countries, but my goal is very much to work here but I do think that there is much that I gained from working there [abroad]." Shelley also prefers to work in Canada and noted that international experiential learning opportunities "made me much more resolved to work in Canada ... I really like it here." Alice said,

> [I am] more interested in community development [in Canada], more local, more here, because I feel one thing I struggled with while I was away was being able to relate and understand and so I feel like working in

a community and in a system that you understand ... I feel like I can understand the society and the system ... So, I feel like I can better relate to that than working in international development, where I have to go learn literally everything. Where[as], at least I've grown up in this system so I understand the system better.

The findings from our interviews with Canadian youth demonstrate that international experiences have become an important benchmark of achievement or résumé-building. The experience abroad was important for many of the participants in terms of looking good on a CV, getting into grad school, and/or finding employment primarily as a result of the skills learned on experiential learning programs. Many of these skills learned abroad, however, could also be learned in a local context. As the participants in this study have argued, the degree of learning or speed in which the learning took place, was what was more significant in an international placement. Language acquisition remains a key skill learned in immersion in other cultures and for those who saw language training as crucial to their careers, travelling abroad was very important. There was a recognition among the participants, though, that much of what they learned abroad could be learned in Canada and this raises questions about the value of international service learning, particularly in countries where poverty rates are high and the cost of hosting international "guests" can be challenging. A related finding in this study is the overwhelming interest in applying their international experience to local community work and a desire to work in local Canadian communities. Given the interest in working "at home" rather than abroad in their desired careers, why does the international volunteer/learn abroad option hold so much appeal? I would argue that the desire for a particular kind of experience is central to the motivation for international experiential learning. Specifically, the kind of experience Canadian youth crave is one that offers potential for adventure and travel, while also improving their employability.

Conclusion

Most participants agreed that their experiences have affected their career goals in some way. More often than not these experiences have exposed them to the practical side of development work and enabled them to make choices for the future about which path they would like to pursue based on their personal capacity, their goals, ethics, new skills learned, and interests. Almost all respondents agreed that their overseas experience has or will help them find employment. Interestingly, even those without related jobs were positive that international experiential learning would one day assist with finding meaningful employment and they have stayed true to the belief that eventually they would have the position they were looking for as a result of their overseas experience. Many respondents considered their current employment related to their experience abroad, although, often in indirect ways.

In terms of the skills learned while participating in international experiential learning programs, most participants thought they learned "cultural" or "personal" skills rather than "technical" skills during the time spent in their short-term placement. Most participants said the personal skills they learned from being in an overseas context were distinct while separating them from the professional skills which some said they would have been able to learn in Canada if they were given an opportunity. Other participants said if they were placed in another community within Canada they would have been able to learn the same skill set as they did during their short-term placement overseas.

The empirical findings suggest, therefore, that international experiential learning holds a particular appeal for young Canadians, particularly in relation to motivations of cross-cultural understanding and testing a career choice or academic background. Universities, governmental and non-governmental organizations alike are promoting international experiential learning as a valuable educational opportunity that promotes skills development and contributes to career advancement. Langdon and Agyeyomah (chapter 3 of this volume) reflect on this phenomenon in the context of the "neoliberal marketplace for professionalization." Building on Langdon and Agyeyomah's assessment, the findings from the empirical study demonstrate an emphasis on employability rather than citizenship, and not the "thick" version of global citizenship Cameron describes in this volume.

The findings raise important questions about the ethical implications of using the Global South as a laboratory or testing grounds for a career choice for Canadian youth. When the Global South becomes an extension of the classroom space, it runs the risk of being treated as a laboratory for trying out international development work, often without the appropriate skills, training, and preparation by the Canadian youth who take part in international experiential learning programs.

The emphasis on personal gain by the Canadian youth who are motivated by career aspirations and employability speaks to the "thin" forms of global citizenship articulated by John Cameron in this volume. The empirical findings from my study suggest that more Canadian youth between the ages of 18 and 30 are driven by superficial global citizenship ideals than by the "thick" conceptions of global citizenship that are characterized by acts of solidarity and a deep level of engagement and long-term commitment to social justice and equality. How we might address this observation, improved models and frameworks for a more deeply engaged global citizenship, and the pre-departure/ return orientation required for improving international experiential learning are examined in the chapters that follow.

NOTE

1 The author would like to thank the IDRC for its generous support. While I do not cite them here, I have published various aspects or sections of the research findings as articles and chapters in a variety of publications.

REFERENCES

Baaz, Maria Eriksson. (2005). *The paternalism of partnership: A postcolonial reading of identity in development aid*. London: Zed Books.

Child, K.P., & Manion, C. (2004). A survey of upper-year students in International Development Studies. *Canadian Journal of Development Studies, 25*(1), 167–186. http://dx.doi.org/10.1080/02255189.2004.9668965

Dwyer, M.M. (2004). More is better: The impact of study abroad program duration. *Frontiers: The Interdisciplinary Journal of Study Abroad, 10*, 151–164.

Hannigan, T.P. (2001). The effect of work abroad experiences on career development for U.S. undergraduates. *Frontiers: The Interdisciplinary Journal of Study Abroad, 7*, 1–23.

Heron, Barbara. (2007). *Desire for development: Whiteness, gender and the helping imperative*. Waterloo, ON: Wilfrid Laurier University Press.

Lough, B., McBride, A.M., & Sherraden, M. (2009). Perceived effects of international volunteering: reports from alumni. *CSD Research Report 09–10*, Washington University in St. Louis. http://csd.wustl.edu/Publications/Documents/RP09-10.pdf

McBride, A.M., & Sherraden, M. (2007). *Civic service worldwide: Impacts and inquiry*. New York: ME Sharpe.

Mohajeri Norris, E., & Gillespie, J. (2009). How study abroad shapes global careers: Evidence from the United States. *Journal of Studies in International Education, 13*(3), 382–397. http://dx.doi.org/10.1177/1028315308319740

Pires, Mark. (2000). Study-abroad and cultural exchange programs to Africa: America's image of a continent. *African Issues 28*(1–2), 39–45. http://www.jstor.org

Plewes, B., & Stuart, R. (2007). Opportunities and challenges for international volunteer co-operation. Paper presented at the IVCO Conference, Montreal, Canada.

Powell, S. & Bratović, E. (2007). *The impact of long-term youth voluntary service in Europe: A review of published and unpublished research studies.* AVSO & ProMENTE Social Research, Brussels, Belgium. Retrieved from http://www.academia.edu/2893624/The_impact_of_long-term_youth_voluntary_service_in_Europe_A_review_of_published_and_unpublished_research_studies

Roschelle, A.R., Turpin, J., & Elias, R. (2000). Who learns from service learning? *American Behavioral Scientist, 43*(5), 839–847. http://dx.doi.org/10.1177/00027640021955630

Salisbury, M.H., Umbach, P.D., Paulsen, M.B., & Pascarella, E.T. (2009). Going global: Understanding the choice process of the intent to study abroad. *Research in Higher Education 50*, 119–143.

Sherraden, M.S., Lough, B., & McBride, A.M. (2008). Effects of international volunteering and service: Individual and institutional predictors. *VOLUNTAS: International Journal of Voluntary and Nonprofit Organizations, 19*(4), 395–421. http://dx.doi.org/10.1007/s11266-008-9072-x

Simpson, K. (2005). Dropping out or signing up? The professionalisation of youth travel. *Antipode, 37*(3), 447–469. http://dx.doi.org/10.1111/j.0066-4812.2005.00506.x

Stukas, A.A., Clary, E.G., & Snyder, M. (1999). Service learning: Who benefits and why. *Social Policy Report: Society for Research in Child Development 13*(4), 1–19.

5 Uncovering What Lies Beneath: An Examination of Power, Privilege, and Racialization in International Social Work

LAHOMA THOMAS
AND UPPALA CHANDRASEKERA

Internationalism is rooted in colonialism and imperialism, especially when the production of knowledge and other academic gains flow from North to South. Hegemony is therefore inherent in our pedagogy, practice, education and attempts at globalization.

– Sherene Razack (2002, p. 255)

Introduction

Social work can be viewed as a transnational profession as it is taught and practiced in most "developed" and "developing" countries (N. Razack, 2002). International social work ranges from practising social work in other countries, to working domestically with individuals who originate from outside the local context, to collaborating with international organizations. International practicum placements are becoming increasingly more accessible to social work students in North America and "schools of social work across Canada have been focusing more attention on international field placements" (N. Razack, 2002, p. 257). A central learning principle for the social worker is their experiences (Goldstein, 2001); learning is conceptualized as a narrative process that is both active and experiential (Goldstein, 2001, p. 17). Social work education comprises a three-step process: One learns to be a social worker deductively (when grounded knowledge is imparted or acquired), inductively (when knowledge is developed from experiential observations and participation), and vicariously (when one learns empathetically through the perceived or narrated experiences of others) (Goldstein, 2001, pp. 17–18). International practicum placements are perceived to provide the opportunity for all three forms of learning. International experiential learning is seen as an opportunity for the social work student to broaden their cultural horizons, better understand who the client is and the changing multicultural nature of Canadian society (Webber, 2005 as cited in Wehbi, 2009), as well as meet the demands of a more globally cognizant student body and faculty.

International social work, broadly, and international social work practicums for students, more specifically, operate as a form of *professional imperialism* (Midgley, 1981). As Cameron notes in chapter 2, neither students nor academics equate international experiential learning with global justice. Instead, students see the international practicum experience in terms of advancing their inductive and vicarious learning as social workers, as well as "fulfilling" the moral and helping imperative that underscores the discipline. Research on volunteer abroad programs reveals that students' motivations to participate in internationally based projects are rooted in a desire to see the world, to have a practical educational experience, to develop their careers, and to discover personal learning and growth (Tiessen, 2007, 2012; Tiessen & Heron, 2012). Positioned as a means to enrich the student's learning experience, international social work placements often reinforce and reproduce the historical hegemonic power dynamics between the North and the South, "the First World" and "the Third World." This is demonstrative from an institutional and individual level. From an institutional perspective, the international practicums are structured as a unilateral knowledge transfer – the movement of students from the North to the South, from the developed nations to the underdeveloped. Langdon and Agyeyomah, in chapter 3 refer to this as the "unstated knowledge hierarchy," a framing process that suggests that the pathway to societal betterment is the purview of Western scholars and students alike. From the individual level, the presumption of Northern hegemony is reflected in how social workers engaged in the global social justice project reinforce stereotypes of less developed nations and perpetuate racialization and racism in their social work practice.

Critical race theory (CRT) and Black feminist thought (BFT) form the theoretical basis for this chapter as both offer a deeper theoretical analysis on power relations within international social work practice. CRT facilitates a critical examination of the hegemonic pedagogical practices embedded in the discipline of social work, while BFT provides a complementary interactive model that examines the ways in which power relations among other intersecting systems of authorization normalize a hierarchy of privilege (Wane, 2009, p. 67). With a lens conversant to the historical and contemporary production of colonialism and imperialism, both theoretical frameworks provide insights into how the structural and cultural aspects of international social work can recreate the power dynamics and inequities embedded in relations between the North and South. In this chapter, we discuss how racialization[1] and racism are reproduced in the context of international social work, both at home and abroad. To illustrate how professional imperialism manifests in the practice of international social work, we present a reflexive analysis of our experiences with international social work in Canada as well as the Global South.

A central tenet of social work education and practice is the notion of becoming an ally. Allies are defined as individuals who belong to the dominant social group who intentionally and actively resist oppression and take action against discrimination and social injustice (Bishop, 2002; Lopes & Thomas, 2006). As Chandrasekera and Thomas (2013) explain, allies from the dominant group, working in conjunction with minorities, can function as agents of social change rather than agents of oppression. The intent of this chapter is to interrogate the notion of developing allies in the context of international social work and to examine the role and behaviours of the social work ally in the context of international development. We do this by expanding on the writings of Anne Bishop (2002) who characterized individuals engaged in social just initiatives as "the allies," "the guilty," and "the backlasher," and Amy Rossiter (2001) who identified "the socially innocent." We reconceptualize these key concepts and propose two distinct categories of allies: *the Apathetic Ally* and *the Authentic Ally* (Chandrasekera & Thomas, 2013).

In this chapter we present our Ally Model, which examines the wide spectrum of allies in the context of international social work, which includes the Apathetic Ally comprised of *the Socially Innocent*, *the Passive Backlasher*, and *the Guilty*, and the Authentic Ally (Chandrasekera & Thomas, 2013). This chapter explores the role of allies in international development work at the institutional and individual level. At the institutional level, we examine how social work education and practice can engender systemic forms of oppression. At the individual level, we examine how the international social worker holds and utilizes their privilege(s) in conscious and unconscious ways; we examine the motivations for participating in international development work and how privilege can be tied to the subordination of others. We also discuss how the Ally Model can assist on the path to developing anti-oppressive principles and practices in international social work, by challenging the social work agent to examine their privileged position and facilitate a self-reflexive dialogue about how they respond to incidents of discrimination and oppression.

This chapter begins with a description of our entry points into the discussion of the social work profession and international development work. Next, we present a short, theoretical discussion on racialization and its impact on international development work. This is followed by our self-reflexive narratives and observations of racialization in the international social work context, as well as the identification of Apathetic Allies encountered in the field. The conclusion highlights the need to engage the action-oriented practice of anti-oppression, and proposes a strategy for conducting authentic anti-oppressive and anti-racist international social work.

Entry Point into the Discussion of Racialization in International Social Work

Our discussion is informed by our experiences as social work practitioners in Canada and in the Global South. In this chapter, we use the term "the Global South" to refer to nations around the world that are rooted in the history of colonization and Western imperialism, and consist mainly of racialized citizenry. Our analysis is grounded in our lived experiences and our autoethnographic accounts of racialization in the international social work context. Chandrasekera's narrative as a South Asian Canadian illustrates her encounters with the experiential learning environment of Canadian social work academia. Her observations as a racialized female social worker offer a unique perspective of the professional imperialism exhibited by Canadian social workers engaged in international development work. Thomas's narrative illustrates her experiences as a Black Canadian development/social worker in the context of Tanzania and Uganda. Her identity as a racialized woman and as a Canadian expat offers a unique position, what Patricia Collins (1986) refers to as the "outsider-within," to observe the contradictions in social justice principles and values espoused by Canadian development workers and their interactions with the Indigenous populations.

International Social Work as Development

The existing literature on international social work placements focus on the description and experiential learning objectives of the international practicum programs, the improvement in students' cross-cultural communication post placement, and the students' experiences of their practicums (Razack, 2009; Wehbi, 2009), while other scholars focus on students' experience upon their return (Heron, 2007; Pawar, Hanna, & Sheridan, 2004). The emphasis on the debriefing of the student post-placement signals the primacy of the student's experience abroad in terms of their educational and personal learning. Wehbi (2009) cites the reasons students choose to undertake international social work placements: a fascination with other cultures, liking people of another country, the perception that their work will have a larger impact in the Global South – making a difference one cannot make in their home country, and the desire to "give back" (by students who are originally from the country of destination) (Wehbi, 2009). Wehbi (2009) discusses how these reasons, although appearing in many ways as innocuous, have the potential to be fuelled by cultural imperialism and voyeurism; homogenize the citizens of a country, thus erasing the cultural diversity and heterogeneity of a nation; and reinforce "the helpless victim" narrative of people in the Global South.

A striking lacuna in social work literature on international practicums is how students understand their identity in relation to their placement; for example, how their social location (race, citizenship, class, education, gender, and sexual orientation among other social locations) shapes their work in the international context. Nor does the literature provide a critical examination or assessment of the utility and impact of student's activities on the host organization (Pawar, Hanna, & Sheridan, 2004; Wehbi, 2009). As a result, we know little about the impact of the practicum on the local population. This absence is troubling because it suggests the discipline views little merit in assessing how the practices and attitudes of students from the Global North can reproduce existing social orders of domination and transcultural power relations. In addition, it speaks to the ideological assumption that the social work student's presence, alone, is a value added to the host organization in the Global South. Nancy Cook's (2007) ethnographic study on female development workers in Pakistan reveals a telling picture of how the subjectivities of Western volunteers is constituted through discourses of imperialism, cultural superiority, gender, race, and class. Her study documented the regularity of ethnocentric discourses that portrayed the Indigenous population, women specifically, in ways that presumed, perpetuated, and augmented the volunteers' own racialized sense of distinctiveness and superiority (p. 98). Cook's (2007) findings echo the observations made by other scholars about the entrenchment of power and privilege in the logic of development praxis (Heron, 2006; Iffe, 1999; Kapoor, 2004; Razack, 2009).

Power, Privilege, and Race in International Social Work

The theory and practice of development, generally, and international social work, specifically, is not short on critiques (Barry-Shaw, Engler, & Jay, 2012; Heron, 2007; Oliver-Smith, 2010). Inherent in development practice is the presumption that the Global South is lagging behind and requires Western expertise to catch up. Thus, the development project itself is derived on the presumption of economic, socio-political and cultural superiority. In practice, the North regulates the type of development interventions employed in the South, which is demonstrative in the unilateral transfer of knowledge from North to South, that effectively ignores the value of existing Indigenous knowledge systems (Huag, 2005; Midgley, 1990). In his analysis of international development interventions, Dei (1993) observes that development policies are constructed in the interest of the North industrial capital. We, further, argue that the day-to-day application of international social work projects, especially the relational dynamics between Western "experts" and the local population, mirror the sociocultural hegemony inherent in the North-South power dynamics.

The Western British model of social work dominates the practice in "developing" countries (Huag, 2005; Iffe, 1999; Midgley, 1990; N. Razack, 2002, 2009). The universal application of Western models of social work is inappropriate to other socio-political cultures as it assumes an ahistorical and apolitical element to the practice of social work and marginalizes Indigenous practices (Midgley, 1990, 2001; Razack, 2009). Huag (2005) argues that international social work is "blind not only to their perpetuation of a paternalistic framing of non-Western cultures, knowledge systems and social care traditions, but also to the elitism and exclusion within this ostensibly global conversation" (p. 127). In his discussion of the application of international social work in East Timor, Iffe (1999), who works in the area of social work and human rights, describes the "assisters" as engaging in colonial behaviour. He cautions social workers that claim to be working in the best interest of someone else, reminding them that this way of thinking has led to the most oppressive and disempowering practices on marginalized populations. He further points out that the presumption of working in the best interest of someone else implies that the *helper* better knows what the *helpee* needs (Iffe, 1999).

This ideological understanding of the role of the social worker derives from the way in which social work is taught and practiced. On the surface, the social work curriculum is centred on the concept of anti-oppressive practice[2] (AOP); however, in its application, social work education can produce an oppressive learning environment for racialized students. Although the social work academic environment may speak about race, it avoids naming racism. This inability to name racism and address issues of racialization is not unique to academia, rather it is endemic across the social services sector (Chandrasekera & Thomas, 2013). Although there now exist countless numbers of initiatives and programs, both academic and community-based, that are dedicated to providing education and addressing issues of oppression, race, and racism have been casually subsumed under the umbrella of "access and equity" and any focused discussion on the existence and impact of racism is significantly diminished (Lopes & Thomas, 2006; Chandrasekera & Thomas, 2013).

Often, the existing discussions concerning racism are dominated by overt acts of racism and there is little discussion regarding covert, institutionalized, and systemic racism in the domestic or international context. Lopez (2003) speaks to the silence on race in the academic context:

> They ignore it because they believe the topic is too unpleasant, because they feel that racism is a thing of the past, because they do not see themselves as "raced" individuals, or because they feel that the race problem is not theirs to solve. Others feel that because they, as individuals, do not hold racist beliefs, then the topic is somewhat external in their daily lives. (p. 82)

This inability and/or unwillingness to speak about race and name racism within academia fosters an environment of culture conflicts for students, staff, and faculty of colour, leading to their alienation, while simultaneously contributing to and protecting the existing white power and privilege in academia (Sue, 2004, p. 766).

In our observations of social work academia in the Canadian context, racialized individuals are rarely presented as educated professionals with "expert" knowledge. Instead, racialized bodies are presented as "survivors" of the social services system. Often, the "expert" voices are white, university educated, graduates of a Master of Social Work (M.S.W.) program (read: social work *professionals*); thus, their social work knowledge is determined to be official and academic. Conversely, the racialized "survivors" are presented as victims (read: social work *clients*), and any knowledge they offer is deemed unofficial, un-academic personal stories of their struggles within the social services system.

This depiction of racialized bodies in the academic social work envi-ronment perpetuates the existing stereotypes in society that continue to pathologize people of colour. Yee and Dumbrill (2003) observe that "the production of social work knowledge and the delivery of social work services remain primarily a white, European enterprise" (p. 101). Simi-larly, Huag (2005) observes that the small body of published literature on international social work is a reflection of the political, economic, cultural, and ideological dominance of the United States international-ly. The authorship and framing of the discourse, he adds, is predomi-nantly by "privileged male academics of European heritage" (p. 12). This dichotomous framing of the social worker as white and the client as racialized is first learned in the academic social work environment and remains with the social worker as they move into the field of prac-tice, both at home and abroad.

Allies in the International Social Work Context

The core objective of the social work discipline is to facilitate social change, and the vehicle of that change is embodied in the work of the individual. Thus, in order to adequately engage in the social justice project, domestically or internationally, we must start with the role, val-ues, and practices of the individual. We argue that this process begins with acknowledging how we experience the world, understanding our role in the global social justice project, and interrogating how we may inadvertently reproduce oppressive relations. This is particularly sa-lient within the international context where, as a profession, social workers are operating within a system that perpetuates inequities and a discipline that produces epistemic violence.

"The Ally Model" (see Figure 5.1) and the "Becoming an Authentic Ally: A Self-Reflection Checklist" (see Figure 5.2) offer individuals in-terested in the social justice project (domestically or internationally) a starting place for self-reflection (Chandrasekera & Thomas, 2013). As Cameron notes in chapter 2, thick global citizenship requires that students, academics, and development workers research and analyse the implications of their everyday actions, both at home and abroad, and its impacts on the citizens of the world. Therefore, by locating oneself within the Ally Model, one can genuinely assess how their espoused commitment to human rights and social justice is actualized in their practice.

This model consists of two distinct types of allies: the Authentic Ally and the Apathetic Ally. The Authentic and Apathetic Ally possess an understanding of the historical ways in which privilege(s) (gained historically through colonization and presently through intersecting social locations such as whiteness, citizenship, formal education, class, sexual orientation, and gender among others) have been used to oppress others and push them to the margins of society. Both Authentic and Apathetic Allies have a desire and perceive themselves as being *true* allies; yet, their similarities end there as their actions differ drastically. Although the Apathetic Ally acknowledges the historical impact of colonialism and oppression, they are unable to acknowledge, or they deny how they continue to benefit from their privilege and how those privileges infringe upon marginalized groups (Sue, 2004). The actions of the Apathetic Ally can be classified into three distinct categories: the Socially Innocent, the Passive Backlasher, and the Guilty.

In the vignettes below, we provide autoethnographic accounts of our lived experiences and observations to illustrate the three types of Apathetic Allies who commonly engage in international social work.

The Socially Innocent

The Socially Innocent understand the process of colonization and oppression that has occurred throughout human history and understand its lingering impact on the twenty-first century, locally and internationally. Yet, they are unable or unwilling to acknowledge that they may also be contributing to the oppression of others in the present day. This failure is in part due to their involvement in the social justice project because it facilitates the misperception that engaging in social justice oriented initiatives makes them exempt from the perpetuation of oppressive behaviours. Furthermore, as Cameron notes in chapter 2, "the casual linkages between actions in one part of the world and suffering elsewhere are complex, indirect and often hidden"; the Socially Innocent do not intentionally and actively interrogate these complexities; therefore, they are unable or unwilling to realize the oppressive consequences of their actions.

Here Chandrasekera recalls an encounter with social innocence in the Canadian social work environment:

During one of my practicum placements for the M.S.W. program, I was working at a large healthcare organization. One day, as I walked through the lobby of the agency, a colourful display caught my eye. There was a woman standing next to the display that I recognized as a social worker in the agency. She greeted me and motioned for me to come over so that she could explain the display.

The social worker was raising money to support her upcoming trip to India for a two-week international development project. She was hoping that the display would generate enough interest from agency staff, clients, and visitors to drum up donations to support her trip. With enthusiasm and excitement, she explained her display to me. She had woven a "sleeping mat" using pieces of used milk bags, grocery bags and garbage bags. "This sleeping mat is for the children living in the slums of Mumbai," she said, "so they have something comfortable to sleep on."

I reached out and touched the sleeping mat. I *cringed*. It felt rough, course to the touch, and scratched against my skin. It was, after all, made entirely from used plastic bags. How is anyone, *especially children*, expected to sleep on something so uncomfortable?

The social worker did not notice my gut reaction. Grinning from ear to ear, she said, "Isn't this great? I've found an easy way to help the poor children in India. I'm using something that we throw away every day in this country, and I've created something that the children can benefit from. I thought *you* would get a kick out of this."

This narrative exemplifies the dichotomous thought process of the Socially Innocent: that to be racialized (to be Indian) is to be poor and in need of assistance, and to be white is to be in a position to assist. There was no interrogation of the way in which the Socially Innocent assist others. In this case, the social worker was congratulating herself for helping the poor children of India by giving them something that the Western world has discarded, something constructed entirely out of garbage. Furthermore, the social worker did not interrogate her assumption that Chandrasekera is of Indian origin. This vignette depicts the ease in which the social worker can accept her identity as *the helper*. It also demonstrates how the social worker is less readily able to acknowledge how her privileges (race, nationality, and profession) will impact her work abroad; as such, the social worker simultaneously embodies the role of helper and oppressor.

Accordingly, Thomas reflects on her encounters with Apathetic Allies in international development:

> As a Black female Canadian, my racial identity and citizenship positioned me as the "outsider-within." My "Canadian-ness" fostered relationships with the larger expatriate community in both Tanzania and Uganda. In many ways, my Canadian citizenship in the international context granted me access into exclusively white spaces. This access allowed me to be privy to the conversations and observations expatriates made about the local communities.
>
> The majority of my fellow expatriates were American and Canadian students or recent graduates in fields related to social work or development studies. For the majority of them, it was their first experience working and living outside the context of North America, which meant that it was the first time that they were within a context where their whiteness was not the socio-cultural norm. This reality was frequently expressed through comments such as, "I am always being stared at!" and "Can you believe that I was the only white person in the room?" What was often not reflected upon was how their whiteness afforded them privileges; for example, how their suggestions and recommendations in program meetings overshadowed those of local staff, or how their intersecting identities of privilege, whiteness, citizenship, foreign education, class, etc., permitted them authority in many professional and social interactions within the local communities.
>
> As much as whiteness functioned as a privilege, affording the expatriates a form of socio-political currency not granted to the local community, instances arose when their identity as white expatriates did not function as a privilege. Two such examples come to mind, the Passive Backlasher and the Guilty.

The Passive Backlasher

The Passive Backlashers are the individuals who behave as though we live in a post-race society (Dei, 2008). They acknowledge that racism was a reality of the past, such as the historical impact of colonization on Indigenous and Black communities. Yet, they believe that racism is no longer a fact that affects racialized communities, nor a continuing factor that creates barriers for daily life. Passive Backlashers are those who deny the existence of racism while simultaneously proclaiming the existence of "reverse-racism" (Dei, 2008). Due to their belief that we live in a racism-free society, they fail to act in the moments when racism and oppression do occur, and worse, they fail to interrogate when they are themselves complicit in the act of oppression. Accordingly, Thomas recalls:

> I witnessed a verbal altercation between a colleague and a *boda boda* (motorcycle) driver in Uganda. We had both reached our destination and were preparing to pay our respective *boda boda* drivers. My colleague called out to me and asked how much I was charged, and realized that her *boda boda* driver quoted her an inflated fare. She then proceeded to yell and verbally assault the driver calling him a "lying dirty African," a "yarn head" and a "thief." As I attempted to intervene and diffuse the situation, she repeatedly stated that she was the victim of "reverse racism" and it was "not fair that she was being lied to because of the colour of her skin." The irony of her comments was not lost to me in that moment.

As this narrative illustrates, Passive Backlashers fail to acknowledge the moments when they are in the role of the oppressor. In this vignette, the development worker recognized that the source of her unfair treatment was her race, yet she did not recognize her enactment of racism through her comments and behaviour. She intentionally engaged in racism towards the driver, whom she felt was deserving of her verbal assault. Through her racist language, she not only perpetuated racism towards the local citizens but also towards her racialized colleague.

The Guilty

The Guilty are comprised of individuals who are capable of naming their power and privilege; for example, these individuals are able to articulate that men have more power than women, the rich have more power than the poor, and citizens of the North have more power than those in the South. However, the Guilty are resistant to identifying the implication of this power, for example, how their identities continue to contribute to the oppression of others. The Guilty understand the impact of oppression and colonization, but as Bishop (2002) asserts, because the Guilty can view themselves as the oppressor their engagement in a racial discourse halts here. The experience of guilt associated with their privileged identity has a paralyzing effect on their analysis of oppression and racism. This particular group feels overburdened by the complexities of oppression and discrimination, and as a result, they actively disengage from anti-oppressive practice and dialogue because it fosters feelings of guilt. Ironically, this act of avoidance in itself exemplifies the power differential between those with privilege and those without, as the Guilty have the opportunity and ability to *choose* to ignore and avoid discussions about oppression and discrimination.

As such, Thomas recalls another incident in the field:

> I was present at a dinner outing with a fellow Canadian white expatriate and a number of our local colleagues. At some point during the dinner, the conversation turned onto the reality that numerous Northern interventions in the Global South have not only been ineffective, but have exasperated living conditions in local communities. One local colleague directly challenged the utility of our work and raised a number of relevant questions about the effectiveness and sustainability of our work in facilitating change. Further, he made an analogy between international development projects and colonial practices. After dinner, once my Canadian colleague and I were alone, she burst into tears. She expressed outrage that "her sacrifices in coming to Uganda were not appreciated" and stated that she felt she was being equated with colonial practices, which she thought was "unfair" because, as she explained "she wasn't even alive then." When I tried to explain that I interpreted the discussion as a larger systemic critique of the field and attempted to engage her in a discussion about the historical material realities of international development projects, she dismissed my comments and stated that I would not understand because the "attack" was more pronounced for her because she was white and I was not.

The conversation during dinner presented a rich dialogical forum to examine how power relations are perpetuated in post-colonial sites through international development initiatives. However, my Canadian colleague's feelings of guilt took primacy and derailed her ability to engage in a critical conversation about the complex tensions and contradictions within international development. This example illustrates how feelings of guilt are triggered in the Guilty when their privileged identity is implicated in the subordination of others. In addition, their emotional experience of guilt is prioritized and disables their capacity to critically engage in activist forms of practice.

The duplicitous nature of Apathetic Allies – the Socially Innocent, the Passive Backlashers, and the Guilty – is that their espousal of anti-oppressive practice and commitment to broader international issues of social justice leaves their work unexamined and obscures how their beliefs are incongruent with their actions. Razack (2004) refers to this as "the Paradox" – when individuals think that they are doing good, when in reality, they are perpetuating racism and oppression. This paradox exists within the field of international social work.

Both Wehbi (2009) and Drucker (2003) note that students engaged in international social work placements hold the belief that they are going to "help" and "save" others. A narrative reflective of the discipline, as a whole, stems from what Martinez-Brawley (1999) describes as *benevolent imperialism*. Within this narrative the social worker participating in the international project is constructed as benevolent and caring. Accordingly, one of the guiding images that informs popular understanding of the importance of international development work is the relentless portrayal of the poor destitute African and/or South Asian woman or child whose relief from suffering is alleviated when she is the recipient of the assistance offered by the Western development worker. Thus, the development worker, as the bearer of relief, is cast solely as the heroic figure (read: selfless, innocent, and honourable). This representation reinforces the Eurocentric masculinist practices in development and fosters an ideological justification for the presence and practices of the development worker, thereby serving to justify and sanitize their behaviour. In this way, international social work functions as a form of professional imperialism.

The Authentic Ally

Unlike the Apathetic Ally, the Authentic Ally understands, acknowledges, and engages in self-reflection regarding the power and privilege that they wield in the world. These are the characteristics of the *true* allies in Bishop's (2002) writings. The Authentic Ally not only acknowledges but validates others' experiences of marginalization and oppression. Furthermore, Authentic Allies engage in multilateral learning, so that both the oppressor and the oppressed can be educated about the causes and impact of oppression, without placing blame. The most important characteristic of Authentic Allies is that they engage in the *action-oriented practice* of anti-oppression and anti-racism. Contrary to the Apathetic Allies, Authentic Allies intentionally and actively resist the moments when their privilege forces others to the margins; they do not remain silent in moments when discrimination and racism occur. Authentic Allies intentionally and actively use their privileged social location to advocate for the anti-oppressive and anti-racist social justice project.

As Chandrasekera recounts here, she encountered an Authentic Ally in the Canadian social work environment:

In class, I was engaged in a small group discussion with a few other social work students. Several of the students had just returned from completing an international placement and we were sharing and debriefing on some of the experiences. One student shared her thoughts about her recent placement in Sri Lanka. She said that the one thing that had surprised her was everyone's need to know where she was all the time; her Sri Lankan supervisor had always inquired about her transportation to and from work and her host family had always wanted to know her whereabouts. She said she was annoyed by this, and then turned to me with a laugh and said, "I don't know why everyone from your country is so *paranoid*."

I was shocked by this statement; I did not know how to respond; I felt so caught off-guard. Seeing my reaction, the student sitting next to me spoke up immediately. He reminded the female student that she was making sweeping generalizations, and those types of comments are inappropriate. Further he challenged the female student to consider the reasoning behind everyone wanting to know her whereabouts; could it be that it's not a matter of paranoia, rather a genuine concern for safety, especially in a country that has experienced civil war for many decades. He commented that the feeling of safety is something that we take for granted in Canada: it's a privilege that we have that is not afforded to many countries around the world.

Similarly, Thomas recalls an encounter with an Authentic Ally in the international social work context:

I was among a team of Canadian medical and psychological trauma specialists invited to facilitate a training workshop for nurses, social workers, and counsellors at a gender recovery centre in Uganda. On the last day of the workshop, the staff had gathered to thank the team for our work. At this time, one of the directors of the organization made a speech thanking us for our time and commenting to the staff that "we had volunteered our time without compensation" and questioned why that was a "quality only exhibited in people from the West and not those of us with this skin" as he motioned to his dark complexion. I was completely taken aback by this statement. One of my white colleagues, immediately, responded to his statement by highlighting my presence on the team, followed by her observations on the tireless efforts of the staff, and closed by attributing her own ability to volunteer her time to the organization was due to her position and privilege in Canada.

The characteristics of the Authentic Ally are evident in both of these examples. In Chandrasekera's situation, the male social work student was the Authentic Ally. He identified and named the inappropriate comments made by his classmate and did not remain silent in the moment. Further, he named the privilege that his classmate, and other Canadians, possessed that was not afforded to citizens of other nations. Similarly, in Thomas's situation, the program director's comment exposed the normativity of the construction of the development worker as white, benevolent, and altruistic, and the Indigenous population as not. In that moment, Thomas's colleague's comments not only shone a spotlight on Thomas's presence, thus deconstructing the identity of the development worker, she also challenged the disparaging comments directed at the local staff by locating her own ability to volunteer with the organization in her socioeconomic privilege. The actions of Thomas's colleague embody that of the Authentic Ally, an individual who intentionally and actively resists and challenges moments of oppression.

Conclusion

As a whole, the field of international social work requires systemic reflexivity on the professional hegemony of the North over the South. This requires social workers to question the ways in which we reproduce oppressive North-South relations while working within the international context. From the institutional level, international social work and development programs need to problematize the utility of employing Northern values and approaches to addressing social concerns in Southern countries. This approach subordinates and ignores the indigenous methods of addressing local needs. In addition, the perpetuation of the universality of Western social work practices reinforces paternalistic North-South power relations, perpetuates a unilateral transfer of knowledge, and inadequately prepares the student to work as an Authentic Ally in their international practice. At the individual level, the Ally Model and Self-Reflection Checklist encourages the individual to investigate their power and privilege, highlights the dangers of a non-reflexive practice, and illuminates how our practices may be reinforcing the oppressive relations that we seek to dismantle. The Ally Model provides a starting point for deconstructing the professional imperialism perpetuated by international social work education and practice. This model is a strategy for engaging in authentic anti-oppressive and anti-racist social work, both within the Canadian and international contexts. It is a strategy for advancing the global social justice project.

AUTHENTIQ
CONSULTING

Authentic Allies

MINDSET
- Believe that they are allies
- Have the desire to be allies

BEHAVIOURS
- Acknowledge and reflect on their unearned privilege(s)
- Dialogue on how their behaviour/privilege(s) contributes to the oppression of others
- Validate the experience of oppression of others
- Engage in multilateral learning
- Actively encourage others to reflect and change their unearned privilege(s)

Apathetic Allies

MINDSET
- Believe that they are allies
- Have the desire to be allies

BEHAVIOURS
- Unable to acknowledge their unearned privilege(s)
- Resistant to dialogue about how their unearned privilege(s) perpetuates oppression
- Learn off the backs of marginalized people (absence of multilateral learning)
- Delegitimize/silence voices of the marginalized

VS

THE GUILTY

MINDSET
- Recognize that their privilege oppresses others, however, cannot move past the feelings of guilt associated with their privilege

BEHAVIOURS
- Stay silent during acts of overt/covert racism and other discrimination
- Disengage from dialogues of oppression

THE SOCIALLY INNOCENT

MINDSET
- Cannot view themselves as the oppressor or refusal to acknowledge how they oppress others

BEHAVIOURS
- Unable to recognize when they are taking part in overt/covert racism and other discrimination
- Do not acknowledge the differential impact of racism and other discrimination

THE PASSIVE BACKLASHER

MINDSET
- Belief in the notion that we reside in a society with race neutrality, meritocracy, and equal opportunity
- Belief in the existence of "reverse discrimination"

BEHAVIOURS
- Active refusal to acknowledge or validate experiences of oppression of others
- Problematize the individual who experienced oppression

WHAT TYPE OF ALLY ARE YOU?

Our work expands on the writings of Anne Bishop (2002) who defined "the allies", "the guilty," and "the backlashers," and Amy Rossiter (2001) who coined the term "socially innocent". We have expanded on these concepts by critically examining the spectrum of allies that exists from the Guilty, to the Socially Innocent, to the Passive Backlasher. We propose that there are two distinct types of allies: the Apathetic and the Authentic. We believe that in becoming an ally, one cannot wax and wane – either you are an ally or you are not. There is no middle ground between an Apathetic Ally and an Authentic Ally; for one cannot simultaneously be both. What type of ally are you?

Figure 5.1. The Ally Model (developed by Chandrasekera and Thomas)

AUTHENTIQ
CONSULTING

authentiqconsultants.com

Becoming an Authentic Ally

A SELF-REFLECTION CHECKLIST

An Authentic Ally is an individual who:

- Recognizes that diversity, equity, social justice, and anti-oppression work is an action-oriented practice;
- Validates other people's experiences of oppression and does not stay silent in the moments when discrimination occurs;
- Engages in multilateral learning so that the person(s) who engaged in discrimination and the person(s) who experienced discrimination can benefit from the transfer of knowledge; and,
- Uses their position of privilege to advocate for equity.

The following is a series of questions to assist you to self-reflect and assess whether you are an Authentic Ally:

UNDERSTANDING INDIVIDUAL IDENTITY

○ Are you educated about your own heritage and your social group (i.e. gender, age, race, religion, disability, etc.)?

○ Do you feel good about and take pride in your social group membership?

○ Do you understand the privileges and disadvantages associated with your social group?

○ Do you agree that in order to create an equitable society, we need to collectively learn and unlearn our oppressive beliefs and practices (i.e. our assumptions of others based on stereotypes)?

UNDERSTANDING "OTHERS"

○ Do you educate yourself on the heritage, history and culture of the marginalized group members in our society?

○ Do you actively listen, acknowledge and respect the experiences of marginalized group members?

ADDRESSING "THE ISMS"

○ Do you use your position of privilege to disrupt incidents of discrimination?

○ Do you use your position of privilege to challenge persons and organizations that engage in discrimination?

○ Do you challenge others in your social group to reflect on their positions of privilege?

WHEN FACED WITH AN INCIDENT OF OPPRESSION AND/OR DISCRIMINATION:

○ Did you take action in the moment (i.e. speak out in solidarity) or did you remain silent?

○ Did you validate the experience of the person(s) who experienced discrimination?

○ Did you use your position of privilege to challenge the person(s) and/or organization(s) that engaged in discrimination?

© 2010 UPPALA CHANDRASEKERA & LAHOMA THOMAS

Figure 5.2. Becoming an Authentic Ally: A Self-Reflection Checklist (developed by Chandrasekera and Thomas)

GLOSSARY OF TERMS

Ally: an individual who belongs to the dominant social group who intentionally and actively resists oppression and takes action against discrimination
and social injustice (Bishop, 2002; Lopes & Thomas, 2006).

Authentic Ally: an individual who understands, acknowledges, and engages
in self-reflection regarding the power and privilege that they wield in the
world. The Authentic Ally not only acknowledges but validates others'
experiences of marginalization and oppression, they engage in multilateral
learning, so that both the oppressor and the oppressed can be educated
about the causes and impact of oppression, without placing blame. The
most important characteristic of the Authentic Ally is that they engage in
the *action-oriented practice* of anti-oppression and anti-racism; they intentionally and actively resist the moments when their privilege forces others
to the margins.

Apathetic Ally: an individual who possess an understanding of the historical
ways in which privilege(s) (gained historically through colonization and
presently through intersecting social locations such as whiteness, citizenship, formal education, class, sexual orientation, and gender) have been
used to oppress others and push them to the margins of society; however,
they are unable to acknowledge, or they deny how they continue to benefit
from their privilege and how those privileges infringe upon marginalized
groups. The actions of the Apathetic Ally can be classified into three
distinct categories: the Socially Innocent, the Passive Backlasher, and
the Guilty.

Anti-Oppressive Practice (AOP): is an umbrella term for a number of social
justice-oriented approaches to social work, including feminist, Marxist,
postmodernist, Indigenous, post-structural, critical constructionist, anti-
colonial, and anti-racist. These approaches draw on social activism and
collective organizing as well as a sense that social services can and should
be provided in ways that integrate liberatory understandings of social
problems and human behaviour (Baines, 2007, p. 4).

Racialization: refers to the inequitable distribution of power and the process
by which racial categories are constructed as different and unequal in ways
that have social, economic, and political consequences (Galabuzi, 2006,
p. 251).

The Global South: refers to nations around the world that are rooted
in the history of colonization and Western imperialism, are often
referred to as "developing countries," and consist mainly of racialized
citizenry.

NOTES

1 Racialization refers to the inequitable distribution of power and the
   "process by which racial categories are constructed as different and
   unequal in ways that have social, economic, and political consequences"
   (Galabuzi, 2006, p. 251).
2 Anti-oppressive practice (AOP) has become the cornerstone in social
   work education and practice because it recognizes the existence of
   intersectionality, whereby an individual can experience multiple, intersecting oppressions all at the same time (Galabuzi, 2006). In *Doing Anti-*
   Oppressive Practice: Building Transformative Politicized Social Work, Baines
   (2007) writes, "Rather than a single approach, AOP is an umbrella term
   for a number of social justice-oriented approaches to social work,
   including feminist, Marxist, postmodernist, Indigenous, post-structural,
   critical constructionist, anti-colonial and anti-racist approaches. These
   approaches draw on social activism and collective organizing as well as
   a sense that social services can and should be provided in ways that
   integrate liberatory understandings of social problems and human
   behaviour" (p. 4).

REFERENCES

Baines, D. (2007). Anti-oppressive social work practice: Fighting for space,
   fighting for change. In D. Baines (Ed.), *Doing anti-oppressive practice: Building*
   transformative politicized social work, (pp. 1–9). Halifax: Fernwood.
Barry-Shaw, N., Engler, Y., & Jay, D.O. (2012). *Paved with good intentions:*
   Canada's development NGOs from idealism to imperialism. Winnipeg:
   Fernwood.
Bishop, A. (2002). *Becoming an ally: Breaking the cycle of oppression in people*
   (2nd ed.). Halifax: Fernwood.
Chandrasekera, U., & Thomas, L. (2013). Exposing the apathetic ally: An
   examination of diversity and race in health and social service organizations.
   International Journal of Organizational Diversity.
Collins, P.H. (1986). Learning from the outsider within: The sociological
   significance of Black Feminist Thought. *Social Problems, 33*(6), S14–S32.
   http://dx.doi.org/10.2307/800672
Cook, N. (2007). *Gender, identity, and imperialism: Women development workers*
   in Pakistan. New York: Palgrave Macmillan. http://dx.doi.org/10.1057/
   9780230610019

Dei, G. (1993). Sustainable development in the African context: Revisiting some theoretical and methodological issues. *Africa Development/Afrique et Developpement*, *18*(2), 97–110.

Dei, G. (2008). SES1921Y Principles of Anti-Racism Education Course Lecture Notes (1–82) (Unpublished lecture notes). Ontario Institute for Studies in Education, University of Toronto.

Drucker, D. (2003). Whither international social work? *International Social Work*, *46*(1), 53–81. http://dx.doi.org/10.1177/0020872803046001596

Galabuzi, G.E. (2006). *Canada's economic apartheid: The social exclusion of racialized groups in the new century*. Toronto: Canadian Scholar's Press Inc.

Goldstein, H. (2001). *Experiential learning: A foundation for social work education and practice.* Alexandria, VA: Council on Social Work Education.

Heron, B. (2006). Critically considering international social work practica. *Critical Social Work*, *7*(2), n.p.

Heron, B. (2007). *Desire for development: Whiteness, gender and the helping imperative*. Waterloo: Wilfrid Laurier University Press.

Huag, E. (2005). Critical reflections on the emerging discourse of international social work. *International Social Work*, *48*(2), 126–135. http://dx.doi.org/10.1177/0020872805050204

Iffe, J. (1999). Report of assessment mission to East Timor. International federation of social workers. Retrieved from http://ifsw.org/resources/report-of-assessment-mission-to-east-timor.

Kapoor, I. (2004). Hyper-self-reflexive development? Spivak on representing the third world "other." *Third World Quarterly*, *25*(4), 627–647. http://dx.doi.org/10.1080/01436590410001678898

Lopes, T., & Thomas, B. (2006). *Dancing on live embers: Challenging racism in organizations*. Toronto: Between the Lines.

Lopez, G.R. (2003). The (racially neutral) politics of education: A critical race theory perspective. *Educational Administration Quarterly*, *39*(1), 68–94. http://dx.doi.org/10.1177/0013161X02239761

Martinez-Brawley, E.E. (1999). Social work, postmodernism and higher education. *International Social Work*, *42*(3), 333–346. http://dx.doi.org/10.1177/002087289904200307

Midgley, J. (1981). *Professional imperialism: Social work in the third world*. London: Heinemann.

Midgley, J. (1990). International social work: Learning from the third world. *Social Work*, *35*(4), 295–301.

Midgley, J. (2001). Issues in international social work. *Journal of Social Work*, *1*(1), 21–35. http://dx.doi.org/10.1177/146801730100100103

Oliver-Smith, V. (2010). *Defying displacement: Grassroots resistance and the critique of development*. Austin: University of Texas Press.

Pawar, M., Hanna, G., & Sheridan, R. (2004). International social work practicum in India. *Australian Social Work, 57*(3), 223–236. http://dx.doi.org/10.1111/j.1447-0748.2004.00150.x

Razack, N. (2002). A critical examination of international student exchanges. *International Social Work, 45*(2), 251–265.

Razack, N. (2009). Decolonizing the pedagogy and practice of international social work. *International Social Work, 52*(1), 9–21. http://dx.doi.org/10.1177/0020872808097748

Razack, S. (2002). Introduction: When place becomes race. In S. Razack (Ed.), *Race, space and the law: Unmapping a white settler society* (pp. 1–20). Toronto: Between the Lines.

Razack, S. (2004). *Dark threats and white knights: The Somalia affair, peacekeeping and the new imperialism.* Toronto: University of Toronto Press.

Rossiter, A. (2001). Innocence lost and suspicion found: Do we educate for or against social work? *Critical Social Work, 2*(1), 1–9.

Sue, D.W. (2004, Nov). Whiteness and ethnocentric monoculturalism: Making the "invisible" visible. *The American Psychologist, 59*(8), 761–769. http://dx.doi.org/10.1037/0003-066X.59.8.761 Medline:15554844

Tiessen, R. (2007). Educating global citizens? Canadian foreign policy and youth study/volunteer abroad program. *Canadian Foreign Policy Journal, 14*(1), 77–84. http://dx.doi.org/10.1080/11926422.2007.9673453

Tiessen, R. (2012). Motivations for learning/volunteer abroad programs: Research with Canadian youth. *Journal of Global Citizenship and Equity Education, 2*(1), 1–21.

Tiessen, R., & Heron, B. (2012). Volunteering in the developing world: The perceived impacts of Canadian youth. *Development in Practice, 22*(1), 44–56. http://dx.doi.org/10.1080/09614524.2012.630982

Wane, N.N. (2009). Canadian feminist thought: Perspectives on equity and diversity in the academy. *Race, Ethnicity and Education, 12*(1), 65–77. http://dx.doi.org/10.1080/13613320802650964

Webber, R. (2005). Integrating work-based and academic learning in international and cross-cultural settings. *Journal of Education and Work, 18*(4), 473–487.

Wehbi, S. (2009). Deconstructing motivations: Challenging international social work placements. *International Social Work, 52*(1), 48–59. http://dx.doi.org/10.1177/0020872808097750

Yee, J.Y., & Dumbrill, G.C. (2003). Whiteout: Looking for race in Canadian social work practice. In K. Al-Kronan & J.R. Graham (Eds.), *Multicultural social work in Canada: Working with diverse ethno-racial communities* (pp. 98–121). Don Mills: Oxford University Press.

6 Secondary School Experiential Learning Programs in the Global South: Critical Reflections from an Ontario Study

KATHRYN FIZZELL AND MARC EPPRECHT

Introduction

Students are increasingly entering the post-secondary education system in Canada seeking out international experiential learning opportunities. The programs cited as most in demand are those that involve travel to less developed countries, most of which include some form of voluntary work. University and college administrations also increasingly tout such programs as markers of their internationalization, the better to prepare students for careers in the globalized market. These programs have been the subject of considerable critical enquiry. Studies point out, for example, a raft of questionable benefits for students from the Global North, plus concerns over local labour replacement in the Global South, resource consumption by volunteers, gender and racial tensions between volunteers and host community members, the use of imagery of the developing world that reinforces notions of "otherness," "incompetence," and "need," and a range of other often quite disturbing ethical and pedagogical concerns. The critique has led to some innovative responses that emphasize critical pedagogy, where the taken-for-granted benefits of volunteering abroad are questioned in relation to the role that power plays in framing relationships and representations.[1]

Little attention, however, has thus far been paid in this critical scholarship to the ways that these programs are evolving within Canada's secondary school system. As a result, we lack an understanding of the types of learning abroad experiences that students may have already had when they enter post-secondary institutions. We therefore know little about how this may impact their expectations for future programs, or how it shapes their conceptualization of global relations and their own positionality within our highly inequitable world. There is also little evidence amongst the academic literature that school boards in Ontario are engaged in debates around the role that critical pedagogy should play in relation to international experiential learning programs that take place in the Global South, or factors that may impede that objective such as the involvement of private, for-profit corporations.

This chapter aims to address aspects of these gaps in the scholarship. It asks: What types of international experiential learning experiences are being offered in secondary schools in Ontario? To what extent have secondary school teachers considered the potential ethical issues that may arise from running these trips in the Global South? And how can more critical forms of pedagogy and better understandings of the concept of experiential learning mitigate the ethical issues encountered and enrich the transformative potential of the experience? Our argument is based principally on data collected by the primary investigator, a secondary school teacher with prior, mixed experiences with her own experiential learning program in Costa Rica.[2] The study involved semi-structured interviews with ten individuals employed in the Greater Toronto area in both public and independent secondary schools and acting as facilitators of international experiential learning programs. The goal was to gather perspectives of the teachers who facilitate these programs on such questions as why they were running them, what they hoped to achieve, what practical problems or ethical dilemmas they encountered, and how they understood the potential impacts of these programs on their students and the host communities within which they volunteered.

The overall argument being put forth in this chapter is that international experiential learning does indeed have the potential to be transformative as envisioned by Kolb (1984), Meizrow (2000), and Huish (in chapter 8 of this volume), each of whom build off the work of Paolo Freire. Freire (2000) sees education as a realm within which the oppressed – teachers and students alike – can work together, through action and reflection, to transform their understanding of the world and hence transform the very knowledge base and structural systems which have sustained their oppression (p. 126). The findings of our study showed that teachers were able to identify, on occasion, specific ethical issues that may arise in this transformative vein. They also sometimes sought to encourage students to deconstruct power relations enacted both within the community and embedded more broadly in mainstream, hegemonic systems of knowledge (as proposed as pedagogical goals by, for example, Brookfield, 2000; OISE, 2011; and Desrosiers & Thomson in chapter 7 of this volume). However, there was very limited discussion or awareness of the types of normative ethics or "hidden curricula" in the programs. Indeed, participants often answered questions put to them by questioning themselves. Our hope is that post-secondary educators and administrators can therefore reflect on the conclusions drawn in this study: (a) that teachers need to be provided with more training in relation to development studies, experiential learning models, and critical pedagogy techniques; and (b) that the concerns raised about the privileging of the student experience over those of the host community raised in the scholarship on post-secondary learning are transferable to any context that involves volunteers from the Global North travelling to the Global South.

The Structure of International Experiential Learning Programs in Ontario Secondary Schools

The international experiential learning programs described by the participants in this study fall into two categories: credit-bearing programs linked to an Ontario curriculum and those (the majority) that are non-credit bearing and take place outside of the student's and teacher's regular academic course load. Considerable variety can be found in each category. The longest and best-developed program is a unique international cooperative education program where students spend eight months preparing for a three-month placement in a South American country, followed by a final month of debriefing activities. Grade 10 Spanish is a prerequisite, while prior to departure students must complete independent and classroom-based academic work to achieve three grade 12 university preparation credits in the subject areas of geography, politics, history, and economics. Much of the latter is student-led learning specifically focused on the host country and region. Alongside academic learning, the teacher of this program also emphasized the importance of teaching students how to stay safe and healthy while abroad and preparing them for the differences they would encounter in day-to-day life in the host country.

The community work experience in this program itself earns an additional three cooperative education credits. Students participate in an orientation camp upon arrival and are then placed in different communities where they live with a host family and work with various local businesses or organizations. Students are under the supervision of the local host organization for the first six weeks of their time in the host country, at which point the teacher facilitator travels to meet with students, host families, and work placement supervisors.

This program clearly holds the most potential to offer students a transformative learning experience where critical pedagogy techniques could be applied to the program design and implementation. The program is longer-term in nature, is directly connected to curriculum, and involves a high degree of collaboration between the individual teacher facilitator, the sending organization, and the host communities. In this particular case, the teacher is fluent in Spanish, meets with each of the students' host families and work placements, and provides specific feedback to everyone involved in the program. With this combination of factors, the program offers a foundation upon which a teacher could embrace the ethos of "critical" or "thick" global citizenship referred to by Cameron in chapter 2.

Shorter-term credit-bearing trips are clearly more limited from the perspective of the learning model advocated by Crabtree (1998, 2008), which emphasizes the importance of designing a curriculum-related project in conjunction with the host community, and of creating a concrete experience upon which students can be guided towards critical reflection. The courses generally take place in the summer (two to four weeks), with in-class preparatory sessions being held either at monthly intervals or during one week of full-day classes before the trip begins. The students earn between one and two credits in these programs, on top of the six to eight credits normally earned during the school year. The curriculum expectations for these related credits may or may not create opportunities to address current issues faced by the host country, and none include any language-learning component. Moreover, the teachers in this study who facilitate these short-term credit-bearing programs were not directly involved in the design of a community service project that would meet both the predetermined curriculum expectations and the specific needs of the community. Nor do their programs provide an extended period of critical reflection after the trip, which is considered a crucial aspect of the learning experience (Epprecht, 2004).

The seven non-credit-bearing programs in this study (the majority, as appears to be the case in Ontario, generally) are better understood as a form of voluntourism because of their short time frames (one to two weeks), the group-based nature of the volunteer work, and the additional elements of tourist-related activities structured into the experience. Numerous problems have been identified with this model, however, which falls far short of the transformative goals sought (and often touted) in learning abroad programs. To be fair, when considering these problems we must keep in mind that the application of the service learning model in high school settings is extremely challenging for the teacher because it takes a considerable investment of time and energy beyond the everyday demands of a regular teaching load (Billig & Root, 2006). When this experiential learning model is then extended to experiences in the Global South, the reality of a full-time secondary school teacher working in participatory-style development projects is simply unrealistic. As one participant noted, teachers do not have the time, training, or supports to reflect critically upon global inequalities, let alone develop international service learning experiences that use participatory style development practices, as is suggested as a best practice by Crabtree (2008). As one participant notes:

> I mean I think that if you look at these trips as development work, it kind of highlights that most teachers are not equipped to facilitate development work. I wasn't equipped, that's a particular skill set that I think is very far off from the world of teaching, in a lot of ways, but in a lot of other ways, it's actually where teaching should be, right? Because teachers should be able to highlight things around power and relationships between Global North and Global South and how people are racialized and gendered or classed – but it's just not the way our educational system is set up. We just don't have those bodies and those rules … So it was kind of a tricky dance for me, to sort of figure out, okay how much of the cultural difference crap can I do, and how much can I talk about power? (P7)[3]

While several participants noted their lack of theoretical understandings of development, many commented that even when they did try to engage students in conversations around these issues they were met with a lack of interest by both students and fellow staff. The more critically minded participants noted the need to skirt around sensitive issues about power by using vague language or emphasizing culture and practical goals. This could create a profound sense of frustration and missed opportunities, although it certainly adheres to the "avoid controversy" model that predominates in the Ontario secondary school system. As one facilitator reflected on a trip to West Africa:

> I was profoundly disturbed by the level of just … okay, I'll give you an example. Every night we would have dinner at one of the two houses where the kids and faculty were staying, and the [local] NGO staff would

have dinner with us. And these were just an amazing group of guys who basically decided that they weren't going to go the route of working in a bank in [name of city omitted] to make a lot of money, but they're going to work in the villages and help their communities. So, at dinner, the kids had access to ask these guys questions, and they wouldn't engage them at all. They were more interested in talking about their lives at [name of school omitted], and the other staff thought this was totally fine. And I was like, "you know you guys, you have to ask, you can't leave here without asking why he does what he does and how he came to do this, right?" And I didn't want to force it and stage it and make it happen; I wanted them to do it, and he left, and then nobody ever asked. And I was just like, you know, there were so many little things like that I found extremely frustrating. (P7)

Trip Rationale and Perceived Benefits

When asked about the overall rationale for the trip, participant responses conformed to the widely observed trend that international experiential learning programs are generally discussed in relation to the benefits to the volunteers (Guttentag, 2009; Raymond & Hall, 2008; Plater, Steven, Bringle, & Clayton, 2009; Tonkin, 2011). Throughout the interviews, the benefits to the host community were pushed to the background, almost to non-existence in some cases. Participants focused instead on encouraging students to feel good about helping others, to appreciate other cultures, to develop interpersonal skills, to learn more about themselves as Canadians, and, finally, to experience a transformation of perspectives on the world around them that neither classroom learning nor standard tourism and travel can offer. The facilitator/teacher introduced the trip to the students as follows:

So the way we word it is this is an alternative to a spring break trip. [We ask the students:] Do you want to do something substantial for a community that doesn't have a lot? Do you want to feel good about your trip and still experience something in a new trip? Then let's go and do that. They come back changed. (P5)

This conceptualization (and its vagueness) speaks to Tiessen's findings (chapter 4 in this volume) where she notes that an international learning experience is increasingly considered a benchmark achievement for Canadian youth, although we do not know (and indeed the teachers and students themselves often do not know) its exact value when it comes to acceptance into post-secondary institutions or the future job market. To be sure, some participants did try to articulate exactly what experience, empowerment, or feeling good meant in relation to their students' personal growth. For one, it meant that the students might come to recognize their privilege and be more appreciative of their material wealth. It should be noted that, based on our own interpretation of the response, the following quote from a participant is not referring to privilege in terms of the difference between the Global North and Global South but rather in terms of their position within Canadian society, as students who attend a fee-based independent school:

> And although it sounds kind of corny or hokey, the experience they get from it – they are different people and you see a side of them you've never seen before. And probably, the most important thing is that it opens their eyes to another culture and another way of life. And not a slam against these students at all, but they're privileged, they have lots of money, they've got a nice way of life, so it really makes them appreciate what they have. (P4)

Another participant described the personal growth he witnessed amongst his students as follows:

> [There was] an increased sense of cultural sensitivity and an increased respect for people in general. [The students gained a] respect for parents in Canada and what they've done for them [the students], [and] a respect for and an appreciation for Canadian health care, [and] Canadian education. (P6)

It would be difficult to claim that there is anything wrong with teaching Canadian youth to be respectful and appreciative of their families or to teach them some of the benefits of living in Canadian society. However, Simpson's (2004) arguments related to the potential for this way of thinking – to lead volunteers to develop a form of "lotto logic" – must be considered. Simpson (2004) argues that when students focus primarily on their own position in relation to the various forms of poverty they encounter while abroad, they run the risk of associating this difference with the so-called "luck" of being born in one place rather than another. This decreases the opportunity for students to question the structures and systems within which we all live that contribute to these conditions of inequality, and may demotivate students from future engagement with social justice initiatives. Furthermore, focusing on an appreciation of Canada may lead students to make sweeping generalizations about what it means to be Canadian. This is another key avenue for teacher-led reflection, where students could be challenged to question both how and why their experience of being Canadian may differ from those of less privileged Canadians. If students are not challenged to develop a more critical understanding of Canadian society, including domestic inequality, poverty, and the "missionary tradition" both in Canadian relations with its aboriginal populations and in Canadian foreign policy, the potential to develop a simplified, binary understanding of the Global North as rich and the Global South as poor is increased (Rennick, 2012). To reach this level of thick or critical reflection, it is of course necessary for teachers to have some awareness of critical theories related to colonialism, global political economy, and international development.

In a similar fashion to Desrosiers and Thomson's (in chapter 7) observation that their students had difficulty articulating exactly what type of change they had undergone, teachers did not often specify what exactly it was about the experience that was eye-opening or life-changing – it seemed to be assumed that to witness poverty was automatically a perception-altering or transformational learning experience. Yet there is a powerful critique of "poverty tourism" that alerts us to several problems here. Poverty tourism is a form of travel where the desire to observe and interact with impoverished places actually reproduces or enhances the sense of distance and separation between the tourist and the poor (Simpson, 2004). Even more troubling is when poverty tourism becomes a marker of status when the traveller gets home. Two participants working in the independent school system drew attention to the growing expectation that all students will have completed an international learning experience by the time they graduate from high school. For many independent schools in Ontario, the international experiential learning opportunities on offer are a defining element of the school's brand. One of these participants drew specific attention to the monetary value associated with completing one of these trips:

> In the independent industry it's huge ... But I don't think there's a real sense of the value that they get in terms of being able to put that on your resume [or that it] has a monetary value. (P7)

When pressed to elaborate on their understanding of the phrase "personal growth," responses began to fall into the critical pedagogy end of the spectrum. This included discussion of a form of empowerment that was not solely related to feeling good about doing good for others, but rather through having to work through challenges or problems in a more independent manner than they would at home. Another facilitator commented:

> I think there's a great improvement in maturity and that comes from problem solving, not relying on your parents to solve your problems, [and] not having your parents, which is a blessing for many kids – they get a bit of freedom. There's lots of well-meaning parents out there who choke their kids and don't let them take the responsibility they're very capable of taking. (P6)

In another case, a teacher invoked Meizrow's (2000) concept of transformational learning by noting that the experience abroad initiated a change in their students' desire to engage in new behaviours that focused on giving back to others:

> But then to see that [learning] transform itself into a student that then takes [it] upon themselves, and has their own initiative to give back, then I think that's a program that's been successful. (P9)

The issues of taking initiative and giving back are not, of course, necessarily or inherently transformative. As Baaz (2005) and Heron (2007) point out, volunteer work in the developing world is often more about the search for self-identity, often through the amelioration of unanchored feelings of guilt, than it is about challenging the sources of the inequality that creates the conditions that enable individuals to perceive themselves as helping others. Heron (2007) refers to this phenomenon as the "helping imperative." The extent to which these theories can be applied to students at such a young age is outside the scope of this study; however, one participant expressed uncertainty over how to address charity-oriented attitudes that reflect the helping imperative.[4]

> Yeah, that's a challenge for me too, and I don't know whether to address it. I've done it both ways and I don't know which is better – to address it from the start, or to let them have this [idea] we'll change them, or we'll fix them, or *we're* going to be the saviours. Do I address this from the beginning so that they're aware of it all the way through, or do I let them have that "I'm going to go change them" and then at the end lead them to "Did

you change them?" "Can you change them?" "Do you want to change them?" So I don't know, that is a challenge on a theoretical level I guess, [deciding] what's the better way to address it. (P1)

A further tension arose from the prevalent assumption that all experiences can lead to personal growth. The tension arises from uncertainty amongst teachers and facilitators as to whether the nature of that growth is dependent on the student's disposition or guided learning strategies. For example, one participant said the following:

But I struggle with that [idea of personal growth] too, because like I said before, I think the journey is different for every single person and I don't think we get to dictate the direction of personal growth ... I would say [students are] adaptable, in that your perceptions going in might not be – like you need to be willing to be changed, essentially, or have your perceptions shifted, sometimes gently, sometimes not. (P8)

One participant set herself apart by expressing a sophisticated theoretical understanding of the assumed individual responsibility for personal growth:

The personal growth is important and I wouldn't want to deny that piece, but the minute that you said that, a whole bunch of red flags go up for me, because, in that kind of framing, a lot of times bodies can be used as objects for other people's personal growth and I think that happens a lot, particularly in a racialized sort of context where it's about your own humanity, or the student's humanity, and it's presumed that because it is about personal growth that it's good. And that you don't really have to look at what's happening ... But I think that it's the way that we fail to set the conditions, and the way that we fall into the neoliberal project of self-realization as being the ultimate goal and it's so atomized, so individualized, do you know what I'm saying? ... So I think, okay sure, we can talk about personal growth, but is that personal, is that just about you? And who does that include and who does that exclude? And why? And what is your growth at the expense of? You know? I think you could do it in a way that's more contextualized for example. (P7)

Of course teachers will always be learning through experience themselves, but this participant's comments reaffirm the importance of developing theoretical understandings of notions related to "helping" and "change" as rationales when purposefully creating learning experiences through interactions with communities in the Global South.

Tourist-Related Activities

Although all of the participants described the trip portion of the program as centring on the volunteer work, all of the programs incorporate some element of tourist activity. This included excursions to an urban centre, days at the beach, and visiting nature reserves and/or historical/educational sites. The amount of time dedicated towards tourist activities seemed to vary according to the overall goals of the trip and the interests of the teacher. Sometimes tourist activities were framed as "adventure," and they were understood as an element of travel with the potential to push students out of their comfort zones; hence they became an additional impetus for personal growth and learning. In other cases, tourist activities were discussed as a way to take a mid-volunteer break from the community in order to recuperate and reflect on the experience before returning to complete the volunteer work. The addition of tourist-related elements, and the rationale for their inclusion, complicates the potential of these trips to reflect on truly reciprocal relations with the host communities.[5] Indeed, if the activities are cost-prohibitive to the communities within which students are interacting and the students' privilege goes unexplored or unquestioned, the potential for a truly transformational learning experience is lost. Again, we find that teachers are aware of the importance of the reflective component, yet they sometimes fail themselves to critically reflect on the contradictions inherent in these program models.

The exploitative and resource-wasteful nature of "typical tourist stuff" (P7) can create challenges for teachers when working on program design in collaboration with other staff and/or sending organizations. As the following quote alludes, one participant's perception of how she was received by her colleagues as a nuisance for raising these issues speaks to arguments made by McQuaid (2009) and Kahn (2011) on the need for the teaching profession as a whole to be engaged in a form of self-reflective learning that questions relationships of power and knowledge construction:

But also, that [typical tourist] stuff isn't really debunked either, in terms of what it means to be a tourist, and the gaze of a tourist, and that's a part of it, too, that doesn't get taken up ... I was so disturbed to see the treatment of the elephants on the fun tourist day ... I was actually pissed off at the other leaders because they thought it was totally fine, and I went back to the school, basically, and said that I didn't think this was appropriate to support, for one thing, and they just thought I was being a pain in the ass, right? So there were things like that that did affect my relationship with other teachers on the trip too. (P7)

The tourist gaze has much in common with what Clost (in chapter 12 of this volume) refers to as the "visual economy of volunteering abroad," which tends to exoticize the "other" and to emphasize binary differences between the Global North and Global South (see also Roman, 2003; Guttentag, 2009). For example, one participant, while describing the type of learning that was taking place during the trip commented:

Yeah, definitely, I mean even just things like seeing the climate, seeing the roads, seeing the geography of the country, seeing the attitude of the people – you know they [the locals] don't have that North American "go-go-go" attitude there, so I think it really opened their [the students] eyes as to why it's very difficult to make changes. And they [students] understand that you can't just go into someone else's country and start changing things as to what you think is right. So I think that was huge for them. (P4)

Students coming to the realization that they cannot change others can be considered an important learning goal. However, likely without realizing it, this participant is implying that there is something inherent in the North American culture or lifestyle that brings about a higher standard of living than that of the host community. The result of framing the situation in this manner is that the poverty students are observing becomes understood as a product of some unspoken, implicitly negative quality amongst the local people, which then eliminates the potential for students to develop a more critical understanding of how North Americans, and their way of life, may contribute to the very conditions they are observing while abroad.

Discussion of what it means to be a tourist would by necessity require careful deconstruction of the imagery used to sell the Global South (and in many cases the experiential opportunity itself) to consumers in the Global North. The plain fact is that images of traffic jams, malls, and other banalities of life in the Global South are not effective recruitment tools compared to zebras, temples, and pristine beaches. While we did not have the opportunity to examine recruitment materials for the specific programs in this study, the widespread use of exoticizing imagery is anecdotally observable and, indeed, evidently structured into the business model of popular sending organizations.[6]

Of course, the issues related to the inclusion of tourism in these types of experiences are not black and white and it may happen that relatively politically conscious students from the Global North encounter frustration with consumerist, middle class partners in the Global South. Yet even when discussions of power are included in reflective exercises around tourism, the extent to which they challenge global power dynamics remains in question. As is pointed out by Langdon and Agyeyomah (chapter 3 in this volume), we must be careful to ensure that an *acknowledgment* of the differences in privilege and power held by program participants from the Global North when compared to their counterparts in the Global South is not mistaken for a critical examination of the structural causes of these differences. The following participant, for example, reflects on a discussion he had with his students about power in relation to the leakage of tourist dollars out of the host country back to the Global North, and the differences between spending money on "mass tourism" versus "local tourism":

> So I think you look at something like that [power] with students, and they get a better understanding of "oh, okay, if I have power, and I can choose where I spend my tourism dollars, cause I'm going to spend tourism dollars, I'm going to travel again, whether it's with my family or by myself as a backpacker or whatever – how can I use that power?" I think a lot of people don't understand that they have power in the first place – the shirt you wear, where does it come from? The chocolate you buy – is it child labour chocolate or is it fair trade chocolate? What does that mean? (P6)

In this case, the reality of individuals from the Global North continuing to travel to the Global South is acknowledged, and the participant addresses the concept of power. Yet he does so from a stance that is related to individual consumption patterns. As such, the notion that students hold power is not questioned or deconstructed. It is what they do with that power that is challenged, rather than why they have that power in the first place. Given the current structure of the majority of the international experiential learning programs discussed by the participants in this study, this is hardly surprising. Moreover, even the inclusion of global citizenship rhetoric in the Ontario secondary school curriculum may undermine the objective of critical reflection on power, due to its presentation of global themes as matters of national self-interest, including economic benefits, while failing to make room for the "views" or "visions" of people in the South (Schweisfurth, 2006; Evans, Ingram, MacDonald, & Weber, 2009).[7] This approach to global citizenship reflects the "conceptual vagueness" referred to by Cameron in chapter 2, and provides further evidence that global citizenship and international experiential learning programs are not necessarily associated with global justice.

Pedagogical Methods

Given the conceptual vagueness noted above, it is not surprising to find a lack of careful attention being paid to critical pedagogy at all three points in the learning experience. At the preparation stage for the non-credit-bearing trips in particular, teachers are generally focused on health and safety, cultural differences, student expectations, emotional preparedness, and fundraising. One participant specifically mentioned a method that involved exposing students to dramatic images of poverty. Of course there are compelling reasons for such an emphasis given the young age of the students and the need to assuage the worries of anxious parents and administrators. The obvious risk in this, however, is to represent the host country in a one-dimensional manner, as this facilitator described:

> ... She [team leader] showed a lot of pictures, like very raw graphic ... what you are going to see: kids living in a garbage heap, old people with no teeth ... [They gave] kind of the shock value that you need to give teenagers so they know where they're going. And I mean it was tough on them, but I don't think any of them was underprepared. (P4)

Another participant expressed a similar concern over the way that issues of health and safety positioned the host country (and people) as a threat:

> So that piece [of health and safety] disturbed me, because I found a lot of it, like the very first thing kids on the trip had to do, and faculty too, was get their inoculations ... and to me that framed it around the whole level of invasion, of potentially, just on the level of sickness and harm

physically, when I didn't feel like – I felt that the teachers really supported that framing of it. (P7)

To be sure, several teachers showed an awareness of the need to move away from the invasion or "saving others" mentality. Most schools, however, lacked the in-house capacity to deliver a well-rounded, critical alternative. As noted above, with the one exception of the long-term international co-op model, none of the programs provided location-specific pre-departure materials that would help students develop a nuanced understanding of the history of the host community or the current socio-political climate in which they would be immersed. By necessity, teachers had to rely upon the expertise of the sending organization, which may or (more commonly) may not prioritize critical pedagogy. The following participant explains his frustration with that conflict of interest:

P2: So the presentation [by the sending organization] was [promoting that] they were really going to change the lives of the people in this village. While they're there, they can feel – they can actually see the progress of walls going up, a roof going on, so there was a real sense of accomplishment.
KF: For the students?
P2: For the students – yeah, that's really important. And it's a sales pitch – for all the travel carriers there's a financial bottom line.
KF: Like even if they're an NGO?
P2: Yeah, like it has to make sense. An NGO's not going to be sending kids and footing the bill, so they need to get customers, or volunteers.

Pedagogy during the trip stage of the program focused primarily on encouraging students to reflect on their individual work and living experiences, primarily through journal writing and group discussion. As discussed earlier, reflection is indeed deemed to be one of the most important aspects of any experiential learning model (Kolb, 1984; Brookfield, 2000; Meizrow, 2000; Ash & Clayton, 2004; King, 2004). All three of the participants who facilitate credit-bearing trips appreciated this point, and emphasized that reflection both during and after the field experience was very important to their programs. Based on Brookfield's definition of "critical" reflection as one that incorporates some analysis of power relations, however, participant descriptions of their pedagogy stopped rather short of that goal. In the following example, not only is there no discussion of the sharing of observations in relation to a specific course content that addresses issues of power, but the teacher seems to abdicate any leadership *as a part* of the pedagogy:

> Reflection is one of the things I value most. Being able to talk about and being able to say, what did you see versus what did I see? We reflect on all those things. They keep a trip journal to reflect as well – there's all that type of reflection. They experience it, they go as deep as they are willing to, and they bring back what they need. So it's really neat, that it's not something that I have to check off the list, or check it off the curriculum, like okay, they know that because they can regurgitate two plus two, but they take back something. What it is they will describe in their debriefs and in their reflections and how much they bring back will be up to them so it's a neat way to teach. (P5)

Many of the teachers noted that, whatever their pedagogy was in theory, in practice they were generally overwhelmed by the day-to-day logistics of managing students. They were consequently less focused on the potential educational components of the trip than they would have preferred. One participant specifically discussed the barriers to her ability to facilitate reflection while on the trip: "If I'd had time to plan ahead and know exactly what I was focusing on, I think it would have been a bit easier to teach the students something while we were there" (P3). Another participant expressed a strong desire to move her international experiential learning programs into the realm of critical pedagogy, yet expressed frustration at how she could go about doing this within the constraints of the field:

> …Reflection is good, and the idea of experiential education is good, but how much does it become a naval gazing exercise? Like when does it get to issues of power? And I just find that, it just takes so much time, and so much knowledge, knowledge isn't the right word, but so much sensitivity to structure these things in a way that it does get to power. (P7)

Some of these concerns could of course be addressed in a post-trip stage. The most prevalent concern raised by the participants in relation to reflection, however, centred precisely on the barriers to facilitating such debriefing. Four of the participants specifically noted that when the trips were not embedded in coursework (i.e., most of them), it was difficult to get students to attend post-trip meetings. The framing of post-trip meetings as a celebration of the experience was mentioned by three of the participants, with one noting that this was a tactic she used to have the students commit to showing up, at which time she would be able to engage in the type of reflection she thought was essential for the students. It may be a risky tactic. One participant expressed a kind of dismay at the ways the students describe/celebrate their experiences abroad:

> P7: I find it really bizarre how they then took it up when they got back. It was almost like there was this narrative – like they knew the story. With the before, and the middle, and now with how they're expected to talk about it afterwards. Which makes the reflections more difficult. They know the words. They know the whole story and they're just telling you the story.
> KF: And what's usually at the centre of that, do you think?
> P7: It's their own subjectivity as someone who makes a difference. Someone who does good in the world. And so a lot of the tensions and ambiguities and contradictions are elided in that story.

In light of the many constraints noted so far, the tendency is to dampen down expectations. Teachers (if not administrators) want to impart an appropriately modest sense of what the students can actually achieve while away. Yet, as is echoed by Huish in this book (chapter 8), framing these trips outside the discourse of development or structural inequality is also problematic. It often leads to a mentality that since we are not trying to pretend these experiences are related to development, then we do not have to think about the socioeconomic differences between the students and the host communities. As one participant put it:

> Certainly we have courses that deal with developmental economics and those kinds of issues. But really the stress for all the trips is to get the most out of that one experience, you know … they don't get too macro – like what are the factors that led us all here? (P9)

This approach greatly diminishes the potential to have students self-reflect on their own positionality in relation to the host community, and this may impact their behaviour and attitudes in future endeavours related to interactions with people in the Global South. It does not mean that the project has to be labelled as "development work." However, to ignore or to strategically blur the relationship of these programs to the history or context of development, as the majority of the participants in this study seemed to do, makes it impossible to frame these trips as an opportunity to develop a more critical understanding of global inequalities. Why, for example, are volunteers in the Global North in the position to volunteer or "serve" those in the Global South in the first place? How might the student/host relationship be seen as perpetuating inequality in the world rather than alleviating it? Without asking these questions, we fail to consider whether the learning experience may be causing harm in some way.

Challenges related to assessing these changes in behaviour illuminate the complicated intersection between trip rationale and critical pedagogy practices. It is not entirely clear whether participants' use of the terms transformation or personal growth really extends to the type described in the literature. It is clear, however, that the desired type of transformation is not something that can be easily quantified or evaluated. The following participant, for example, reflects on the types of changes he has seen in students that reinforce the reasons why he runs these trips:

> Yeah, I think that [assessing behaviour is] like anything in high school – you've got teenagers, adolescents – even if they're young adults. How do you – it's more like seed planting, you're really laying a foundation, I hope, you know, so it's hard if you never hear back from them. But we've got students like Jane Smith [student's name changed by participant], going off to medical school. She's finished her second or third year at [name of university omitted] and that's one you hear back from. And they've started their own [fund-raising] dinner at [name of university omitted] for the prison. They've been doing a holiday dinner, so they've taken a local example, so it hasn't changed her career focus, but global citizenship might change the context of why [she's] a physician or what [she's] doing as a physician – I don't know (laughs). (P2)

This quote is interesting because when the participant laughs it signals an awareness of the difficulty of trying to measure the impact these experiences have had on the students. The theory behind both experiential and transformational learning models claims that the learning process should culminate with some evidence of a conscious decision to either make a change in attitudes or behaviours or not. Because the evidence of these changes may not be immediate, teachers must rely on their own potentially self-interested perceptions of the changes that occur within their students plus anecdotal evidence from those few students who keep in contact with them to confirm the beneficial impact these programs have had.

Finally, it has been recognized that gendered learning styles play a significant role in how students move through the cycles of Kolb's (1984) experiential learning model. Indeed, one teacher in this study noted that he and his colleagues struggled with the issue of getting male students in particular to reflect: a common frustration amongst teachers at his all-boys school. Bearing in mind Heron's observations on the highly gendered nature of the "helping imperative," this is an obvious avenue of further investigation, and an issue that could be addressed through gender-differentiated instruction techniques.

Perceived Ethical Challenges

Many of the authors cited so far raise concerns about the ethics of international experiential learning programs from the Global North to the Global South, and indeed, such concerns were a motivating factor for the present study. To put it bluntly: Are international experiential learning programs at the secondary school level exploitative? Are they, under the guise of "helping," perpetuating Orientalist images of the Global South and emphasizing egoistic notions of "do-goodism" and personal growth in the Global North? Are these problems intrinsic to the structure of the programs or can effective steps be taken to mitigate them?

During the interviews, the participants were never directly asked about ethical issues related to their programs. We felt that to ask the participants directly would be to imply that these issues were well known, or that they would suggest negligence or culpability on the teachers' part. Terms such as "challenges" and "drawbacks" are less threatening, and thus create more room for the participants to explore their own feelings towards their practices and conceptualizations of these trips. The question was designed to explore whether or not, and how exactly, some of the ethical issues discussed in the literature were on the "radar" of the participants in this study, even if not in a conscious or explicit manner.

When asked to discuss some of the challenges they faced in their role as facilitators of international experiential learning programs, participants overwhelmingly responded first in relation to the challenges faced by students, such as adjusting to a new culture, staying safe and healthy while abroad, and overcoming language barriers. It is safe to say that teachers were closely aware of and aspired to the highest standards of professional ethics in this regard. The emphasis on safety and liability, however, created dilemmas for the participants. Most commonly, they felt obliged to use the sending organizations that administrators, parents, and teachers felt most comfortable with based on proven track records related to safety. The public school teachers in particular were constrained to choose from their school board's pre-approved list of travel carriers. Yet there could be conflicts of interest or ideology between the sending organization and the desire of the teachers for a critical and ethical learning experience for the students. As one participant expressed it:

> We had a lot of trouble; there was a real disconnect, or we had trouble finding out who [was] staffing this school, what kind of facilities [there were], who's going to be paying the utilities? So, it's almost like you were being sold an aid trip when we were looking for a volunteer trip. We didn't want to sell to the students: "Here's an aid package where we're going to change a community." With a little bit of research, we could not justify that. We could not find the evidence or data that would back that up ... but hopefully the host community's receptive, and (hesitates) happy I guess to have students come in and volunteer their time. I think it's also made very clear, I hope it's made very clear to the community, that students and the staff from [name of school board omitted] are not coming in to make their life better, or (laughs) – there's no revolution, there's no – that kind of stuff. (P2)

The institutionally embedded focus on potential risks associated with travel to the developing world also "implicitly references old colonial tropes" such as the fear of contagion (Heron, 2007, p. 790). This can diminish the potential for students to develop a sense of injustice in regards to the reality that the locals whom they encounter during their time abroad are equally (or more) vulnerable to these risks. The fact that only one participant expressed concern over this emphasis in preparatory sessions demonstrates that these types of more theoretically based ethical issues tend to fly under the radar of the average teacher facilitating international experiential learning in Ontario.

What ultimately emerged as more problematic – and hence more interesting to explore in this section – were discussions that centred on the impact of these programs on the host community. To begin, all of the participants acknowledged that the community had to benefit from the experience in order for it to be a worthwhile endeavour, yet three specifically mentioned their uncertainty as to how to go about assessing these benefits. For example, one participant addressed a concern that the volunteers have their experience in the community but then move on, which may invoke negative feelings amongst the community:

> You go to Kenya and you meet these students who are exactly the same age as you and they put on a huge dramatic production at the end that is unbelievable and you don't want to leave and you don't want to say good-bye and everyone's crying. But then you realize that those students that are in that scenario in Kenya – they have to do that again, three weeks later, with another group – and is that healthy? There's so many things that come with volunteerism that are good, but who does it benefit? Is it us? (P5)

This notion of community burnout was also expressed in relation to host family living situations: two participants thought that there need-ed to be continual re-evaluation of the benefits of these arrangements to the family. Yet that goal will be difficult for a teacher facilitator to real-ize unless they are actively engaged in the program planning. That was only the case with the international co-op program teacher and the one independent school teacher who works in a department of global edu-cation – both of which are full time positions related to facilitating these types of trips. In all of the other cases, the role as facilitator is either done in a voluntary capacity, running trips as extra-curricular activities, or as summer school positions, meaning that trip planning is done while still carrying a full teaching load during the regular school year. In these cases, teachers are structurally constrained not only by the time they have available to invest in exploring sending organization options but also by the increasing emphasis by schools and school boards on safety and liability. The need to fulfil so many different roles all of the time necessitated a compromise, or a performance – a kind of triage that sidelined time-consuming critical pedagogy methods. For one of the participants, this in itself became an ethical question. As she aptly put it:

> I think there's an ethical obligation, it's not just the impact on the develop-ing community, there's an ethical obligation to the kids that we're taking on these trips to give them better conceptual tools, to give them better language, to give them better instruments to understand the experiences

that they're having. I think that's a huge ethical obligation that's being totally missed. (P7)

Another participant raised questions over the type of preparation the community received – a question that is difficult to answer when the teacher works through a sending organization located in the Global North:

> I think, too, we get a lot of education on our end, but does the community where these trips are taking place in – did they get any information about who these people are, why they are doing it, what they gain from it? So I think it's probably more on the other end – like what do they think when a bunch of white kids show up and start fixing their stuff ... I'm sure there are communities that get helped that don't really want, or need – it must be frustrating for some people who are like, why are you coming to our country or sending kids to our country? But it's an interesting question. (P4)

One of the more complex reflections a participant offered during the interviews was concern expressed over the impact of having female students living in host families in a rural community where teacher or staff supervision is limited:

> So we're sitting here going, hmm, you've got a host community that sees a group of Canadians come in, and what are they learning? They're learning that it's worthwhile to push and see if you can fulfill the stereotypes of Hollywood that North American women are sexually easy and they'll sleep with you on a moment's notice. And are those the stereotypes that you want to pursue? And beyond that, some of the people in this community, as it opens up more to foreigners, have migrated to England or whatever, because they've married a foreigner. And, we study international migration, but are we supporting international migration? You've got economic challenges and social challenges in [this] small rural community along the coast – is one of the ways to deal with that to get shacked up with a foreign female and have it develop into migration papers to another country? For the individual, it may be perfectly fine, but as a model of development, as a model of how your youth are looking at what do I need to do to make my community work? Is that what we want to support as a model? (P6)

This type of analysis of a situation that seems to be evolving is further evidence that teachers do not take their impact on the host community lightly, but that it does take a certain level of commitment or repeated visits to a particular community to really understand the potential impact that a group of North American students might be having. While some teachers might focus their concerns solely on the repercussions of this type of behaviour on the female student, it is worth noting that this participant holds a degree in Development Studies and so approaches the issue from a more global perspective. These types of incidents not only illuminate the potential ethical dilemmas that arise from these types of programs but also demonstrate how crucial it is that teachers have at least a baseline understanding of global dynamics in order to assess the impacts these programs have on the host communities.

Conclusion

Freire (2004) reminds us as teachers that in order to truly engage in a transformative process of learning we must be willing to recognize that our own assumptions about the world might inhibit our ability to see how our actions may be contributing to the oppressive conditions we wish to reverse. As this study has shown, this is not an easy process when it comes to our roles as facilitators of international experiential learning programs. Mainstream thinking, institutional structures, and curriculum and policy documents act as powerful barriers to our ability to see the conditions by which Freire would argue we are oppressed.

This study has shown that secondary school international experiential learning programs in Ontario that are focused on volunteer work in the Global South are generally short-term in nature and, with the exception of a few very distinct and locally developed programs, are not embedded in course curricula. As such, teachers tend to conceptualize these trips as beneficial experiences for the personal, rather than intellectual, growth of their students. Despite evidence of a desire to engage in more critical forms of education around these experiences, teachers are limited by their lack of educational background in both development studies and experiential learning theory. There are as well a number of structural restraints. As a result of limited time frames, limited commitment on the part of the students, and the reliance on sending organizations to plan the experience abroad, teachers are not able to engage consistently in the type of critical pedagogy practices advocated for by advocates of thick or critical global citizenship education. Secondary students participating in these programs are not pushed to think about their place in the global political economy, nor are they systematically encouraged to evaluate their impact on the community in any other than a "helping" role. Ethical dilemmas related to our negative moral obligations to do no harm are generally ignored in the pedagogical models being used to facilitate these programs in Ontario at this time. By failing to take a more critical stance on the role that Canadians play in the global political economy, it seems likely that these trips do more to reify the Canadian mythology of a helping nation than they do to develop students' understanding of the sources and causes of both domestic and international poverty and inequality.

Does this mean that we should give up on the possibility that we can intervene at the secondary school level in an ethical manner that seeks to redress social injustice globally? As the other contributors to this section have outlined, there are in fact international experiential learning models that do practice more critical forms of pedagogy. Overall, our research supports this potential. It provides strong evidence of the need for teacher training informed by critical forms of global citizenship education and transformational learning theory.

By adopting a post-colonial perspective and raising issues related to power, global structures, and inequalities in our world, secondary school teachers could take an important first step in challenging mainstream understandings of relations between the Global North and Global South. However, it would require system-level changes to infuse this type of thinking into the theorizing around international experiential learning programs at the level of those who facilitate these programs. Given the current fiscal and political climate that tends to emphasize "efficiency" or "austerity" in public service, it seems unlikely that such changes could be expected soon on a top-down basis. Bottom-up pressures from the participants themselves are equally unlikely to affect change. Our hope is that studies such as this one, which included participants willing to openly share their thoughts and feelings regarding how they conceptualize these trips and this form of learning, will open the door for professional dialogue amongst teachers who want to provide their students with rich learning opportunities that do not privilege their students' learning over the well-being of people encountered while abroad.

NOTES

1 See, for example, Tiessen and Epprecht (2012); Epprecht (2004); Simpson (2004); Heron (2005); Crabtree (2008); Lewis (2006); Tiessen (2008); Lewin (2009); Zemach-Bersin (2009). See also Huish, chapter 8, and Thomson and Desrosiers, chapter 7 in this volume.
2 Fizzell (2012), from which this chapter was adapted in an iterative process with the co-author.
3 Interview participants in this study are referred to as P1 to P10 throughout this chapter. Data was collected by recording the face-to-face, semi-structured interviews conducted with each of the research participants. Interviews lasted approximately 35 minutes to 75 minutes in length and were transcribed using basic wordprocessing software. All participants were provided an opportunity to review and withdraw any or all portions of their interviews from the study.
4 For further research it may also be worth considering the intellectual and emotional capacity of adolescents to engage in this type of theoretical analysis of their own position in the world. In the authors' experience in Global Development Studies at Queen's University, even highly accomplished first-year undergraduates often struggle emotionally to take in this critique.
5 See, for example, Epprecht (2004); Chieffo and Griffiths (2009); Simpson (2004); Gray and Campbell (2007).
6 Accessed 1 June 2013. See, for example, Zemach-Bersin (2009), and http://blytheducation.com/blyth-international/future-students/programs-and-courses/locations/south-american-programs/
7 For examples of the type of global citizenship curriculum being referred to by Schweisfurth (2006) and Evans, Ingram, MacDonald, and Weber (2009), see http://etfo.net/globaled/Educating4GlobalCitizenship.pdf

REFERENCES

Ash, S.L., & Clayton, P.H. (2004). The articulated learning: An approach to guided reflection and assessment. *Innovative Higher Learning, 29*(2), 137–154. http://dx.doi.org/10.1023/B:IHIE.0000048795.84634.4a

Baaz, M.E. (2005). *The paternalism of partnership: A postcolonial reading of identity in development aid.* London: Zed Books.

Billig, S.H., & Root, S. (2006). Maximizing civic commitment through service-learning: Case studies of effective high school classrooms. In K.M. Casey,

G. Davidson, S.H. Billig, & N.C. Springer (Eds.), *Advancing knowledge in service-learning: Research to transform the field* (pp. 45–63). Greenwich, CT: Information Age Publishing.

Brookfield, S.D. (2000). Transformative learning as ideology critique. In J. Meizrow (Ed.), *Learning as transformation: Critical perspectives on a theory in progress* (pp. 125–148). San Francisco: Jossey-Bass.

Chieffo, L., & Griffiths, L. (2009). Here to stay: Increasing acceptance of short-term study abroad programs. In R. Lewin (Ed.), *Handbook of practice and research in study abroad: Higher education and the quest for global citizenship* (pp. 365–380). New York: Routledge.

Crabtree, R.D. (1998). Mutual empowerment in cross-cultural participatory development and service learning: Lessons in communication and social justice from projects in El Salvador and Nicaragua. *Journal of Applied Communication Research, 26*(2), 182–209. http://dx.doi.org/10.1080/00909889809365501

Crabtree, R.D. (2008). Theoretical foundations for international service-learning. *Michigan Journal of Community Service Learning* (Fall), 18–36.

Epprecht, M. (2004). Work-study abroad courses in international development studies: Some ethical and pedagogical issues. *Canadian Journal of Development Studies, 25*(4), 687–706. http://dx.doi.org/10.1080/02255189.2004.9669009

Evans, M., Ingram, L.A., Macdonald, A., & Weber, N. (2009). Mapping the "global dimension" of citizenship education in Canada: The complex interplay of theory, practice and context. *Citizenship Teaching and Learning, 5*(2), 17–34.

Fizzell, K. (2012). *From the teacher's perspective: The complex nature of facilitating volunteer abroad programs in Ontario Secondary Schools* (Unpublished master's thesis). Queen's University, Kingston, ON.

Freire, P. (2004). *Pedagogy of indignation*. Boulder: Paradigm Publishers.

Freire, P. (2000). *Pedagogy of the oppressed* (30th ed.) New York: Continuum.

Gray, N.J., & Campbell, L.M. (2007). A decommodified experience? Exploring aesthetic, economic and ethical values for volunteer ecotourism in Costa Rica. *Journal of Sustainable Tourism, 15*(5), 463–482. http://dx.doi.org/10.2167/jost725.0

Guttentag, D.A. (2009). The possible negative impacts of volunteer tourism. *International Journal of Tourism Research, 11*(6), 537–551. http://dx.doi.org/10.1002/jtr.727

Heron, B.A. (2005). Changes and challenges: Preparing social work students for practicums in today's sub-Saharan African context. *Journal of International Social Work, 48*(6), 782–793. http://dx.doi.org/10.1177/0020872805057088

Heron, B. (2007). *Desire for development: Whiteness, gender and the helping imperative.* Waterloo: Wilfrid Laurier University Press.

Kahn, H.E. (2011). Overcoming the challenges of international service learning. In R.G. Bringle, J.A. Hatcher, & S.G. Jones (Eds.), *International service learning: Conceptual frameworks and research* (pp. 113–124). Sterling, VA: Stylus Publishing.

King, J.T. (2004). Service-learning as a site for critical pedagogy: A case of collaboration, caring, and defamiliarization across borders. *Journal of Experiential Education, 26*(3), 121–137. http://dx.doi.org/10.1177/105382590402600304

Kolb, D. (1984). *Experiential learning: Experience as the source of learning and development.* Englewood Cliffs, NJ: Prentice-Hall, Inc.

Lewin, R. (2009). Introduction: The quest for global citizenship through study abroad. In R. Lewin (Ed.), *The handbook of practice and research in study abroad: Higher education and the quest for global citizenship* (pp. xiii–xxii). New York: Routledge.

Lewis, D. (2006). Globalization and international service: A development perspective. *Voluntary Action, 7*(2), 13–26.

Meizrow, J. (2000). Learning to think like an adult: Core concepts of transformation theory. In J. Meizrow (Ed.), *Learning as transformation: Critical perspectives on a theory in progress* (pp. 3–33). San Francisco: Jossey-Bass.

McQuaid, N. (2009). Learning to 'un-divide' the world: The legacy of colonialism and education in the 21st century. *Critical Literacy: Theories and Practices, 3*(1), 12–25.

Ontario Institute for Studies in Education (OISE). (2011). The Transformative Learning Centre. Retrieved from http://tlc.oise.utoronto.ca/About.html

Plater, W.M., Steven, G.J., Bringle, R.G., & Clayton, P.H. (2009). Educating globally competent citizens through international service learning. In R. Lewin (Ed.), *Handbook of practice and research in study abroad: Higher education and the quest for global citizenship* (pp. 485–505). New York: Routledge.

Raymond, E.M., & Hall, C.M. (2008). The development of cross-cultural (mis) understanding through volunteer tourism. *Journal of Sustainable Tourism, 16*(5), 530–543.

Rennick, J.B. (2012). The new mission field: International Service Learning in Canada: A socio-historical analysis. *Journal of Global Citizenship and Equity Education,* Special Edition, 2(1), 1–16.

Roman, L.G. (2003). Education and the contested meanings of "global citizenship." *Journal of Educational Change, 4*(3), 269–293. http://dx.doi.org/10.1023/B:JEDU.0000006164.09544.ac

Schweisfurth, M. (2006). Education for global citizenship: Teacher agency and curricular structure in Ontario schools. *Educational Review, 58*(1), 41–50.

Simpson, K. (2004). 'Doing development': The gap year, volunteer-tourists and a popular practice of development. *Journal of International Development, 16*(5), 681–692. http://dx.doi.org/10.1002/jid.1120

Tiessen, R. (2007). Educating global citizens? Canadian foreign policy and youth study/volunteer abroad programs. *Canadian Foreign Policy, 14*(1), 77–84. http://dx.doi.org/10.1080/11926422.2007.9673453

Tiessen, R. (2012). The contours and debates of international experiential and global citizenship education (Unpublished paper).

Tiessen, R., & Epprecht, M. (2012). Introduction: Global citizenship education for learning/volunteering abroad. *Journal of Global Citizenship and Equity Education,* Special Edition, 2(1), 1–11.

Tonkin, H. (2011). A research agenda for international service learning. In R.G. Bringle, J.A. Hatcher, & S.G. Jones (Eds.), *International service learning: Conceptual frameworks and research* (pp. 191–224). Sterling, VA: Stylus Publishing.

Zemach-Bersin, T. (2009). Selling the world: Study abroad marketing and the privatization of global citizenship. In R. Lewin (Ed.), *The handbook of practice and research in study abroad: Higher education and the quest for global citizenship* (pp. 303–320). New York: Routledge.

7 Experiential Learning in Challenging Settings: Lessons from Post-Genocide Rwanda

MARIE-EVE DESROSIERS AND SUSAN THOMSON

Our chapter examines some of the challenges of experiential learning in settings like post-genocide Rwanda, where managing former – also often ongoing – socio-ethnic divisions and undertaking post-conflict reconstruction is at issue and/or where the political realm is controlled by a select group of elites. We qualify Rwanda and societies with similar trajectories as "challenging" because post-conflict societies face the daunting task of rebuilding not only infrastructure and state institutions but also social relations. While their landscape is beset with often obvious physical scars of combat, emotional and psychological scars also lie below the surface and demand great sensitivity on the part of researchers, teachers, and students. We also include in "challenging settings" authoritarian states where political power is centralized in the hands of specific political, bureaucratic, or military elites.[1] This centralized leadership is often controlling, exercising restraints on legislatures, courts, the media, social institutions, civil society, and even private citizens, which also has an impact on the space for experiential learning activities. Such settings are challenging as they represent realities that are distant from the lived experiences of students, teachers, and scholars, while also raising important ethical and human dilemmas that require precautions, preparation, and training.[2]

Learning in these settings can be unsettling or frustrating for Western-born students, especially if they have never lived the material and emotional constraints as well as the lack of personal freedom, that characterize these challenging settings. With this said, experiencing these settings can also be intellectually and personally rewarding. It provides insight into the lived realities of a significant portion of humanity, considering that more than 2.5 billion people live under an authoritarian regime, to which we could add the numerous others who live in post-conflict countries not categorized as authoritarian, such as Colombia and East Timor.[3] Just as important, these environments push our boundaries in terms of how we map, understand, and analyse social and power relations. Because things are rarely straightforward in post-conflict or authoritarian settings, they can teach students, teachers, and scholars alike to think differently and with a different degree of self-reflectivity than other destinations. Indeed, the international experiential learning literature does not distinguish by regime type (Che, Spearman, & Manizade, 2009; Heron, 2003; Langdon & Agyeyomah, chapter 3 in this volume; Lantis & DuPlaga, 2010), but we firmly believe that the settings we qualify as "challenging" demand a different look because of the specific challenges they present and significantly different learning opportunities they afford.

This chapter chronicles our experiences as teachers preparing and accompanying senior undergraduate students in study abroad courses (Desrosiers) or advising those doing internships and other residency-based learning activities (Thomson) in post-conflict and authoritarian settings – contemporary Rwanda in particular. We work with our students before, during, and after their study abroad period (averaging three to six weeks in length) to help them reflect on how they engage, learn, and grow in their new setting. Our aim is to help sensitize students to some of the realities they encounter, giving them tools to push their critical reflection, as well as to prepare them for the ethical and human dilemmas they inevitably confront. Our approach follows in the tradition of the pre-departure and post-return self-reflective learning cycle analysed and critiqued by Butin (2010), Epprecht (2004), Fizzell and Epprecht (chapter 6 in this volume), Heron (2006, 2011), and Kolb (1984), among others. We acknowledge that international experiential learning in any setting, let alone challenging ones, can reinforce ethnic and other stereotypes about difference, power, and privilege. It can also lead students to develop simplistic and potentially harmful solutions to complex socio-political problems and to generalize inaccurately about a given location or actors based on limited data (Conrad & Hedin, 1990; Eyler, 2000; Huish, chapter 8 in this volume; Schön, 1983). Just as Cameron (chapter 2 in this volume) points out in his discussion on "thick" global citizenship, we find in addition that students who have experienced post-conflict and other challenging learning environments can sometimes feel morally and ethically superior to their peers about their ability to diagnose and solve the practical problems of the world immediately upon their return home. Finally, we find that within just a few months of returning home, some of our students reflect on their time abroad superficially or cynically. For these reasons, we have worked over the years to improve our approach to sensitizing students to "challenging" settings. Our approach has been an evolving one, and one that we continue to improve in light of our students' and our own engagement with post-genocide Rwanda. This chapter reflects on this evolving process, what we have learned from it, and the current state of our reflection on experiential learning in post-conflict and authoritarian settings.

In the first section of our chapter, we propose a "do no harm" and nuanced self-reflective approach, as well as a learning objectives rubric to help guide students in their learning activities. In the second section, we introduce the lessons learned and strategies we propose to our students, with emphasis on the ways in which we prepare them to experience post-genocide Rwanda as an example of a "challenging" setting. We also briefly discuss some of the re-integration strategies and prompts we use to promote continued learning and reflection upon students' return home. This section includes a description of some of the exercises we do with our students throughout the learning cycle in the hopes that some of their components be reproduced or adapted by others in their preparation for learning in challenging settings. In our conclusion, we reflect on the utility of our approach for students and experiential learning courses or programs.

Introducing "Do No Harm" and Nuanced Self-Reflection

The difference between what we know before we embark on a learning experience abroad and the breadth of what we have learned by the time we return is often significant. According to Rogers (1969, p. 164), students learn best when they participate actively in the learning process and when they have control over its nature and direction. The "hands on" experience of a learning abroad opportunity affords just that. To make sure our students are well prepared for the experience, and especially for challenging settings, we act as guides in the process. Throughout their experience, we mean to get them engaged in "a purposeful and strategic process" of critical reflection rather than a stream-of-consciousness or hyper-subjective reflective process that may lead to superficial or ethnocentric learning (Eyler, Giles, & Schmide, 1996, p. 16; see also Fizzell & Epprecht, chapter 6 in this volume). As Stanton

(1990, p. 185) and Langdon and Agyeyomah (chapter 3 in this volume) note, when reflection on experience is weak, student learning tends to be "haphazard, accidental, and superficial." Because students are unfamiliar with the socio-political realities of challenging settings such as post-genocide Rwanda, they often need guidance and cues to learn to read, engage, and analyse the settings they encounter. Far from providing them with a rigid map or predetermined set of questions, we try to equip our students with some reading keys or flexible, adaptable guidelines to help them make sense of what they encounter, and just as importantly to stimulate their own process of critical reflection, which allows them to raise their own meaningful questions, develop and apply their own critical thinking skills, and confront their own biases.

Our aim, with the onus we put on reflection, is to help foster a more holistic perspective – a "big picture" perspective – through which students become aware of, and try to minimize, their footprint in settings they operate in and which allows them to develop a nuanced understanding of their host society. "Doing no harm" and "embracing nuance" should, in our mind, be the two central reading keys and guiding norms for learning in challenging environments.

According to Butin, experiential learning is more easily assimilated when external threats to others and to oneself are at a minimum (2010, p. 108). Going a step further, the maxim "do no harm" implies understanding the impact of our presence or actions abroad and deploying conscious efforts to minimize negative emotional and physical risks to the people we meet and societies we visit, including learning to avoid getting involved altogether if risks are too high (Anderson, 1999; Mertus, 2009; Thomson, 2009, 2013; Wood, 2006). Even when going into experiential learning with the best intentions, we can still behave in ways that cause harm (Huish, chapter 8 in this volume). As a result, it is essential to take the time to think about what doing no harm means in the specific context of a field experience and to keep reflecting on it as the experience unfolds. Just as importantly, once we are aware of potential risks involved with our presence, we have a duty to try and develop strategies to minimize these risks. Awareness and sensitivity should be "practiced," especially in challenging settings, where respecting boundaries people put up as a result of trauma, fear, social and political taboos is essential.

At the same time, we insist on nuance. Beyond thinking critically, self-reflection should also imply a more nuanced understanding of the local realities we encounter. In light of their complexity, post-conflict and authoritarian societies demand attention to detail. Considering how dramatic people generally take conflict and authoritarianism to be, they tend to become too often the primary filters used to read post-conflict and authoritarian societies at the cost of nuance. But not everything has been transformed by conflict in a post-conflict setting, nor is everything political in an authoritarian setting. It becomes important to make these distinctions, as well as to seek a nuanced understanding of socio-political dynamics at both the macro- and micro-levels of society. It means understanding how individuals are differently situated vis-à-vis power and the different types of knowledge various actors possess, whether they are elites, members of the middle-class, or so-called powerless peasants. Not only can reflecting on these issues help our students relate in a more meaningful manner to the actors they encounter but it also allows them to reflect on their own power, privilege, and status, abroad and at home.

Mindful of the fact that students travel to challenging settings for different reasons and that we each have different emotional and intellectual capacities, we also promote three broad learning objectives: research skill development, intercultural learning, and personal growth. To illustrate more concretely our approach and these learning objectives, we propose a learning objective rubric based on the work we do to prepare students for experiential learning in post-genocide Rwanda (see Table 7.1). This rubric is adapted from Thomson's work preparing students for residency-based learning and is meant to guide and encourage a "do no harm" stance and the nuanced self-reflection imperative throughout the experiential learning cycle.

This rubric is indeed designed to allow for sufficient time for self-reflection at all stages of the experiential learning process (pre- and post-departure, as well as being in country). It lets students work at their own pace, helping them avoid or work through the "information overload" common to being immersed in a foreign location. The timing and pace of this rubric also gives them ample opportunity to think critically about information they obtain. This is particularly important in post-conflict and authoritarian settings like Rwanda where making sense of local realities that are not only different than our own but also often not as straightforward as what we are accustomed to can only occur when we take a "step back" and try to piece the "puzzle" together through structured learning activities.

Table 7.1 Learning Objectives Rubric: Cumulative Experiential Learning

Meta-Goal: Sensitize to Socio-Political Realities in Country	Academic Skill Development	Intercultural Learning	Personal Growth
Learning Objective Level	*Students learn academic skills and/or the research cycle*	*Students learn that other societies operate differently and, to the extent possible, how these societies operate*	*Students grow through awareness of self and of the learning environment (including do no harm and nuance)*
LO 1: Identify	Identify your academic objective and/or research question and the way you intend to find answers	Identify the key actors (government, civil society, individuals, etc.) in post-genocide Rwanda, and their role (or lack thereof), as well as key social and political structures and relations	Reflect on what it means to "do no harm" to others, other societies, and yourself, as well as on where you situate yourself with regard to others and your new settings
LO 2: Apply	Apply your understanding (academic theory, previous empirical readings, pre-departure training) to your experience in Rwanda	Apply your understanding of actors, structures, and relations to realities on the ground	Apply your understanding of "do no harm" and nuanced self-reflection in the broader socio-political context of post-genocide Rwanda
LO 3: Analyse (usually concurrent with LO 2)	Compare and analyse the similarities and differences between your initial understanding and practical realities on the ground in Rwanda (what you see, what you read, what you are told, or what you sense – see more on "reading between the lines below")	Compare and analyse your understanding in light of Rwanda's post-conflict nature and authoritarian state structures	Analyse the sources of harm and misreadings of post-genocide Rwanda and compare with your understanding of what it means to do no harm and to reflect in a nuanced manner on local Rwandan realities

Table 7.1. Learning Objectives Rubric: Cumulative Experiential Learning (*Continued*)

Meta-Goal: Sensitize to Socio-Political Realities in Country	Academic Skill Development	Intercultural Learning	Personal Growth
LO 4: Synthesize	Develop your own model or understanding, in other words your own answer, to your puzzle or question about post-genocide Rwanda	Develop an enhanced, context-sensitive understanding of Rwanda's social and political realities in light of your experience	Develop an enhanced awareness and sensitivity towards people you meet, societies you engaged, and develop a better understanding of your relationship with them
LO 5: Evaluate	Critically evaluate your understanding (answers) of Rwanda's post-genocide environment	Critically evaluate post-genocide Rwanda in terms of long-term sustainable peace, political stability, and development	Critically evaluate your strategies to "do no harm" and for nuanced self-reflection over the long term, both academically and personally

Lessons Learned and Strategies

There is no overemphasizing the need to prepare prior to undertaking international experiential learning in a challenging setting. Students should take the time and be encouraged to read up on their host society and the challenges that may confront them. Local blogs, newspapers, policy briefs, human rights reports, academic books, and articles help give a sense of local dynamics, current debates, and broader trends in society. And though these accounts may not always paint an accurate portrait of local realities, they nonetheless help students realize that things can operate differently in post-conflict and authoritarian settings. These preliminary encounters help students to be receptive, to have an open mind in regard to differences they will encounter, which is necessary for critical thinking and self-reflection. The lack of appropriate preparation may have the opposite effect. For example, due to unforeseen circumstances, Desrosiers was unable to offer pre-departure sensitization on post-conflict and authoritarian conditions to a group of students she took to Rwanda in 2010. Once in Rwanda, most students began expressing within a week significant frustration about lectures received locally, complaining about what they perceived to be lecturers' untruthfulness or naïveté. Some students had difficulty making links between what lecturers said and the authoritarian context in which they gave their lectures. Students who receive pre-departure training can also express similar sentiments, though, in Desrosiers's experience, less frequently.

While preparing is essential, over-preparation can also be an issue, however. Preliminary readings can lead students to form a strong opinion of the realities they encounter, which may end up shaping their interpretation once on the ground. In the case of authoritarian settings, this can be particularly problematic. Since much of the available work may be focused on contesting the authoritarian state and its practices, students may become hyper-politicized with regard to the settings they visit. While there is nothing wrong with taking a political stance, in the field it can lead students to overemphasize political aspects to the detriment of other important realities and dynamics. But it can also become an issue in terms of access or even security if an openly critical stance is adopted, leading to greater scrutiny on the part of local authorities.

When available, pre-departure sessions and continued prompts throughout the field experience are also good opportunities to stimulate students' reflection and raise their awareness to analytical, ethical and human issues they encounter while in post-conflict and authoritarian settings. These pre-departure sessions may help supplement the lack of literature on these issues. While a few good contributions have been published recently on conducting research in post-conflict settings (Sriram, King, Martin-Ortega, & Herman, 2009; Thomson, Ansoms, & Murison, 2013), teaching students to appreciate the politics of authoritarian rule is difficult as there is really no place in the academic literature for them to start. In particular, there are few examples of life under authoritarian rule since the literature tends to be divided into two broad categories, democratization or transitions from authoritarianism and the authoritarian personality, rather than on the system itself.

To introduce her students to authoritarianism as context, Thomson uses specific exercises to help them understand exclusion and oppression. Rather than overwhelming students with the literature on "the white savior complex" (Goudge, 2003; Heron, 2007) or assigning more theoretical readings from texts like Havel's (1985) *The Power of the Powerless* or Wedeen's (1999) *Ambiguities of Domination* on the intricacies of authoritarian forms of power, Thomson sets up small groups of students to act out in the classroom critical incidents from one or more of these texts without students knowing that they will later read from these sources. The purpose of having small groups of three or four students act out specific scenes from a text is to get them thinking about where power is located in a given context, whether in a challenging setting (where they want to go) or in Canada or the United States (where they grew up) through the lens of the experience of being excluded or oppressed. Thomson then uses a bullying framework – where students play the roles of bullied, bully, or bystander – developed by Coloroso (2007) to ask her students to reflect on that experience from a different perspective than the one they grew up with and to think about different subject positions. At this point, Thomson introduces the concept of "powerlessness," assigning Young's chapter "Five Faces of Oppression" (from *Justice and the Politics of Difference* 1990) to get students thinking about the ways that powerlessness accounts for differing conditions of oppression based on gender, race, and class. Thomson also introduces the concept of "domination" through Scott's chapter "The Infrapolitics of Subordinate Groups" (from *Domination and the Arts of Resistance* 1990) to get students thinking about the ways in which the relationship between the powerless (often assumed to be the citizens in authoritarian settings) and the powerful (meaning government officials and other state agents) are laden with deception. In this way, their minds are opened to the idea that power in authoritarian settings operates differently than it does in liberal democratic ones. Students also gain insights on the various ways one's position in the socio-political hierarchy affects life chances. In thinking through how relationships can be power laden, students become aware of their own relative position of power when they are learning in a challenging setting like postgenocide Rwanda.

While it is important to be sensitized to field settings, students should also be equipped with the right tools to make sense of them. Considering the constraints they have imposed or continue to impose on those who live them, challenging settings often lead people to behave and in particular to speak in ways that we may not think straightforward. Because the wrong words or "careless talk" can have dire consequences, and because in authoritarian environments expectations of "proper behavior" are often explicit, people can develop strategies to navigate these conditions: giving in to oblique behaviour, disengagement, posturing, evading answers pertaining to sensitive topics, vagueness, answering through non-answers, or reverting to "official" or accepted "safe" scripts. While this may confound or frustrate outsiders, it offers a glimpse into the different universes post-conflict and authoritarian settings constitute, an opportunity to look at the social changes their structures can impose in terms of behaviour, and a look at the ways in which people manage and adapt to them. It calls on students to learn to read the "story behind the story" they are told. It means, more specifically, being sensitive to or learning to decode, to the extent a foreigner can, what is left unsaid by paying attention to particular behaviours – even possibly contradictory ones – accompanying speech, as well as some of the hidden meanings or cues found in straightforward language. Without falling into the trap of over-interpreting or assuming all is "hidden text," engaging post-conflict or authoritarian settings means students need to hone their skills at reading conscious and unconscious subtext presented by the people they interview or encounter. Similarly, students should also learn to perceive discomfort or apprehension, transpiring in some forms of avoidance or silences, for example. By becoming better at decoding some of the signals people send, students can also become better at respecting people's boundaries. Overall, students need to develop their observation skills, often adopting the role of "active listener" more than that of a communicator – the role we are more accustomed to adopt as Westerners, particularly in North America.

To help her students become aware of multi-level messages or "hidden scripts," Desrosiers works prior to departure with her students on the concept of "meta-data," as applied to post-conflict settings by Lee Ann Fujii (2009). After having assigned Fujii's chapter, the concept of "meta-data" is then discussed in class to help students realize that the shape answers take during interviews and the way people behave is also worthy of study. Body language, silences, deceptions, and so on can reveal significant things. Failing to answer a question directly may not necessarily mean one does not know the answer, for example, but meta-data can signal an interviewee's discomfort with the topic or reveal a taboo. Similarly, the choice of specific words may also be very revealing, such as referring to the events of early 1990s in Rwanda as "genocide," "war," or, commonly, "the events," for example. To help make the concept more concrete, Desrosiers encourages students to give real or imagined examples of "meta-data" (taken from Fujii's text, from other texts they may have read, or even from encounters in their own lives). She prompts them by asking them to give examples of and reflect on "a story behind the story," "a story behind the absence of story," "a story behind the story when many or all tell the same story," "a story behind the choice of certain words," or a "story behind avoidance and silences." Desrosiers then opens the discussion to the broader topic of how context can influence what people say, especially the political context and existing networks of power relations and people's position in them. She also leads students to discuss the similar or different impacts violence may have on how people behave or what they say.

We have also come to realize that students need to develop their ability for critical introspection to help them realize and acknowledge when they lapse into stereotypical thinking or stereotyped comparisons. Stereotyping and comparing are natural human reflexes. They are – often unconscious – strategies we employ to make sense of complex or abundant information by collapsing information around simpler notions, ideas, or renderings or comparing it with something that is already known. Considering the information overload that often accompanies travelling to very different locations, we should not be surprised that we tend to revert to stereotyping and simple comparisons. The tendency to stereotype and compare often accompanies the "cultural dissonance" – what used to be referred to as "culture shock" – and related emotions many of us experience when travelling to a foreign country. Whether positive, where students may be elated about what they discover, or negative, where differences are seen negatively, possibly even harshly, this state of "cultural dissonance" tends to impact perceptions and interpretations, possibly leading to simplifications, crude comparisons, and stereotypes about people, relations, structures, habits, and social and cultural modes of functioning encountered abroad. Common assumptions about foreign societies, especially in the South, include assumptions of their "communitarianism" and their larger sense of solidarity, as well as a romanticized ideal of the "simpler life" they represent. While these images may resonate with common renderings of everyday life in the global South, they are nonetheless misleading simplifications. There is also a tendency to "globalize" categories, speaking for example of Rwanda or "Rwandans," and glossing over personal, regional, religious, class, gender, and urban/rural distinctions found in all societies.

Problematic assumptions exist about challenging settings, too. For example, in post-conflict settings, it can be easy to adopt a simplistic distinction between perpetrators of violence and victims, where perpetrators are necessarily portrayed as malevolent and victims as passive pitiful individuals. This glosses over the complex motives actors have to take up arms or to refrain from fighting. But it is also important to remember that the distinction between aggressor and victim in conflicts is more complex than often assumed. Victims can aggress and aggressors can be victims. Similarly, it would be an oversimplification to assume that all authoritarian leaders are ill intentioned, driven by nothing else but power, when many also believe they are doing what is good for their country. Some of their policies may even have positive impacts on society. In addition, people who refrain from opposing an authoritarian government are not necessarily converted to the authorities' precepts nor are they naïve. Many assumptions also surround the greater display of weapons in many post-conflict and authoritarian settings. From security guards to regular armed forces, seeing people carry "big guns" in public can be unsettling. Many of our students have expressed their discomfort, even a feeling of insecurity, at the number of weapons publicly displayed in Rwanda. Here again, it is important to avoid jumping to conclusions about the meaning of these weapons. And this display of "big guns" is not limited to post-conflict or authoritarian settings.

It is therefore crucial that students reflect upon their assumptions about what it means to live in post-conflict and/or authoritarian settings. A common assumption that we ask our students to examine is the notion that everything is political in challenging settings like post-genocide Rwanda. Students often assume that power in authoritarian settings operates in a binary relationship pitting elites as dominant actors over a largely passive citizenry. Seeing socio-political power as one-sided leads many students to misread the sources of power and authority in a given society. To encourage students to reflect upon the sources of power in society and how individuals are positioned by it, we teach our students the distinction between "politics" and "the political" as a means to illustrate the various points of conflict and unity in a given society from the perspective of different actors. Some students intuitively understand that politics is about who decides the distribution of resources in a given society, about "who gets what." Others interpret politics to mean the activities of government and the functioning of the institutions of the state. We push students to think about "the political" as a way to look beyond day-to-day decision-making and party politics to appreciate the broader socio-economic and historical context in which actors – both elites and ordinary folk – participate in political relations. It means encouraging our students to think about how people partake and engage these broader political relations, raising issues of power, rights, and voice, and their different forms. Taking an explicit political approach encourages students to identify and understand the politics of all actors, from the president down to the subsistence farmer, as well as to be made more aware of their own politics as an outsider.

In order to develop a sense of "the political," Thomson tries, through a pre-departure exercise, to raise her students' awareness to stereotypes and simplifications and to break down some of their assumptions about life under authoritarian rule. She assigns her students a text by An Ansoms (2009) which analyses the vision and ambitions of Rwanda's post-genocide political elite to re-engineer rural society in ways that go against the interests of the rural peasantry. Once students have read Ansoms's article, Thomson assigns to each student the role of one of the various actors Ansoms identifies in her article (government ministers, local officials, subsistence farmers, widows of the genocide, and unemployed male youth). Students begin to research post-genocide agriculture and land policies from the perspective of the actor they have agreed to represent. Students embrace the opportunity to embody the actor they have been assigned, with those playing government officials coming to class in suits and ties with briefcases, an attitude of bravado, and a sense of self-importance. Those playing peasants perform barefoot, mindful not to look government officials in the eyes, while casting knowing looks of their deception of not planting government-ordered crops at those who share their socio-economic and sometimes marginal lot in life. Students who play widows of the genocide cower in the corner, highlighting that these Rwandans rarely get the psychosocial and economic support they need to rebuild their lives. What emerges in the classroom is a rich portrait of life under authoritarian rule from a variety of perspectives. The exercise reveals the differences in personal resources and autonomy Rwandans have to shape their own lives and livelihoods. As an assigned reading, the power of Rwanda's elites to re-engineer society seems abstract, and perhaps even exaggerated. As lived experience, the reach of the authoritarian state in everyday life cannot be ignored. It also shows students that making a difference, and doing so ethically is not as simple as they may have imagined. The imperative of "doing no harm" comes to life when students listen to a range of voices, learn to empathize with people different than themselves, and learn to understand the techniques of censorship and citizen dissimulation that characterize authoritarian settings.

While learning to make some sense of the setting visited is important, students should not neglect themselves throughout their international experiential learning activities, especially from an emotional standpoint.

We are often accustomed to think about our physical security when we travel and it is undoubtedly an issue that should be given great consideration. We are rarely encouraged, however, to think about our emotional security. This is the case despite the emotional challenges field experiences entail, especially in challenging settings. We both dedicate significant time to working with our students to prepare them for the emotions that arise when living and learning in post-conflict or authoritarian settings. By "emotional security," we mean the ability and willingness to acknowledge both negative and positive emotions stemming from the field experience as a form of self-protection against the roller coaster of emotions that is normal and expected, particularly in challenging settings. Ensuring one's emotional security also means thinking about and developing strategies to manage difficult or unexpected emotional states. Our primary task is therefore to raise student awareness to issues surrounding emotional security.

We start by letting students know that the range of emotions they might feel in country are valid and worthy of reflection, however positive or negative their experience. Some of Desrosiers's students reported feeling strange because they did not feel shocked or saddened when visiting one of Rwanda's primary genocide memorial sites, Murambi, where the bodies of individuals killed in the genocide are on public display. Some of Thomson's students shared post-return feelings of regret in going to Rwanda in the first place because they felt that Rwanda was "too complicated" and it was a place they would "never understand so why bother in the first place." These anecdotes from our students mirror some of Tiessen's (chapter 4 in this volume) empirical findings on the impact of study abroad placements on career placements.

We encourage our students to tap into such emotions – whether about themselves or Rwandans – through self-reflective writing exercises which should be undertaken before, during, and after their period of study. Through journaling, we encourage students to embrace their negative emotions rather than deny them, which is the impulse of many. Their acknowledgment of negative emotions associated with "cultural dissonance," for example, is an important part of their personal growth and intellectual development. By reflecting on these emotions, students can learn a lot about themselves as individuals and their privilege in the wider world, but they can also learn from local social dynamics. Journaling exercises allow students the safety and security of working through "cultural dissonance" and other emotional stressors through their own means, while pushing through the challenge of staying curious, open-minded, and tolerant despite fatigue and a recurring tendency to get frustrated. Students often realize how much emotional learning they do through journaling, how it allows them to reflect on and work out some key emotional challenges, and become quite fond of their journal. In addition, we find that pushing students to journal about the positive and negative emotions that their daily in-the-field encounters raise encourages them to negotiate a variety of social situations. They begin to critically accept and evaluate "negative" differences. They also begin to learn how to address people in different social groups, how gender roles affect social relationships, what constitutes acceptable behaviour in a range of everyday situations, and how gestures and body language differ from their own community. The process of gaining cultural literacy, which their journal helps them in part gain, results in higher quality critical thinking that moves students from descriptive, first person accounts to a more in-depth assessment of socio-political realities in Rwanda.

Finally, while people often focus on what happens abroad, the learning process does not stop when returning home. It is often a few weeks after the return home, with a bit of distance from the intensity of field experience, that many "streams of thought and analysis" come together to form a "big picture" perspective. We believe, as a result, that it is fundamental that we continue to work with our students beyond the field. We help integrate what students learned before and during their international experience into a global post-experience reflection through journaling, a final essay or in-class oral presentations, and discussions.

Given the stresses and strains of learning in a challenging setting like post-genocide Rwanda, our post-return self-reflection focuses on a number of elements. We especially work with our students to ensure they do not neglect the feelings they have when they return home, including coping with "reverse cultural dissonance." Many of our students have a difficult time adjusting to everyday life in Canada or the US because of the strong positive or negative emotions they just experienced abroad. We give our students one to three weeks to adjust to life back on campus. We then organize a meeting with them to discuss and analyse in seminar format what they felt during their time in Rwanda, as a way to enhance their self-reflection and to get them thinking about ethical conundrums they confronted in the field. In conversation, students reflect on the assumptions and expectations they brought to their experience in Rwanda, with a particular focus on how the experience made them feel at different times during their stay abroad. We also ask our students to discuss how they handled their emotional reactions (whether positive, negative, or neutral), and whether or not they would have handled themselves differently in hindsight. Through this identification and explanation of personal assumptions and expectations, students begin to think more articulately about the ways they did well in a particular situation (like meeting widows of the genocide, or visiting genocide memorial sites), and what personal characteristics helped them weather particular challenges (patience, empathy, active listening, etc.).

We ask our students to reflect in the same manner on their return home and feelings it may have triggered. Many of our students come back expressing negative emotions about their own society after having experienced a different one. Others may come back with a new perspective, looking positively on their society through the filter of what they lived abroad. Many of our students report coming back from Rwanda as "changed individuals," though with a vague idea of what this change entails. Some, with a clearer idea of this "transformation," embraced the roller-coaster ride that is studying in a challenging setting and are ready to keep working on issues they experienced first hand. Others fully reject the idea of continuing to research and write on Rwanda from their home country. We encourage students to engage these emotions and analyse the ways in which they themselves shape their learning, and more broadly their world view, through these emotions, as well as their perceptions and lived experiences. This opens up a fruitful discussion on how students' own personality and characteristics matter. One of the most fundamental lessons learned over the years is, as a matter of fact, that no student is alike and that they all engage experiential learning in challenging settings differently. Self-awareness or learning to "listen to oneself" is therefore an essential key to self-reflection and engagement with others and other settings, a lesson we continue to teach our students throughout the experiential learning cycle, including when they return home.

Conclusion

Though rarely acknowledged in the literature, challenging settings entail their own set of dilemmas, ethical and human, for international experiential learning endeavours. They undoubtedly demand their specific precautions, preparation, and training. They also afford, however, incredible learning opportunities, proving an eye-opening, deeply enriching academic and human experience, as our work with students reminds us on a regular basis. Convinced of the utility of experiential learning in challenging settings, we have worked over the years to develop – and continue to develop, as we learn with and from our students – an approach based on "doing no harm" and nuanced self-reflection, on which we base our pre- and post-field exercises and discussions, as well as our in-the-field guidance. We have also learned important lessons, which we happily share with our students, recognizing that both our approach and these lessons are reading keys or suggested guidelines to be adapted to situations and individuals. We believe these tools to be also adaptable to students preparing for their own international learning opportunity in a challenging setting or programs considering such an experience.

Students, teachers, and coordinators of experiential learning courses or programs can benefit from our approach in a variety of ways. Working with the precept of "doing no harm," through personal reflection and discussions or programmed exercises, raises awareness to students' impact on their host settings and the people they meet locally. It stresses the importance of creating respectful personal relationships, respecting boundaries, and engaging people and settings on their own terms. The adoption of the "doing no harm" maxim is therefore a tool to learn to tread lightly in host societies, to minimize one's footprint, to reduce the potential harm to people and societies visited. "Doing no harm" can also be thought of as raising awareness to how the field may impact students, including its emotional impact. While traditional ethical training focuses on physical safety, challenging settings may call on students in a deep emotional manner. It is important to work with them, throughout the learning cycle, to help them be aware of their emotional state, to "listen to themselves" and take the time to work through these emotions or find apt strategies to engage them. Focused on nuance, our approach is also a tool for students, their teachers, or coordinators to push the boundaries of how we apprehend foreign realities. Our approach to experiential teaching and advising underscores the inherent challenges and rewards of working in ways to promote a subtler understanding of local realities. It teaches students to examine then undo the generalizations and stereotypes about actors and power relations often found in challenging settings. In so doing, such an approach not only helps students identify and learn from some of the social, political, and economic dynamics that characterize everyday life in a challenging setting but also leads them to re-evaluate their own place in the world, their relation to others, and even to their own society. Overall, students, teachers, and course or program coordinators can therefore employ our approach, including the proposed learning objectives rubric, to help harness the potential of experiential learning in a challenging setting, which holds the promise of not only generating conventional academic learning (articulating questions, confronting bias, examining causality, contrasting theory with practice) but also deepening much needed and often neglected ethical and human learning (reflecting on impacts and consequences of actions on others and self, challenging stereotypes and generalizations, inviting alternative perspectives and explanations).

NOTES

1 Authoritarianism should be understood as a "range" or "scale," as the ability of states to centralize power and control the public realm varies significantly. The shape authoritarianism takes as well as the means and practices such regimes employ to control state and society also varies widely. With regard to Rwanda, it has consistently been categorized as "autocratic" by the Polity IV project in recent years, as "authoritarian" by the Economist Intelligence Unit's *Democracy Index 2010*, as well as "not free" by Freedom House's *Freedom in the World 2012* report. Polity IV data is available online at http://www.systemicpeace.org/polity/polity4.htm, the *Democracy Index 2010* at http://graphics.eiu.com/PDF/Democracy_ Index_2010_web.pdf, and Freedom House's *Freedom in the World 2012* report at http://www.freedomhouse.org/report/freedom-world/ freedom-world-2012, retrieved 28 August 2012. Scholars studying Rwanda have also regularly commented on the current government's authoritarianism. See, for example, Reyntjens (2011) and contributions to Straus and Waldorf's recently edited volume (2011).

2 We work with our students to recognize human dilemmas as well as ethical ones in order to stress the fact that we often encounter circumstances, situations, or events that call upon us as human beings to tap into our compassion and ability to empathize. Though these dilemmas often have an "ethical answer," they also have emotional and social components that we try to teach our students not to ignore. In addition, while we do not address this specifically, we advise students to look into local procedures and requirements for research or study programs – including costs – well ahead of departure. Authoritarian governments may require scholars to

obtain specific authorizations before studying in their country or conducting certain types of projects. While this is generally also the case in
non-authoritarian settings, the length of the authorization process, as
well as some of the dilemmas it may raise if the project touches on issues
judged sensitive by the government, may complicate the process.
3 Drawing on the 2010 Democracy Index, http://graphics.eiu.com/PDF/
Democracy_Index_2010_web.pdf, retrieved 6 June 2012.

REFERENCES

Anderson, M.B. (1999). *Do no harm: How aid can support peace - or war*. Boulder,
CO: Lynne Rienner Publishers.

Ansoms, A. (2009). Re-engineering rural society: The visions and ambitions of
the Rwandan elite. *African Affairs, 108*(431), 289–309. http://dx.doi.org/
10.1093/afraf/adp001

Butin, D.W. (2010). *Service-learning in theory and practice*. New York: Palgrave
MacMillan. http://dx.doi.org/10.1057/9780230106154

Che, S.M., Spearman, M., & Manizade, A. (2009). Constructive disequilibrium:
Cognitive and emotional development through dissonant experiences in
less familiar destinations. In R. Lewin (Ed.), *The handbook of practice and
research in study abroad: Higher education and the quest for global citizenship*
(pp. 99–116). London: Routledge.

Coloroso, B. (2007). *Extraordinary evil: A short walk to genocide*. New York:
Nation Books.

Conrad, D., & Hedin, D. (1990). Learning from service: Experience is the best
teacher—or is it? In J. Kendall and Associates (Eds.), *Combining service and
learning* (pp. 87–98). Raleigh, NC: National Society for Internships and
Experiential Education.

Epprecht, M. (2004). Work-study abroad courses in international and
development studies: Some ethical and pedagogical issues. *Canadian
Journal of Development Studies, 25*(4), 687–706. http://dx.doi.org/10.1080/
02255189.2004.9669009

Eyler, J. (2000). What do we need most to know about the impact of service-
learning on student learning? *Michigan Journal of Community Service
Learning*, Special Issue, 7, 11–17.

Eyler, J., Giles, D., & Schmiede, A. (1996). *A practitioner's guide to reflection in
service-learning*. Nashville: Vanderbilt University Press.

Fujii, L.A. (2009). Interpreting truth and lies in stories of conflict and violence.
In C.L. Sriram, J.C. King, J.A. Mertus, O. Martin-Ortega, & J. Herman

(Eds.), *Surviving field research: Working in violent and difficult situations* (pp. 147–162). London: Routledge.

Goudge, P. (2003). *The whiteness of power: Racism in third world development and aid*. London: Lawrence and Wishart Ltd.

Havel, V. (1985). The power of the powerless. In J. Keane (Ed.), *The power of the powerless: Citizens against the state in Central-Eastern Europe* (pp. 10–59). London: Hutchinson.

Heron, B. (2003). *Report on research: Preparing Canadians to work in Africa* (Unpublished report). Toronto: York University, School of Social Work.

Heron, B. (2006). Critically considering international social work practica. *Critical Social Work, 7*(2). http://www1.uwindsor.ca/criticalsocialwork/critically-considering-international-social-work-practica

Heron, B. (2007). *Desire for development: Whiteness, gender, and the helping imperative*. Waterloo, ON: Wilfrid Laurier University Press.

Heron, B. (2011). Challenging indifference to extreme poverty: Considering Southern perspectives on global citizenship and change. *Ethics and Economics, 8*(1), 109–119.

Kolb, D. (1984). *Experiential learning: Experiences as the source of learning and development*. Upper Saddle River, NJ: Prentice-Hall.

Lantis, J., & DuPlaga, J. (2010). *The global classroom: An essential guide to study abroad*. Boulder, CO: Paradigm Publishers.

Mertus, J. (2009). Maintenance of personal security: Ethical and operational issues. In C.L. Sriram, J.C. King, J.A. Mertus, O. Martin-Ortega, & J. Herman (Eds.), *Surviving field research: Working in violent and difficult situations* (pp. 165–176). London: Routledge.

Reyntjens, F. (2011). Constructing the truth, dealing with dissent, domesticating the world: Governance in post-genocide Rwanda. *African Affairs, 110*(438), 1–34. http://dx.doi.org/10.1093/afraf/adq075

Rogers, C. (1969). *Freedom to learn: A view of what education might become*. Columbus, OH: Charles E. Merrill.

Schön, D. (1983). *The reflexive practitioner: How professionals think in action*. New York: Basic Books.

Scott, J.C. (1990). *Domination and the arts of resistance: Hidden transcripts*. New Haven, CT: Yale University Press.

Sriram, C.L., King, J.C., Mertus, J.A., Martin-Ortega, O., & Herman, J. (Eds.). (2009). *Surviving field research: Working in violent and difficult situations*. London: Routledge.

Stanton, T.K. (1990). Liberal arts, experiential learning and public service: Necessary ingredients for socially responsible undergraduate education. In J. Kendall and Associates (Eds.), *Combining service and learning* (pp. 175–189). Raleigh, NC: National Society for Internships and Experiential Education.

Straus, S. & Waldorf, L. (Eds.). (2011). *Remaking Rwanda: State-building and human rights after mass violence*. Madison, WI: University of Wisconsin Press.

Thomson, S. (2009). *Developing ethical guidelines for researchers working in post-conflict environments*. Research report prepared for the Program on States and Security, City University of New York.

Thomson, S. (2013). Academic integrity and ethical responsibilities in post-genocide Rwanda: Working with research ethics boards to prepare for fieldwork with 'human subjects'. In S. Thomson, A. Ansoms, & J. Murison (Eds.), *Emotional and ethical challenges for field research in Africa: The story behind the findings* (pp. 139–154). London: Palgrave Macmillan.

Thomson, S., Ansoms, A., & Murison, J. (Eds.). (2013). *Emotional and ethical challenges for field research in Africa: The story behind the findings*. London: Palgrave Macmillan.

Wedeen, L. (1999). *Ambiguities of domination: Politics, rhetoric, and symbols in contemporary Syria*. Chicago: University of Chicago Press.

Wood, E.J. (2006). The ethical challenges of field research in conflict zones. *Qualitative Sociology*, 29(3), 373–386. http://dx.doi.org/10.1007/s11133-006-9027-8

Young, I.M. (1990). *Justice and the politics of difference*. Princeton: Princeton University Press.

8 "Would Flexner Close the Doors on This?" The Ethical Dilemmas of International Health Electives in Medical Education

ROBERT HUISH

An Enormous Double Standard

If you are a medical educator, then you know who Abraham Flexner is and just how important his Carnegie Foundation Report was, and still is, to medical education in North America (Flexner, 1910). For those who do not know, Flexner's infamous study, published in 1910, on the state of professional medical education in the US and Canada set the course for standardizing medical school curricula in rigorous science-based study (Austin, 2001; Beck, 2004; Cooke, Irby, Sullivan, & Ludmerer, 2006). In the early twentieth century there were 155 medical colleges in Canada and the United States. The curriculum varied considerably from school to school. Many of the schools were unaffiliated with universities and almost all were proprietary trade colleges run by a small scattering of faculty. Flexner noted that many students only observed medicine through lecture or text, with little opportunity for practicum, even in hospital settings (Flexner, 1910). He felt there was a lack of rigour in scientific education. It was possible to pass through a two-year degree without ever conducting lab work or dissections. It was an era when many medical schools lacked thoroughness, institutional ethics, and professional confidence. In some cases training physicians came close to treading on quackery (Ober, 1997).

Flexner's report called for strict standardization of medical education so that degrees would take four years to complete, and admission would require students to demonstrate basic scientific knowledge by holding a high school diploma or a bachelor's degree. Most important, Flexner rejected the proprietary nature of medical schools and insisted that medical colleges be affiliated with established universities in order to ensure a professional teaching environment with full-time clinical professors (Flexner, 1910). This recommendation set the professional trajectory for medical education up to today. Medical curricula must be scientifically grounded, comprehensive, and standardized so that students can meet national standards and certification board requirements. Increasingly, schools value problem-based learning in this package (Barrows, 1986). Changes and developments to medical school curriculum are based on findings from the academic literature from peer-reviewed journals like *Academic Medicine*, *Medical Education*, *The Lancet*, *The Canadian Medical Association Journal*, and *The New England Journal of Medicine*. When changes to curricula are proposed, they often go through academic development committees, the school's senior administration, and even state or provincial regulatory bodies. Curriculum changes require the faculty member to identify learning goals and objectives, and to engage problem-based learning practices in order to achieve those goals (Liaison Committee on Medical Education, 2012). In sum, medical education in North America is strictly standardized, rigorously scientific, heavily structured, and overly bureaucratized. Except for one popular and ever-growing area of study: global health.

In 2011, one out of every three medical graduates took on a global health experience, (formally referred to as International Health Elective – IHE) before they graduated (Chase & Evert, 2011). That number is expected to increase to two out of every three in the next five years (Huish, 2012). Medical students are ever-increasingly expected to venture overseas to a resource-poor setting to work alongside local health workers. There are also expectations that the students will bring much-needed resources to the under-funded clinics. Desrosiers and Thomson (in chapter 7 of this volume) suggest that "Western-born students, especially if they have never lived the material and emotional constraints", may struggle, rather than adapt well into resource-poor settings. With this said, experiencing these settings can also be intellectually and personally rewarding." Medical students on IHE's must negotiate such tensions throughout their experience, as the very nature of practice in resource-poor settings can be simultaneously hopeless and enriching. In some medical schools there are pre-departure briefing sessions and then some debriefing sessions upon return, which are rarely run by faculty members (Canadian Federation of Medical Students, 2009). Of the eighteen allopathic medical schools in Canada and 126 in the United States, there is absolutely no standardized curriculum for global health or IHEs. At best some schools have established Global Health Offices (or Centres) that coordinate the pre-departure seminars and post-trip debriefing. At worst students take off to an overseas placement with little more than a signed sheet of paper indicating that the trip is for credit. While the norm in Canadian medical schools is for students to brief and debrief each other, there is a slowly growing trend of coordinating these sessions through institutionalized offices (Canadian Federation of Medical Students, 2009). Considering that every detail of medical education is planned and measured with the utmost scrutiny to that of which Flexner desired, how is a it that one of the fastest growing subject areas in medicine is completely unregulated, uncoordinated, and at times unprofessional? As many have argued, with such a rise in popularity it may be time to re-examine the values of global health and IHEs (Kerry et al., 2011; Redwood-Campbell et al., 2011). No other area of medical education would be allowed to continue to train students with such loose standards and guidelines. Failure to adhere to strict standards in medical education can lead to serious consequences. In fact, the Canadian and American medical school accreditors put Dalhousie University on probation for failing to meet 17 out of the 132 standards set in place by the American Accreditation Liaison Committee on Medical Education (Jones, 2012; The Canadian Press, 2009). While there is one clause that requires a risk assessment of elective rotations at a non-affiliated medical school through the dean's office (Liaison Committee on Medical Education, 2012), of these 132 standards, not a single one specifically deals with the ethical dimensions of global health education or how IHEs negotiate uneven socio-economic development in resource-poor countries. Medical schools continue to encourage students to take short-term IHEs in resource-strapped health systems, with only token education in ethics and minimal instruction in processes of international development or political economy (Huish, 2012). It smacks of disregard to socio-economic conditions that govern health care capabilities in resource-poor settings in the Global South.

As the title of this chapter suggests, Flexner would likely flag the current practices of global health education as off side to that of the rigour and integrity of every other dimension of medical education. I am not suggesting that global health education become further rooted in the scientific rigidity that Flexner prescribed over 100 years ago. Interestingly enough, many IHEs already strive towards Flexner's call to use the field experience for scientific clinical education (Valani, Sriharan, & Scolnik, 2011). Rather, the point of this chapter is to identify the enormous double standard of a complete lack of rigour for global health education, in large part because of the continued Flexnerian tradition of valuing scientific knowledge in health care at the cost of overlooking the potential role of social science.

I argue that the lack of moral attention to standardized edification in social theory and ethics within IHEs is in fact a reflection of a pedagogical hubris. This superciliousness within the medical sciences places less value on educational opportunities that should require knowledge and appreciation for social sciences by students and certainly by program coordinators. While IHEs could be a valuable experience for future practitioners to engage in understanding the structural causes of social inequity, resource scarcity, marginalization, and sub-development, many overlook any serious commitment to understanding these processes, and instead turn crowded and resource-strapped foreign hospitals into exotic clinical training grounds. Fizzell and Epprecht (in chapter 6 of this volume) point out that many international experiential learning opportunities bring about, "concerns ... over local labour replacement in the Global South, resource consumption by volunteers, gender and racial tensions between volunteers and host community members." This could not be more apparent than with IHEs as many programs transform resource-poor clinics into training spaces for well-to-do medical students. Underqualified students are being asked to gain clinical experience in underfunded clinics in underdeveloped countries. The result is that the foreign clinic becomes a low-cost clinical learning centre for students who may think that their efforts are really helping to improve the lives of community members, and the clinic is conveniently placed a short distance away from safari or the beach.

The lacking rigour of social theory and comprehensive development within global health education is in part due to the popular assumption that IHEs are in resource-poor countries that are too poor and too poorly organized to ever achieve reliable health care, and hence they will always be in need of aid from wealthier medical schools (Travis et al., 2004). In this chapter I explain how medical school hubris in what is known as "the hidden curriculum" has shaped IHEs into an ethically problematic branch of medical education (Gaufberg, Batalden, Sands, & Bell, 2010). The chapter then makes a case for placing deeper social theory into the heart of global health, especially at the administrative and program design level. The best example to demonstrate this is by looking at the dimensions of Cuban medical education that pays specific attention to the social determinants of health and community dynamics in health practice. Finally, the chapter calls for innovative global health approaches such as that with the non-governmental organization Partners in Health, and also the partnership between Columbia University in New York and Ben Gurion University of Negev in Israel in the Medical School for International Health. Those programs may very well provide the first steps towards a global health approach that seeks to address ethical conundrums of IHEs rather than merely adding to them.

The goal of this chapter is to make an appeal to medical practitioners and educators in global health. While IHEs are a popular and profitable elective for medical schools to offer, many are run in a way that compounds ethical conundrums. The pre-departure and post-trip debriefing sessions generally focus on reflective personal experiences, rather than on structural inequities between health systems (Canadian Federation of Medical Students, 2009). In marginalized communities, the clinics barely have capacity to handle local care needs, and training preference in those clinics is given to wealthy visiting students rather than to local capacity building. There is an urgent need to structure IHEs so that they may address ethical challenges rather than contribute to them (Elit et al., 2011). Solutions do exist, and by working with partners overseas to share medical knowledge, to build local capacity, and to address the structural causes of health care inequity, it will be possible to improve global health education from a loose collection of electives to an established sub-discipline of cooperation and coordination between colleagues and students in the Global North and South alike.

The Two Broad Ethical Conundrums of IHEs

There are two major ethical conundrums with IHEs in their current form. First is that many of the existing global health practicums emphasize clinical-based scientific study at the cost of understanding structural deficiencies in resource-poor health systems. This continues a long-standing tradition of emphasizing scientific knowledge in medicine above all other knowledge (Arawi & Rosoff, 2012). Many structures of medical education are unable to facilitate rich study in social theory and practices of economic development. The result is that social theory is not emphasized in IHEs and students arrive in resource-poor centres to spend time in clinical settings being mentored by local health professionals (Elit et al., 2011). Without dedicated study to health policy, local governance, and the structural roots of inequity, students are

left with only a raw comparison of the clinical settings between resource flush and resource poor. Through this lens global health work
becomes an experience of comparison between differences in services,
practices, and infrastructure. Yet Drain et al. (2007) suggest that students who participate in IHEs will be more likely to enter primary care
or serve marginalized populations (p. 225). Ramsey, Haq, et al. (2004)
also suggest that while there is no causative relationship between IHEs
and career choices, there seems to be a tendency for participants, of a
specific International Health Fellowship Program involving three US
medical schools, to seek career options aimed at community-based
health. Jeffrey, Dumon, Kim, and Kuo (2011) found that the global
health literature reflected a consistency in that "IHE experiences contributed to a more well-rounded training for medical students; students
reported being more culturally competent and were more likely to
choose a primary care specialty and/or a public service career" (p. 21).
While IHEs do vary in quality and consistency (Jeffrey, Dumon, Kim, &
Kuo, 2011), and they have the potential to introduce medical students
to cross-cultural clinical contexts, I would not go as far to say that the
typical IHE experience is a deep exploration of global health ethics,
health system management, or the globalization of health. While the
literature may reflect a link between IHEs and interest in service to the
marginalized, it is unlikely, as this chapter demonstrates, that this interest comes as the result of rich engagement in social theory. The result,
then, is that while medical students may have a deepened interest in
global health and community health for the marginalized, they likely
have a shallow understanding of the nature of social injustice and
structural inequities.

Green, Green, Scandlyn, and Kestler (2009) argue that little research
has been undertaken to understand the value of such programs from
the point of view of the host communities. Green et al. find that the
value of projects varies on a case-by-case basis and cannot be broadly
generalized. In some cases the clinical experiential learning may have
few social benefits, and in others, community members may find positive value through temporary improved access. However, it can be
noted that while particular projects may vary in quality and capacity, a
general trend of under-preparation in global health education continues
unabated.

Bozorgmehr, Schubert, Menzel-Severing, and Tinnemann (2010)
found that in German medical schools "formal preparation beyond

self-study is virtually non-existent amongst [the] sample and the participation rate in courses of tropical medicine or global health is appallingly low. We have identified unmet perceived needs and the demand for more learning opportunities in global health in our sample, urging for reforms to adjust curricula to a globalizing world" (p. 1). Chan, Dillabaugh, Pfeifle, Stewart, and Teng (2011) suggest that curricula should include a broad range of subjects that expose students to global health dynamics beyond the clinical experiential learning components. Topics could include:

> An overview of global health and the global burden of disease; health indicators and an understanding of their use and limitations; economic and social development; institutions and organizations involved in global health, including policy and trade agreements; environmental health, including water acquisition and safety, natural and man-made disasters, and immigration issues; cultural, social and behavioral determinants of health; demography; social justice and global health including an understanding of human rights; personal health and safety during global health field experiences; global health ethics and professionalism, and cultural competency training. (Chan, Dillabaugh, Pfeifle, Stewart, & Teng, 2011, p. 18)

This is an enormous amount of content and knowledge to condense into a brief international rotation let alone an entire undergraduate degree. Some have argued for a more trimmed collection of key topics (Peluso, Encandela, Hafler, & Margolis, 2012). Chan et al. note that it is incredibly difficult to load these topics into medical education and residency programs that are already stuffed full of content (2011, p. 16). The question is not just how to raise awareness of greater social science themes in global health, but how to find time to serve the topics justice by placing them within already compact medical curricula. Laven and Newbury (2011) discuss how a pre-departure program called The Rural Undergraduate Support and Coordination (RUSC) program has managed to address certain dimensions of global health education such as education modules on the burden of global disease, travellers' medicine, and refugee health, but little is mentioned about social determinants of health, organization of health systems, or the role of policy and trade agreements that Chan et al. (2011) recommend. The Global Health Education Consortium and the Association of Faculties of Medicine of

Canada's Global Health Resource Group have developed a core competencies in global health wiki to help establish a standard set of content
for global health education including:

• the global burden of disease
• migration, travel, and displacement
• social and environmental determinants of health
• the globalization of health care
• health care in low resource settings, and
• health as a human right.

> (Arthur et al., 2011; Global Health Education Consortium
> & Association of Faculties of Medicine of Canada, 2012)

While this is an important effort to bring focus to the social, economic, political, and environmental dimensions of global health, the topic
spread is enormous, and it is unlikely that any of these subjects could
be seriously addressed in a period of less than a full academic year, let
alone in a couple of one hour pre-departure sessions. If global health
entails such a broad range of subject matter, and if already overworked
medical students have little space to cover the topics in the sort of explicit detail that they expect of other medical topics, should there even
be attempts made at structuring global health electives in this way so it
condenses such broad theory around a clinical elective? Should the curricula even be aimed at students? Should it perhaps be targeted at program developers? In sum, this may well be a paradox of trying to build
a rigorous global health curriculum into IHEs that are, by design, taken
as peripheral and less important to medical education.

The second ethical challenge within global health programs is the
creation of dependency of resource-poor clinics in the South on affluent
ones in the North. Clinics that receive a steady flow of medical students, researchers, and donated resources come to rely on these external assets in order to facilitate the day-to-day operations (Garrett, 2007,
p. 31). This may provide short-term benefits, but it risks dependency
over the long term in two key areas. First are the risks involved in pro-
curing medical supplies through donations rather than through long-
term aid schemes. It is a classic scene. Medical students are at the airport
with suitcases everywhere, many bursting with medicines, bandages,
and other much-needed supplies. When these bags arrive at the clinic
the pharmacy is stocked, and the supplies are much appreciated. But if
in future trips the suitcases start to get a little light, or if there are delays

in scheduling the elective, it can turn into real resource shortages in the clinic. While there is a certain photogenic value of medical students carrying more suitcases for patients than for themselves, it can be impractical in terms of long-term sustainability. What would be far more useful is the establishment of a monthly monetary donation system to local NGOs and pharmacy distributors who could constantly maintain supply. While it is not as photogenic, establishing a local pharmacy distributor is a valuable global health action.

The second area of dependency involves human resources for health. When under-resourced clinics are in receipt of medical students and residents, they do receive remuneration for offering up their centres for educational purposes. There is also a tendency to cater more teaching attention and administration support to the visiting foreigners than there is for establishing programs to enhance capacity building at the local level (Finch et al., 2011). The clinic becomes an extension of the wealthy medical school as a dedicated training space (Huish, 2012). When the students, residents, and experts return to their home countries so too does the money. Clinics are then pressured to encourage the return of Northern medical students in order to secure more resources rather than seek out less lucrative strategies to enhance local capacity building. There are some circumstances when the remuneration from IHEs can work to fund training at the local level, but this is by no means a standardized practice (Suchdev et al., 2007).

In sum, many IHEs prioritize the resources and capacities of underfunded clinics to act as teaching spaces for wealthy students to experience the clinical setting, but not necessarily to engage in the broader dimensions of global health education. How then can medical educators find ways to operate global health rotations so that they can actually address the ethical issues of hubris and dependency rather than contribute to them? In order to pursue such change, medical educators must address a topic that is well known, that is just as important as the standard curriculum, but rarely discussed: the hidden curriculum.

The Hidden Curriculum

Hidden curricula can exist in any profession. It is understood as skills, traits, norms or values that are unintentionally learned. Often this involves the internal political dynamics of a work environment, or students witnessing the normative behaviour of top educators and professionals. In general this can lead to the tacit influences of mentors on a medical student's long-term career choices (Woloschuk, Wright, & McLaughlin, 2011). Lempp and Seale (2004) identify six cultural dimensions of the hidden curriculum in medical school that students experience that may impact career choices and the general practice of medicine:

- loss of idealism
- adoption of a "ritualised" professional identity
- emotional neutralisation
- change of ethical integrity
- acceptance of hierarchy, and
- the learning of less formal aspects of "good doctoring." (p. 770)

Lempp and Seale (2004) show that some dimensions of the hidden curriculum can work through the "lead by example" approach of good role models facilitating positive outcomes in "good doctoring." However, many of the dimensions reveal the potential for establishing cultural norms in nihilism, questioned ethics, and skepticism among students. Lempp and Seale (2004) identify a noticeably disturbing trend of reinforcing the hierarchies of medicine through public humiliation of students by senior faculty (p. 771). Moreover, the hidden curriculum in medical education can have detrimental effects on building appreciation and collaboration for other non-medical disciplines and non-western cultures (Ewen, Mazel, & Knoche, 2012). As Michalec (2012) notes, "students discuss experiencing disapproval, mistrust, and negative judgment toward laypersons thereby suggesting that this distancing may lend to deleterious effects on students' ability and willingness to connect with others" (p. 267). White, Brownell, Lemay, & Lockyer (2012) show that the expectations of the hidden curriculum reach as far as the application process, which could include emphasizing morals that are thought to be more "traditional" than personally genuine. Babaria, Abedin, Berg, & Nunez-Smith (2012) demonstrate that while there are an increasing number of women entering medical school, there is still a strong presence of harassment and gender discrimination through the education experience. The consequence here is that the hidden curriculum works to influence identity formation and personal career decisions among female students. It may help to explain why there may be more women entering medicine, but also why few go into advanced specializations.

The most troubling evidence of the hidden curriculum may be found in the ways in which it dehumanizes patients, sets false limitations in health care, and encourages students to "act like a doctor" in becoming a physician. Gaufberg, Batalden, Sands, and Bell (2010) discuss some worrisome testimonies from third-year Harvard medical students. Gaufberg et al. (2010) show that students frequently witnessed dehumanizing behaviour of attending physicians to patients. One student wrote,

> There were several times when a patient was called "demented" or "frontal" without having any explanation given to them ... The most horrific thing I saw was when the attending asked the patient to turn over and then proceeded to demonstrate the anal wink reflex to us without warning the patient of what he was going to do. (p. 1711)

If within their own home learning environments there is a tendency to strip patients of their humanity, how is it possible to expect students to transform their normative ethics in foreign and under-resourced clinics to be champions of humanity?

Gaufberg et al. (2010) also show how the hidden curriculum pushes students to disengage from the non-medical dimensions of a patient's well-being, notably through sympathy to suffering or empathy for a patient's personal convictions. One student wrote about the disconnect between the expected medical check-up during a home visit, and the broad social determinants of health:

> True, my patient has a long laundry list of scary health problems, and she deserves counselling about lifestyle modifications and the importance of medication compliance in order to decrease her risk of developing a myriad of future complications. But all of these things strike me as ridiculous in the moment. My patient's problem list, in my opinion, consists of a single item heading: the unimaginable suffering of isolation. (p. 1172)

The message here is that the student recognizes the importance of the social determinants of health, but her evaluation criteria – which matters in obtaining a passing grade – has nothing to do with the impacts of the social determinants of isolation to a patient's health. Again, if the social determinants of health are undervalued at home, how can they be championed abroad?

Finally, Gaufberg et al. (2010) illuminate how many students felt the need to "fake it" as a doctor, meaning that they would change their normative behaviour in order to conform to the manners, habits, and identity of the senior attending physicians. A student explains this "faking":

> I felt vaguely like a child "playing dress-up," and frequently wondered whether patients could see through the cheap costume in order to scrutinize my actual competency. Still, I clung to the white coat as an official uniform, perhaps as proof to reassure both myself and the patient I belonged in the room, that I had the capability to assume responsibility for the lives of patients (who often appeared much older and wiser than I). Even now, the white coat still offers me a sense of validity, of entitlement. It is essentially a façade, but I confess with a visceral twinge of chagrin that it heightens my confidence in my abilities to perform. (p. 1713)

If identity and hierarchy matter enormously in the formation of physicians, how is it possible to remove these power dynamics in experiential learning programs abroad? Combined, a hidden curriculum that belittles patients, undervalues the social determinants of health, and reinforces power dynamics is completely at odds with the desired teaching outcomes of global health education.

Tiessen (in chapter 4 of this volume) notes that "for many of the participants [of experiential learning abroad], the learn/volunteer abroad program served as a litmus test for their career choices; enabling them to decide if they want to continue a career in international work or pursue different and/or Canadian-based poverty-related work. Almost all respondents agreed that their overseas experience has or will help them find employment." This partially holds true in the medical profession. While IHEs can be effective and bolster a medical student's CV, there is little evidence to suggest that IHE participants are more likely to take on medical careers focused on improving access in resource-poor communities or to work towards social justice. Considering that the official medical curriculum necessarily values science-based study above social theory, and that hidden curriculum can reinforce normative behaviour that is incongruent to the values of social justice education through global health curriculum, it seems tantamount to defeat in even attempting to legitimize global health education as anything more than a light-hearted jaunt abroad. To suggest deep reforms to the ethics of global health education would also suggest deep adjustments to both the hidden and overt medical curricula. To the sceptics who see no hope in making such adjustments, there are only two options, and both draw close to danger as with Homer's Odyssey when sailors had to pass through the monsters of Skylla and Charybdis. The Skylla would be to let IHEs carry on as is with the knowledge that the current medical culture presents numerous ethical dilemmas (Elit et al., 2011). The Charybdis is to move towards eliminating the electives altogether. Still it may be possible to avoid a Greek mythological disaster and actually chart a third way for global health education to meet the learning objectives through social theory and to help bolster solidarity between the Global North and Global South. To help chart this path it is important to explore three examples of global health experiences. The first example is found in Cuba's medical education curricula. The second example involves some of the programs run by the NGO Partners in Health, and the third example comes from Ben Gurion University in Israel. There are elements in all three of these cases to show that it is possible, and desirable, to position global health education around addressing ethical challenges rather than contributing to them.

Lesson 1: Cuban Medical Internationalism

Cuba has a long-standing history of medical outreach, cooperation, and collaboration with other resource-poor countries throughout the Global South. Labelled "Cuban Medical Internationalism" (Huish & Kirk, 2007; Kirk & Erisman, 2009) it is a dynamic mix of foreign policy and medical care aimed at producing transformative change within resource-poor settings. Over 110,000 Cuban health workers have been involved in medical missions in 101 countries since 1960 (Huish, 2013). As of 2012, there are roughly 38,000 Cuban health workers in 76 countries. Notably there are close to 19,000 providing health services in Venezuela and another 2,000 working on a rotating basis in Haiti (Huish, 2013). Cuban workers take on contracts that can run between two to ten years, and they work in a collaborative effort with local governments and public health systems with aims of building local human resource capacity (Huish, 2013). In addition to sending human resources for health abroad, the Cuban government also offers complete scholarships for students from other countries in the Global South to come to Cuba to train in several disciplines with the understanding that they will return to their home countries to provide services. As of 2012 there are over 15,000 medical students from 56 countries studying in Cuba. These students are expected to return to their home countries to provide health care in marginalized communities to the best of their ability (Huish & Kirk, 2007).

These programs have helped to warm bilateral relations between Cuba and many other countries in the global South while providing much needed health resources to some of the world's most vulnerable populations. In 1999 hurricanes Mitch and George devastated Central America and the Caribbean. Cuban emergency medical response teams deployed for Honduras, Guatemala, and Nicaragua following the torrential rainfall that resulted in massive mudslides. While the physical destruction was disastrous, many Cuban emergency workers noted that the complete lack of in-country human resources for health in rural areas was catastrophic (Huish & Kirk, 2007). The Cuban government made efforts to increase the number of scholarships offered to Central America, and then created the Latin American School of Medicine (ELAM – *Escuela Latinoamericana de Medicina*), a faculty of medicine that exclusively receives foreign students on full scholarship. The idea was that it was far more effective to build long-term human resource capacity for the region than it would be to interminably send Cuban health workers.

The program of study is six years, with optional pre-medical training years for students who require additional tutoring in sciences or language proficiency. The six-year program provides rigorous scientific curriculum, but so too does it specifically cater to dedicated training in the social and environmental determinants of health. When students first arrive at ELAM, their initial textbooks are in "Health & Medicine" and epidemiology (Álvarez Sintes et al., 2001). They begin by looking at the social, economic, environmental, and power determinants that go into influencing health at the individual and community level, even before study of the human body. It is a radical departure from the entry point of many medical programs in the North that emphasize medical sciences in year one. Moreover, students trained in Cuba learn to chart out community health maps, how to make house calls that involve the collection of health data for tracking, and how to work with other health professionals to establish routines of health promotion and disease prevention. While the Cuban curriculum adheres to the strict scientific rigour to that of medical schools in the North, the continual reinforcement of the social determinants of health is found throughout the curriculum. The result is that when Cuban, or Cuban-trained, health workers practice in resource-poor settings they have not only the medical science training but also highly developed skills in establishing routines of disease prevention and health promotion (Huish, 2013). This makes a world of difference for improving health outcomes in marginalized communities.

The Cuban approach matters enormously for global health education (Evert et al., 2011). While many IHEs in Northern medical schools focus entirely on short-term clinical rotations, the Cuban approach trains graduates for long-term placement for the health management of resource-poor communities. Certainly the Cuban-trained graduates will have competency to work in clinical settings, but the reality of health care throughout the Global South is that there is a paucity of available clinical services in rural and marginalized areas. A clinically competent physician is a tremendously important asset for a marginalized community. An even greater resource is to have trained health workers who can organize, manage, and coordinate health strategies that maintain health and lessen the dependency on underfunded clinics.

To train Northern medical students to work for the long term in rural outposts in the Global South may be unrealistic. And this speaks to another lesson from Cuba. Global health education does not need to accommodate the travel desires of well-trained health workers to resource-poor settings. It can very much involve the travel of resource-poor medical students to well suited settings for education. Certainly medical education programs can benefit from the receipt of students from the Global South and from the establishment of coordinated partnerships with hospitals in the Global South. Many schools do engage in such practice (Goldner & Bollinger, 2012). When it comes to positioning global health education in a way to address pressing health needs and to improve the quality of lives of patients in marginalized communities, is it not morally compelling to seek out strategies that can actually meet these goals? It has been long known in medicine that students from marginalized areas have a much greater chance of becoming effective medical workers in those areas (de Vries & Reid, 2003). If global health education is to make a difference in improving health for the marginalized, then it should include a reverse in the flow of study to build capacity in under-resourced communities rather than using those communities to build capacity for the North.

Lesson 2: Partners in Health

One case where Northern medical expertise went to marginalized communities in the South for the long term is that of Partners in Health. It was founded in 1987 by a group of physicians working in Boston including Paul Farmer, Ophelia Dahl, and current World Bank president Jim Yong Kim. The group's aims are to develop improved access to primary health care in resource-poor areas, notably Haiti, Peru, Rwanda, and certain inner-city neighbourhoods in the United States (Kidder, 2009). Partners in Health focuses specifically on disease prevention and health promotion against health calamities that result from the structural violence of poverty (Farmer, 2005). Partners in Health believes that affordable and accessible primary care is crucial to ensure health as a right to the poor. As well, the group does not shy away from political advocacy and engagement. Where many health-based NGOs, such as Médecins Sans Frontières or the Red Cross and Red Crescent Societies, aim for political neutrality, Partners in Health maintains the importance of political advocacy and activism in speaking out against social, political, and economic structures that systematically marginalize the health of the poor. Combined, it is a program of work that goes well beyond the clinical to actually addressing the very structures of health inequity.

In order to ensure robust primary care and constant advocacy for health as a right for the poor, Partners in Health encourages capacity building of health professionals within and alongside their operations abroad. In Haiti the Zanmi Lasante medical centre is a Partners in Health initiative that includes a 104-bed training hospital and employs over 4,000 people, most of them locals (Partners in Health, 2012). The organization carries this approach into other similar projects operating in Rwanda, Burundi, Peru, Guatemala, Russia, Malawi, Lesotho, and the Dominican Republic. It is not enough to expect that Northern medical students and experts will be able to provide long-term primary care or social advocacy for the global poor. The true strength of such initiatives needs to come from within communities themselves (Kidder, 2009). As a result, Partners in Health does not offer short-term experiential learning visits from students in the North. Instead they encourage students to take on leadership roles within their home communities to raise solidarity and support for Partners in Health operations abroad. Such activities can include the organization of study groups, advocacy groups, and fundraising groups. In 2010, following the Haitian earthquake,

International Development Studies students at Dalhousie University raised over CAD$9,000 for Partners in Health. This money went directly to the community-based operations of the organization, and local experts controlled the allocation of funds. For about the same cost of sending one medical student on a three-week IHE, the student's donations greatly assisted the capacity of Partners in Health to reach out to thousands of people in rural Haiti. Consistent and long-term capacity in rural and outlying areas matters enormously for the provision of quality care. During the cholera outbreak in Haiti, Partners in Health provided over 45,000 vaccinations and established a reliable potable water system in the Haitian plateau to mitigate future outbreaks. None of this required IHEs, but it did require funding and advocacy. The Partners in Health model is not just about clinical care, it is about strengthening community resources for long-term health promotion.

While Partners in Health does not promote experiential IHEs, it does offer students, health professionals, and others the opportunity to get involved with their programs. The organization encourages donations and fundraising activities, the establishment of student chapters on campuses across North America, and advocacy for global health equity. The message from the Partners in Health model is that medical students should be involved in global health, but not in a trivial way. The true strengths and resources of medical students in global health can be applied through advocacy. It is a reminder that global health can very much entail local participation in initiatives that address the structural causes of systematic poverty.

Lesson 3: The MSIH Model in the Negev Desert

Another important lesson comes from the Medical School for International Health (MSIH) located at Ben Gurion University in Beer Sheva, Israel. This is a school partnered with Columbia University to offer students an integrated four-year program in global health. Whereas many medical schools offer global health as an elective, MSIH ties global health study into the entire curriculum, and includes an eight-week rotation to a resource-poor setting. Global health courses are not slotted in as electives. These courses are required rotations. MSIH emphasizes a hands-on approach to global health, which includes clinical experience abroad, but it also addresses dimensions of social theory in its curriculum. MSIH students enter the program to a comprehensive and thorough study of epidemiology as it reflects "a major importance in global health" (Medical School for International Health, 2012). In addition, the biomedical sciences students take global health preparation courses that cover "Demography and Health Indicators, Health Problems in LDC, Cross Cultural Health Beliefs, Maternal and Child Health, the Aged, Primary Health Care, Global Health and Environment, Infectious and Tropical Diseases, International Programs and Projects, and Health Care Organizations" (Medical School for International Health, 2012).

The global health content covered includes:

– History of Global Health and Current Global Health Players
– The Global Burden of Disease and Determinants of Health
– Introduction to Healthcare Systems and MSIH Modules
– The Israeli Healthcare System
– Global Health Economics
– Nutrition and Food Science
– Health Policy and Communication Skills
– Maternal and Child Health
– Disaster Management, Displaced Persons, Refugees and Terrorism
– Aging Populations
– Mental Health
– Poverty and Health
– Primary Care in Global Health
– Environmental Health Issues
                              (Medical School for International Health, 2012)

These topics closely reflect the pillars of global health education that Chan et al. (2011) identify. There is, however, no attempt to cram these topics into a few short lectures. Rather, these themes are explored in depth over two years.

The lesson plans in year two expand on the comprehensive medical sciences, but in years three and four students begin clinical rotations including a global health clinical clerkship. These clerkships may incorporate some of the clinical training experiences that come from other IHEs; however, the two-month placement allows for the incorporation of non-clinical activities that encourage disease prevention and health promotion. Students also have the opportunity to present case reports that analyse the state of health inequity in their placements.

The value of the MSIH model is that global health is not taken as a whimsical elective. It is approached as a rigorous sub-discipline that requires attention to topics beyond pure medical science, and is studied in depth over the four-year period. While the program engages in similar overseas clerkships that IHEs take on, it differs in the level of training and attention it affords students pre-departure. The global health training at MSIH is not just a small package of seminars on behavioural ethics led by fellow students, rather, the school structures entire learning modules around understanding the complex socio-economic dynamics of global health. They routinely bring in leading experts in global health to give a collection of seminars to the students. In a sense, MSIH attempts to integrate the clinical and advocacy elements of global health into a single curriculum. It is an innovative program that stands apart from almost every other medical school's practice of global health in its breadth and depth.

Conclusions

This chapter has shown that the hubris of medical education has devalued global health as an important sub-discipline, and has resulted in the ethically questionable practice of sending underqualified medical students into highly complex clinical settings. This hubris has reduced global health education within faculties of medicine to little more than a short-term clinical elective abroad. IHEs routinely send underqualified medical students to some of the world's most difficult clinical settings for short electives. Without proper educational grounding in social theory and policy, students are left to merely compare the practice of medicine in resource-poor settings to what they take on at home. Without proper resource support, resource-poor clinics transform to meet the needs of well off medical students, rather than build capacity at the local level. In essence, IHEs put both medical students and local community clinics in ethically perilous situations.

This is largely due to medical educators failing to take global health seriously as a dynamic sub-discipline that requires careful attention to social theory, processes of globalization, epidemiology, and other disciplines. Instead, many medical schools have pandered to an obsession with scientific curriculum by making IHEs almost entirely clinical. As this chapter has shown, such a practice does more to reinforce the hubris of the hidden curriculum and dependency of the poor clinic upon the wealthy medical school. It is hardly desirable to do away with global health as a discipline. Likewise, it is hardly ethical to ignore the moral challenges that come with IHEs.

While this chapter proposes no fixed solution to this practice, it does make an appeal to medical educators to seek a third way. To find the path between Skylla and Charybdis, the chapter offers three approaches to global health. Cuban medical internationalism reverses the geographic flow of global health so that it is based on resource poor students travelling to seek education that is meant to better their communities. Partners in Health moves away from IHEs altogether by asking medical students from the North to practice advocacy at home, while the organization works on expanding capacity in the South. The MSIH offers disciplinary rigour to global health by positioning the entire program around advanced training from social theory to political economy to clinical practice. While the specific methods of these programs differ, they all share the capacity to overcome the hubris of the hidden curriculum by valuing social theory in health, building solidarity with the global poor, and offering students dedicated focus to global health challenges. Moreover, this is a chance for program designers to engage these topics and model global health experiences accordingly. If medical educators wonder if a third path is possible, these three organizations show that it is. There is student demand for global health, and there is pressing need to address the health inequities, not just between rich and poor countries but between the rich and poor of all countries. If IHEs fail to adequately serve these demands, then they must be repositioned in order to do so.

This is not a call for every medical school to mirror the curriculum of ELAM or MSIH. Rather, this is a call to realize that real alternatives to the current clinical practice of global health exist. These alternatives are grounded, tested, and go beyond scientific obsession. While Flexner may take exception with curricula going beyond science, he would hardly disapprove of a standardized curriculum that addresses ethical challenges rather than one that contributes to them.

REFERENCES

Álvarez Sintes, R. (2001). *Temas de medicina general integral.* (Vol. I. Salud y Medicina). La Habana: Editorial Ciencias Médicas.
Arawi, T., & Rosoff, P.M. (2012, Jun). Competing duties: Medical educators, underperforming students, and social accountability. *Journal of Bioethical Inquiry, 9*(2), 135–147. http://dx.doi.org/10.1007/s11673-012-9365-z Medline:23180257
Arthur, M.A., Battat, R., & Brewer, T.F. (2011, Jun). Teaching the basics: Core competencies in global health. *Infectious Disease Clinics of North America, 25*(2), 347–358. http://dx.doi.org/10.1016/j.idc.2011.02.013 Medline:21628050

Austin, D. (2001). Special issue: Flexner revisited – Guest editor's foreword. *Research on Social Work Practice, 11*(2), 147–151. http://dx.doi.org/10.1177/104973150101100201

Babaria, P., Abedin, S., Berg, D., & Nunez-Smith, M. (2012, Apr). "I'm too used to it": A longitudinal qualitative study of third year female medical students' experiences of gendered encounters in medical education. *Social Science & Medicine, 74*(7), 1013–1020. http://dx.doi.org/10.1016/j.socscimed.2011.11.043 Medline:22341202

Barrows, H.S. (1986, Nov). A taxonomy of problem-based learning methods. *Medical Education, 20*(6), 481–486. http://dx.doi.org/10.1111/j.1365-2923.1986.tb01386.x Medline:3796328

Beck, A.H. (2004, May 5). STUDENTJAMA. The Flexner report and the standardization of American medical education. *Journal of the American Medical Association, 291*(17), 2139–2140. http://dx.doi.org/10.1001/jama.291.17.2139 Medline:15126445

Bozorgmehr, K., Schubert, K., Menzel-Severing, J., & Tinnemann, P. (2010). Global health education: A cross-sectional study among German medical students to identify needs, deficits and potential benefits (Part 1 of 2: Mobility patterns & educational needs and demands). *BMC Medical Education*, doi: 10.1186/1472-6920-10-66

Canadian Federation of Medical Students. (2009). *CFMS Annual Review*. Ottawa: CFMS.

Chan, K., Dillabaugh, L., Pfeifle, A., Stewart, C., & Teng, F. (2011). Global health education curriculum. In J. Chase & J. Evert (Eds.), *Global health training in graduate medical education* (pp. 16–24). San Francisco: Global Health Education Consortium.

Chase, J., & Evert, J. (2011). *Global health training in graduate medical education*. San Francisco: Global Health Education Consortium.

Cooke, M., Irby, D.M., Sullivan, W., & Ludmerer, K.M. (2006, Sep 28). American medical education 100 years after the Flexner report. *The New England Journal of Medicine, 355*(13), 1339–1344. http://dx.doi.org/10.1056/NEJMra055445 Medline:17005951

Drain, P., Primack, A., Hunt, D., Fawzi, W., Holmes, K., & Gardner, P. (2007). Global health in medical education: A call for more training and opportunities. *Academic Medicine, 82*(3), 226–230.

de Vries, E., & Reid, S. (2003, Oct). Do South African medical students of rural origin return to rural practice? *South African Medical Journal, 93*(10), 789–793. Medline:14652974

Elit, L., Hunt, M., Redwood-Campbell, L., Ranford, J., Adelson, N., & Schwartz, L. (2011, Jul). Ethical issues encountered by medical students during international health electives. *Medical Education, 45*(7), 704–711. http://dx.doi.org/10.1111/j.1365-2923.2011.03936.x Medline:21649703

Evert, J., Huish, R., Heit, G., Jones, E., Loeliger, S., & Schmidbauer, S. (2011). Global Health Ethics. In J. Illes & B. Sahakian (Eds.), *Oxford handbook of neuroethics* (pp. 835–856). Oxford: Oxford University Press. http://dx.doi.org/10.1093/oxfordhb/9780199570706.013.0185

Ewen, S., Mazel, O., & Knoche, D. (2012, Feb). Exposing the hidden curriculum influencing medical education on the health of Indigenous people in Australia and New Zealand: The role of the critical reflection tool. *Academic Medicine, 87*(2), 200–205.

Farmer, P. (2005). *Pathologies of power: Health, human rights, and the new war on the poor: With a new preface by the author.* Berkeley: University of California Press.

Finch, T.H., Chae, S.R., Shafaee, M.N., Siegel, K.R., Ali, M.K., Tomei, R., Panjabi, R., & Kishore, S.P. (2011, May–Jun). Role of students in global health delivery. *The Mount Sinai Journal of Medicine, New York, 78*(3), 373–381. http://dx.doi.org/10.1002/msj.20254 Medline:21598264

Flexner, A. (1910). *Medical education in the United States and Canada: A report to the Carnegie Foundation for the Advancement of Teaching* (Vol. 4). Boston: D.B. Updike, The Merrymount Press.

Garrett, L. (2007). The challenge of global health. *Foreign Affairs, 86*(1), 14–38.

Gaufberg, E.H., Batalden, M., Sands, R., & Bell, S.K. (2010). The hidden curriculum: What can we learn from third-year medical student narrative reflections? *Academic Medicine, 85*(11), 1709–1716. http://dx.doi.org/10.1097/ACM.0b013e3181f57899 Medline:20881818

Global Health Education Consortium & Association of Faculties of Medicine of Canada. (2012). Global Health Competencies. Retrieved from https://session.wikispaces.com/1/auth/auth?authToken=a21b8a7a8a7de7ca9e592eb6609a0dda.htt

Goldner, B.W., & Bollinger, R.C. (2012). Global health education for medical students: New learning opportunities and strategies. *Medical Teacher, 34*(1), e58–e63. http://dx.doi.org/10.3109/0142159X.2012.638008 Medline:22250696

Green, T., Green, H., Scandlyn, J., & Kestler, A. (2009). Perceptions of short-term medical volunteer work: A qualitative study in Guatemala. *Globalization and Health, 5*(4), 4. http://dx.doi.org/10.1186/1744-8603-5-4 Medline:19245698

Huish, R. (2012). The ethical conundrum of international health electives in medical education. *Journal of Global Citizenship and Equity Education, 2*(1), 1–19.

Huish, R. (2013). *Where no doctor has gone before: Cuba's place in the global health landscape*. Waterloo: Wilfrid Laurier University Press.

Huish, R., & Kirk, J.M. (2007). Cuban medical internationalism and the development of the Latin American School of Medicine. *Latin American Perspectives, 34*(6), 77–92. http://dx.doi.org/10.1177/0094582X07308119

Jeffrey, J., Dumont, R.A., Kim, G.Y., & Kuo, T. (2011, Jan). Effects of international health electives on medical student learning and career choice: Results of a systematic literature review. *Family Medicine, 43*(1), 21–28. Medline:21213133

Jones, L. (2012). Dal med undergoes curriculum transplant. Retrieved September 2012, from http://thechronicleherald.ca/thenovascotian/114874-dal-med-undergoes-curriculum-transplant

Kerry, V.B., Ndung'u, T., Walensky, R.P., Lee, P.T., Kayanja, V.F., & Bangsberg, D.R. (2011, Nov). Managing the demand for global health education. *PLoS Medicine, 8*(11), e1001118. http://dx.doi.org/10.1371/journal.pmed.1001118 Medline:22087076

Kidder, T. (2009). *Mountains beyond mountains*. New York: Random House Trade Paperbacks.

Kirk, J.M., & Erisman, H.M. (2009). *Cuban medical internationalism: Origins, evolution, and goals* (1st ed.). New York: Palgrave Macmillan. http://dx.doi.org/10.1057/9780230622227

Laven, G., & Newbury, J.W. (2011). Global health education for medical undergraduates. *Rural and Remote Health, 11*(2), 1705. Medline:21595498

Lempp, H., & Seale, C. (2004, Oct 2). The hidden curriculum in undergraduate medical education: Qualitative study of medical students' perceptions of teaching. *British Medical Journal, 329*(7469), 770–773. http://dx.doi.org/10.1136/bmj.329.7469.770 Medline:15459051

Liaison Committee on Medical Education. (2012). Standards for Accreditation of Medical Education Programs Leading to the M.D. Degree. *Annual Report LCME*.

Medical School for International Health. (2012). Curriculum Overview. Retrieved from http://www.cumc.columbia.edu/dept/bgcu-md/ps/overview.html

Michalec, B. (2012, May). The pursuit of medical knowledge and the potential consequences of the hidden curriculum. *Health (London), 16*(3), 267–281. http://dx.doi.org/10.1177/1363459311403951 Medline:21602249

Ober, K.P. (1997, Jan 15). The pre-Flexnerian reports: Mark Twain's criticism of medicine in the United States. *Annals of Internal Medicine, 126*(2), 157–163. http://dx.doi.org/10.7326/0003-4819-126-2-199701150-00012 Medline:9005751

Partners in Health. (2012). What we do. Retrieved from http://www.pih.org/pages/what-we-do/

Peluso, M.J., Encandela, J., Hafler, J.P., & Margolis, C.Z. (2012). Guiding principles for the development of global health education curricula in undergraduate medical education. *Medical Teacher*, 34(8), 653–658. http://dx.doi.org/10.3109/0142159X.2012.687848 Medline:22830323

Ramsey, A.H., Haq, C., et al. (2004). Career influence of an international health experience during medical school. *Family Medicine*, 36(6), 412–416.

Redwood-Campbell, L., Pakes, B., Rouleau, K., MacDonald, C.J., Arya, N., Purkey, E., & Pottie, K. (2011). Developing a curriculum framework for global health in family medicine: Emerging principles, competencies, and educational approaches. *BMC Medical Education*, 11(46), 46. http://dx.doi.org/10.1186/1472-6920-11-46 Medline:21781319

Suchdev, P., Ahrens, K., Click, E., Macklin, L., Evangelista, D., & Graham, E. (2007, Jul–Aug). A model for sustainable short-term international medical trips. *Ambulatory Pediatrics*, 7(4), 317–320. http://dx.doi.org/10.1016/j.ambp.2007.04.003 Medline:17660105

The Canadian Press. (2009). Dalhousie medical school loses probation appeal. Retrieved from http://www.cbc.ca/news/canada/nova-scotia/story/2009/10/14/ns-dalhousie-probation.html

Travis, P., Bennett, S., Haines, A., Pang, T., Bhutta, Z., Hyder, A.A., & Evans, T. (2004, Sep 4–10). Overcoming health-systems constraints to achieve the Millennium Development Goals. *Lancet*, 364(9437), 900–906. http://dx.doi.org/10.1016/S0140-6736(04)16987-0 Medline:15351199

Valani, R., Sriharan, A., & Scolnik, D. (2011, Jan). Integrating CanMEDS competencies into global health electives: An innovative elective program. *Canadian Journal of Emergency Medicine*, 13(1), 34–39. Medline:21324295

White, J., Brownell, K., Lemay, J.F., & Lockyer, J.M. (2012). "What do they want me to say?" The hidden curriculum at work in the medical school selection process: A qualitative study. *BMC Medical Education*, 12(17), 17. http://dx.doi.org/10.1186/1472-6920-12-17 Medline:22448658

Woloschuk, W., Wright, B., & McLaughlin, K. (2011, Jan). Debiasing the hidden curriculum: Academic equality among medical specialties. *Canadian Family Physician / Medecin de Famille Canadien*, 57(1), e26–e30. Medline:21252122

9 Getting Prepared for International Experiential Learning: An Ethical Imperative

JULIE DROLET

Many years ago I was reminded, while lying in a hospital bed in Southeast Asia, of my privilege. After my "accidental" ingestion of ice cubes in a young coconut juice drink, I experienced severe gastrointestinal problems that required medical treatment. As a Canadian holder of health insurance in a foreign country, I was able to access the best health care that insurance could buy. For three days I was treated with intravenous in a modern hospital that cost a small fortune in the local economic context. Through this experience I learned an important lesson: I was not being treated as an individual deserving of health care. Rather, I was able to access health care because I had the privilege of health insurance. The unearned power and privilege that we carry as Canadians in the Global South requires our critical examination and reflection. Increasingly, Canadian students are going abroad for international experiential learning. Students are encouraged to think and act globally, and to think and act locally, in their journeys to become globally minded citizens. In line with the editors' (this volume) definition of experiential learning as *making meaning out of direct experience in academic, personal, and/or professional terms*, I examine international experiential learning as an avenue for students to apply and to integrate their knowledge and skills "in the field" while challenging their values and the ethical implications of learning/volunteering abroad. This examination grows out of a body of literature questioning the relevancy and applicability of Western knowledge in the Global South (Gray & Fook, 2004). Students who engage in international experiential learning must be conscious of their social location and have an understanding of how their Canadian education can be rooted in Western perspectives and ideologies that affect their practice and their values. Preparing students for experiential learning therefore entails an understanding of the theoretical and conceptual challenges that must be considered and integrated when working towards culturally relevant education and practice. Drawing from many years of working and living overseas, including my own international experience as a former practicum student and as a faculty member and field education coordinator (Drolet, 2012b), this article shares my perspectives and experiences in working with students who engage in international experiential learning in the Global South. International opportunities can provide valuable learning and a broader perspective of local and global practice, and potentially new forms of knowledge in social justice, equity, and rights perspectives, along with practical and ethical challenges that demand our attention.

Experiential learning has long been acknowledged as being among the most powerful and memorable aspects of student learning across many disciplines (Maidment, 2006). The critical role of experience in learning is a theme in the educational literature, and many students and graduates consider this experience to be the most crucial component in their preparation for practice (Bogo, 2010). Based on feedback that students have given me over the years, many students remember their learning/volunteering abroad experiences as sites of pivotal learning. However, as Stacie Travers (chapter 10 in this volume) reminds us, "we learn from experience, but not all experience is educational." Experiential learning offers students the opportunity to "practice" what they have learned in the classroom and to critically reflect on these experiences. Both domestically and internationally, students can acquire highly educational experiences by serving individuals, communities, and organizations under the guidance of a local field instructor or supervisor. As Katie MacDonald (chapter 11 in this volume) notes, student reflective learning can be conceptualized as a form of solidarity "to be with" rather than charity work "to do for" those with whom students work and live while abroad. Many experiential learning programs aim to develop practical competence and prepare reflective, self-evaluating, knowledgeable professionals capable of critical thinking and analysis. However, not all experiential learning programs achieve these goals. In this chapter, I provide some examples of strategies that can be employed to ensure that students strive for solidarity with their host communities and engage in a critical reflection of their participation in learning/volunteering abroad programs.

Understanding the Demand for International Experiential Learning

Students are increasingly confronted with social problems that stem from a plethora of international issues such as global poverty, famine, war, political oppression, pandemics, and natural disasters (Xu, 2006). Anti-oppressive approaches to the study of these international issues require an understanding of global interdependency. What happens in one country impacts another (Drolet & Heinonen, 2012, pp. 4–5). For these reasons, students need to develop an understanding of global issues and practical skills in order to make meaningful contributions in an interconnected and globalized world (Drolet & Heinonen, 2012, p. 5). Students have demanded international experiential learning opportunities in order to more fully comprehend global interdependency. In Tiessen and Huish (chapter 1 in this volume), the authors elaborate on the importance of global competency for well-educated youth and the importance of understanding the world around us. Global competency is particularly valuable today given the realities of globalization and our interconnected and interdependent world.

At the same time, international activities of post-secondary institutions have dramatically expanded in volume, scope, and complexity over the past two decades (Altbach & Knight, 2007). The Canadian Bureau for International Education, for example, applauds the recent report of the Advisory Panel on Canada's International Education Strategy titled *International Education: A Key Driver of Canada's Future Prosperity*. This report encourages all Canadians to embrace the benefits of international education (Canadian Bureau for International Education, 2012). International experiential learning programs now comprise diverse organizational contexts.

According to the Association of Universities and Colleges of Canada (AUCC, 2007), the six main reasons institutions provided for promoting study abroad are: (1) to develop global citizens; (2) to strengthen international understanding; (3) to develop international cultural awareness and skills; (4) to increase job skills and employability; (5) to enhance disciplinary expertise; and (6) to enhance quality of curriculum (p. 2). A critical review of current knowledge about international field education by Nuttman-Shwartz and Berger (2012) discusses the various motives that drive students, faculty, and professionals, the unique challenges in developing curriculum, and the intensive preparation and collaboration between sending and host schools. While international opportunities can provide new knowledge in broader structural issues of social justice, equity, and rights perspectives, and a broader perspective of practice, there are numerous concerns to be considered and it is necessary to question the "assumed" benefits of experiential learning, particularly in light of the growing demand for such opportunities.

Critiques of international experiential learning provide important insights into the ethical challenges of learning/volunteer abroad programs by questioning the supposed benefits, the "helping imperative" (Heron, 2007), neocolonialism, post-colonialism and imperialism, and the one-way flow of benefits (Tiessen & Huish, chapter 1 of this volume). The conceptualization of ethics as an either-or dichotomy is found largely in the Global North or Western countries, with an emphasis on the decision-making and not on the decision-maker (Banks & Nohr, 2012). To enhance our ethical understanding, a reflective process is required, which entails a critical reflection of ourselves and of our actions (Tiessen & Kumar, forthcoming). A starting point for critical reflection, as Narda Razack (2002) suggests, is providing students with the opportunity to engage in discussions of the forces of imperialism, the legacies of colonization, and the profound effect of these processes on identity and location (p. 264) in their field experiences. Professional imperialism persists with "the built assumptions and cultural biases of first world theories and models of practice" (Gray & Fook, 2004, p. 626). Post-colonialism refers to the ways in which the domination of colonies by Western colonial countries did not disappear with the passing of European empires in the period between 1950 and 1970, and how identities, attitudes, and practices are affected and manifested between cultures (Askeland & Payne, 2006). Samantha Wehbi (2009) argues that critical examination of international placements is crucial in fostering internationalization without reproducing oppressive power relations. International experiential learning can challenge one's understanding of oppression and injustice by providing a "world view" of the relationship between the macro and the micro and vice versa. For example, students have shared with me that while they read material on critical Global North-South issues prior to their departure, it was only during their international experience that their eyes were opened to the struggles and pain caused by injustice and oppression in host communities. Yet there is a need for caution given the current context of neoliberalism and globalization that supports the proliferation of internationalism. Razack (2012) demonstrates that theories of "race" and racism, colonization, post-colonialism, white privilege, and their critical insights are essential for engaging in non-hegemonic and anti-imperialistic work with partners abroad. International experiential learning, especially from North to South, may be seen as engaging in a colonizing activity in one's efforts to learn and glean from the "other" (Razack, 2012). The act of "othering" is problematic and raises broader ethical dimensions, which will be examined later in this chapter. International experiential learning programs also provide opportunities for global engagement by providing students with critical skills in participatory rapid appraisals, intercultural problem solving, and learning from local and indigenous voices that may counter dominant hegemonic understandings of local and global realities. MacDonald (chapter 11 in this volume) highlights some of the educational opportunities for students when they have access to new sites of knowledge and different ways of knowing through decolonizing pedagogies.

Rosemary Sarri (1997) identifies three key reasons for students to engage in international experiential learning. For Sarri, the students she refers to are international social work students. However, the reasons she identifies can be applied to any student interested in international experiential learning. First, she argues that international social development widens one's understanding of economic, political, and social welfare systems outside one's own country. Second, international experiential learning introduces a cross-cultural perspective that is very valuable as communities grapple with the impact of multiculturalism and social exclusion on a daily basis. And finally, cross-national collaboration between workers across countries and cultures can foster new knowledge and learning. International experiential learning can further lead to sharpening skills in cross-cultural competencies among students.

Students may develop their own self-awareness by seeking to understand their personal and cultural values and beliefs as one way of appreciating the importance of multicultural identities. Cross-cultural knowledge is enhanced and developed through specialized knowledge and understanding about the history, traditions, values, family systems, and artistic expressions of population groups served. While there are many cross-cultural advantages afforded by international experiential learning programs, the ability to travel for educational purposes is often predicated on an enactment of Western privilege (see MacDonald, chapter 11 in this volume). It is critical to understand how privilege is enacted abroad, how "identities that move" from North to South become unsettled in the process, and how post-colonial realities operate (Razack, 2012).

Relational Ethics

Through international experiential learning, students have an opportunity to integrate theoretical concepts learned in the classroom to actual practice situations within a local agency work environment abroad. Local agency staff members assist students in integrating a theoretical framework into their practice. Internationally, the practice frameworks may be quite different, allowing both staff members and students to engage in dialogue regarding their respective approaches to practice through real-life situations. It is within this relationship that I would like to explore the role of relational ethics. Wendy Austin (2008) defines relational ethics as an approach to ethics that situates ethical action explicitly in relationship. In the field, students are confronted with ethical dilemmas. The question of how we should act or live is one that is discovered not in isolation, but in dialogue with others. Students and their field instructors are committed to a relationship with the people they serve and with each other. This relationship is strengthened by establishing a regular time for supervision and to foster dialogue that includes theoretical discussion and critical self-reflection. The relational space is nurtured and respected if ethical practice is to be enacted, allowing students, for example, to unpack their feelings and experiences. Bergum and Dossetor (2005) identify four major themes in relational ethics: mutual respect, engagement, embodiment, and environment. Mutual respect is described as interactive and reciprocal, with an emphasis on respect for and acceptance of difference. Engagement beseeches a sensitivity that promotes authentic connection using empathy. Embodiment integrates the feeling body with the thinking mind. The theme of environment expands the relational space beyond the individual to consider the relations between the individual and other systems, the community, and the world. Becoming an effective learner requires creating relationships across difference (see MacDonald, chapter 11 in this volume). As Wilson and Hernandez (2012) reflect on their experiences in developing relationships in a CIDA-funded project in Nicaragua, "the best international relationships are those built on a sense of solidarity ... a genuine shared sense that we are all in this together and that what we are working on is intended to benefit us all" (p. 186). Relational ethics considers how we ought to treat each other in particular circumstances and how certain situations facilitate or impede our efforts to do so. Adopting an approach of relational ethics can facilitate an enhanced learning experience.

Effective Learners and Reflective Practice

Students become effective learners by acknowledging their role as participants by "being with" rather than "spectators of" host communities. Wehbi and Straka (2011) found that field seminar activities can reaffirm the importance of reflective practice for knowledge building and for social transformation, and they cite participatory reflection activities to revalue student knowledge and favour students' active involvement in the educational process. Reflective practice is promoted through the use of journals, self-assessment, and group seminar processes. Reflective learning paves the way for cross-cultural competencies in spite of the barriers and challenges confronted in diverse cultural settings. For example, international experiential learning students that I have supervised have demonstrated that in order to become effective learners, they had to become observers and listeners. These students found that they learnt a great deal from their reflective writing and journals. To become a reflective practitioner requires taking time for reflection in order to think, to write, and to dialogue with colleagues, and to examine one's values and check for congruency with one's actions. Field instructors, as reflective practitioners, can foster reflexivity and improved cultural awareness while sensitizing students to issues of difference and equity.

Practical Considerations in Preparation for Experiential Learning Programs

In this section I provide some practical tips and information that can be useful in preparation for international experiential learning programs. The suggestions provided here are based on my experience as an experiential learning program facilitator. First, international experiential learning requires substantial planning, which begins at least four to six months prior to the on-site component of the program. In Canadian universities, some learning programs require that students begin planning up to one year in advance (Drolet, 2012a). Planning well in advance is important for students and faculty to have enough time to make all of the necessary arrangements and practical requirements for the host field agency, post-secondary institution, and related affiliation agreement between the university and agency.

Furthermore, planning for a successful international practicum requires attention to: (1) building and sustaining international field partnerships and relationships; (2) developing mutually agreed-upon learning arrangements; (3) supporting language acquisition and cultural preparation before departure; (4) monitoring the quality of field experiences through ongoing communication between students and faculty supervisors; and (5) engaging in debriefing seminars upon return (Drolet, 2012a).

One of the key elements of preparation, however, is developing an awareness of social location and positionality. This can include self-awareness of one's cultural background, gender, race, class, sexual orientation, and ability status, and the intersection between these identities. Being from the Global North or Global South affects how students are perceived and how they consider their relationships in the field. A relational ethics approach considers "who we are" rather than a simplistic focus on the actions and mechanics of doing the work. Developing an understanding of one's identity, subjugation, dominance, or marginalization is an important component of discussion and learning (Razack, 2001). Critical reflection on positionality lends itself to a greater awareness of asymmetric power relations, and how one's position might impose "harm upon, or have undue influence over, clients" (Banks & Nohr, 2012, p. 65). Students need to be able to tolerate ambiguity and often face struggles to learn cultural meanings throughout their experience (Drolet, 2012a).

International experiential learning opportunities and programs work best where there are long-term sustained partnership agreements between institutions. The importance of relationships emerges in the connections between host and sending institutions, which is the foundation of such partnerships. Support for student learning can be found through respectful relationships between field instructors and faculty, often situated in non-governmental organizations that offer learning opportunities within their development programs and projects, as well as faculty working overseas who can assist in negotiating opportunities for students. A Memorandum of Understanding (MOU) is a document signed between institutions that outlines shared roles and responsibilities in the field placement (Drolet, 2012a). The MOU can be used to clarify roles and responsibilities, to provide service to the community, to engage in joint evaluation of student learning, to share learning resources, and to establish timelines.

The geographic location of a learning site – in a large metropolitan urban centre or small rural and remote community – may also affect what and how a student learns. For example, living in a small community often means that all members perform multiple roles, and rural practice brings together personal and professional lives in a different way. There are many opportunities for learning in a smaller community, where one may be expected to assume dual and multiple roles and work inter-professionally across disciplines. Some rural workers report challenges in managing professional and personal role boundaries, and negotiating availability and privacy on a daily basis (Green, Gregory, & Mason, 2006), which is an attribute for students to consider in their day-to-day obligations and responses to one another.

Student wellness, health, self-care, and well-being are increasingly recognized as important components of practice. There is a need to consider the multiple dimensions of well-being (such as physical, emotional, psychological, and spiritual components) for a holistic and integrated wellness approach. There are many unknowns in the early stages of international experiential learning, and some students experience anxiety and stress in new situations. As a learner moves through the transitional stages of the classroom, through field-based learning and ultimately into practice, it is essential that proper self-care and wellness be implemented into their practice (Hebb, 2012). Students can benefit from the preparation of a wellness plan, recognizing that they may not have access to the same social supports or networks as in their home country. Wellness and self-care is an ethical imperative particularly in light of occupational hazards frequently associated with international experiential learning, such as stress, primary and vicarious trauma, and compassion fatigue (Monk, 2011).

Narrative-based reflection can be an additional practical strategy for international experiential learning. Student narratives dramatically highlight many of the realities, challenges, and opportunities students face during international experiential learning. Writing about their experiences provides students with an opportunity to share workable responses to real and pressing issues. The power of the reflection is in the images, remembrances, and situational immediacy that are conveyed in the writing. Field instructors and faculty get a glimpse of life as it is experienced from the students' perspective. Narratives can provide a window into the often contradictory and ambiguous nature of practice. For example, reflections on personal challenges can include: instances when professional and personal boundaries are blurred; feelings of personal inadequacy as a result of political decisions; discriminatory practices; and the effects of feeling alienated and sometimes isolated on placement (Noble, 2001). The narrative process can be encouraged by providing questions for the students to contemplate as they reflect on their experiential learning (see MacDonald, chapter 11 in this volume).

Conclusion

International experiential learning is a potentially powerful tool for students to become immersed in a cross-cultural environment and to confront different views of human behaviour and perspectives about how things operate (Healy, 2001, p. 254). Increasingly, students are eager to complete an international experiential learning program in order to gain new skills and knowledge that will prepare them to incorporate international perspectives into local practice at home and, for some, to work in international settings (Drolet, 2012a). Students often return from these international experiences and report that their time abroad was life-altering (Healy, 2001, p. 254). During this period of internationalism, students are interested in developing knowledge and skills in international contexts. Yet there is a need for caution and a critical lens to examine student motivations and interests for pursuing international opportunities given the realities of Western imperialism, colonialism, and hegemony. Midgley (1981) cautions that Western forms of knowledge are unsuited to the cultural circumstances and pressing problems of poverty and deprivation found in the Global South. This chapter discusses the role of relational ethics in student learning, and offers some very practical information and strategies that can be used in preparation for, and reflection on, international experiential learning. Additional information on practical strategies for improving international experiential learning programs can be found at online sources listed at the end of this chapter.

REFERENCES

Altbach, P.G., & Knight, J. (2007). The internationalization of higher education: Motivations and realities. *Journal of Studies in International Education*, 11(3/4), 290–305. doi:10.1177/1028315307303542

Askeland, G., & Payne, M. (2006). Social work education's cultural hegemony. *International Social Work*, 49(6), 731–743. doi:10.1177/0020872806069079

Association of Universities and Colleges of Canada. (2007). *Canadian universities and international mobility: Internationalizing Canadian campuses*. Retrieved from http://www.aucc.ca/wp-content/uploads/2011/05/student-mobility-2007.pdf

Austin, W. (2008). Relational ethics. In L. Given (Ed.), *The SAGE encyclopedia of qualitative research methods* (pp. 748–749). Thousand Oaks, CA: Sage Publications. doi:10.4135/9781412963909.n378

Banks, S., & Nohr, K. (Eds.). (2012). *Practising social work ethics around the world: Cases and commentaries*. New York: Routledge.

Bergum, V., & Dossetor, J. (2005). *Relational ethics: The full meaning of respect*. Hagerstown, MD: University Publishing Group.

Bogo, M. (2010). *Achieving competence in social work through field education*. Toronto, ON: University of Toronto Press.

Canadian Bureau for International Education. (2012, Aug 14). *CBIE supports Panel's vision for Canada's international education strategy*. Retrieved from http://www.cbie-bcei.ca/?p=8607

Drolet, J. (2012a). International field placements: New practices for the twenty-first century. In J. Drolet, N. Clark, & H. Allen (Eds.), *Shifting sites of practice: Field education in Canada* (pp. 183–208). Toronto, ON: Pearson Education.

Drolet, J. (2012b). Statement of teaching philosophy: My role as field education coordinator. *Social Work Education: The International Journal, 32*(2), 274–277. doi:10.1080/02615479.2012.717921

Drolet, J., & Heinonen, T. (2012). Introduction. In T. Heinonen & J. Drolet (Eds.), *International social development: Social work experiences and perspectives* (pp. 1–11). Winnipeg, MB: Fernwood Publishing.

Gray, M., & Fook, J. (2004). The quest for a universal social work: some issues and implications. *Social Work Education: The International Journal, 23*(5), 625–644. doi:10.1080/0261547042000252334

Green, R., Gregory, R., & Mason, R. (2006). Professional distance and social work: Stretching the elastic? *Australian Social Work, 59*(4), 449–461. doi:10.1080/03124070600986010

Healy, L. (2001). *International social work: Professional action in an interdependent world*. New York: Oxford University Press.

Hebb, D. (2012). *Wellness plan* (Unpublished manuscript). Thompson Rivers University, Kamloops, BC.

Heron, B. (2007). *Desire for development: Whiteness, gender, and the helping imperative*. Waterloo, ON: Wilfrid Laurier University Press.

Maidment, J. (2006). Using on-line delivery to support students during practicum placements. *Australian Social Work, 59*(1), 47–55. doi:10.1080/03124070500449770

Midgley, J. (1981). *Professional imperialism: Social work in the third world*. London: Heinemann Educational Books.

Monk, L. (2011). Self-care for social workers: A precious commodity, an ethical imperative. *Perspectives, 33*(1): 4–7.

Noble, C. (2001). Researching field practice in social work education. *Journal of Social Work, 1*(3), 347–360. doi:10.1177/146801730100100307

Nuttman-Shwartz, O., & Berger, R. (2012). Field education in international social work: Where we are and where we should go. *International Social Work, 55*(2), 225–243. doi:10.1177/0020872811414597

Razack, N. (2001). Diversity and difference in the field education encounter: Racial minority students in the practicum. *Social Work Education: The International Journal, 20*(2), 219–232. doi:10.1080/02615470120044310

Razack, N. (2002). A critical examination of international student exchanges. *International Social Work, 45*(2), 251–265.

Razack, N. (2012). International social work. In M. Gray, J. Midgley, & S.A. Webb (Eds.), *The SAGE handbook of social work* (pp. 707–722). London: Sage Publications Ltd. doi:10.4135/9781446247648.n46

Sarri, R. (1997). International social work at the Millennium. In M. Reisch & E. Gambrill (Eds.), *Social work in the 21st century* (pp. 387–395). Thousand Oaks, CA: Prince Forge Press.

Tiessen, R., & Kumar, P. (forthcoming). Ethical challenges encountered on learning/volunteer abroad programs for students in international development studies in Canada: Youth perspectives and educator insights. *Canadian Journal of Development Studies.*

Wehbi, S. (2009). Deconstructing motivations: Challenging international social work placements. *International Social Work, 52* (1). 48–59. doi: 10:1177/0020872808097750

Wehbi, S., & Straka, S. (2011). Revaluing student knowledge through reflective practice on involvement in social justice efforts. *Social Work Education: The International Journal, 30*(1), 45–54. doi:10.1080/02615471003739584

Wilson, M., & Hernandez, I.P. (2012). Solidarity, common cause, relationship: A learning journey in social work education. In T. Heinonen & J. Drolet (Eds.), *International social development: Social work experiences and perspectives* (pp. 170–190). Winnipeg, MB: Fernwood Publishing.

Xu, Q. (2006). Defining international social work: A social service agency perspective. *International Social Work, 49*(6), 679–692. doi:10.1177/0020872806069075

ONLINE INFORMATION

Foreign Affairs and International Trade Canada (DFAIT)
www.travel.gc.ca
   This website provide links and information on travel reports and warnings, country profiles, registration of Canadians abroad, and other relevant publications on living, working, and studying abroad.

Intercultures
www.intercultures.ca
This website offers a collection of Internet sites for country information and research. There are "e-thologies" available for over 200 countries.

Canadian International Development Agency (CIDA)
www.acdi-cida.gc.ca
This website provides information, maps, and country profiles for CIDA-supported projects in numerous countries.

Health Info
www.travelhealth.gc.ca
This Health Canada site offers information for travellers, such as travel clinics across Canada and advice for specific countries.

World Health Organization (WHO)
www.who.int
The World Health Organization site offers information on a variety of health topics.

Centers for Disease Control & Prevention (CDC)
www.cdc.gov/travel
The Centers for Disease Control & Prevention website covers topics such as the Special Needs Traveller and Travelling with Children, and provides specific health information for countries and destinations.

Canadian Public Health Association (CPHA)
www.cpha.ca
The Canadian Public Health Association website provides links to other Canadian health associations, and includes health resources such as "Don't Drink the Water" and information from the Canadian HIV/AIDS Clearing House.

Telephone Info
www.infocanadadirect.com
This website provides information about Canada Direct, which is an automated access service. It allows Canadian travellers to call Canada using the Canadian telecommunications network.

Radio Canada International
www.rcinet.ca
This website provides a list of programs, schedules, and other interesting information.

10 Getting the Most out of Studying Abroad: Ways to Maximize Learning in Short-Term Study Trips

STACIE TRAVERS

Introduction

We learn from experience, but not all experience is educational. Experiences do not lead to learning when we cannot extract anything new from them, when we fail to reflect on them, or when we cannot identify lessons learnt (Jarvis, 1994, quoted in Davies, 2008). Studying abroad can be filled with educational experiences. However, not all study abroad programs provide experiential learning opportunities to the same degree. Each program is a combination of various experiences, some educational, some memorable, some valued, and others less transformative, easier to forget, and not as appreciated. As our world becomes more connected and globalized, opportunities to study abroad are growing and the programs that facilitate these opportunities will likely continue to increase in number. The preceding chapters have helped think through deconstructing these programs. We have questioned their value, weighed their supposed benefits vs. their local impact, and cast a critical lens on their pedagogies and claims. The criticism and debate surrounding studying and volunteering abroad are mainly concerned with the length of time abroad (Kauffmann, Martin, & Weaver, 1992; Chieffo & Griffiths, 2009); the true impact of these programs, including the link between them and the creation of global citizens (Tiessen & Heron, 2012); and more recently the ethical considerations related to these types of programs surrounding the self-centred nature of participant motivations (Tiessen, 2012) and the unbalanced distribution of benefits, which include a real risk of doing more harm than good (Epprecht, 2004). Although discussion and debate of study abroad continues, as pointed out in this volume's introductory chapter, it seems these types of program are here to stay. We therefore need to point to possible models and methods that will minimize harm, distribute benefits more evenly, and encourage meaningful learning and future action.

In this chapter I argue that study abroad programs are not by definition examples of experiential education. I address the critical elements of experiential education, elements that are often lacking in such programs. By exploring experiential learning theory – its natural, but not guaranteed, link with study abroad programs – and drawing on a 2010 case study, I then suggest ways to design study abroad programs so that they are true examples of experiential education.

Study Abroad and Experiential Education: Natural Partners but Not One and the Same

The reason for temporarily dropping the use of the term "international experiential learning" is because I argue that studying abroad is not experiential learning by definition. In other words, simply going abroad with the objective of learning does not always qualify as experiential learning. Lutterman-Aguilar and Gingerich (2002) point to the abundance of study abroad programs that fail to put the principles of experiential education into practice. An example of this often-cited gap between theory and practice in experiential education is captured by Kolb, who writes:

> Many experiential education programs emphasize that reflection is an essential element of the experiential learning process and yet practitioners leave little time for debriefing, journaling, group discussion, counseling, or other forms of reflection. (In Breunig, 2005, p. 110)

There is a noted tendency to choose action over reflection and a subsequent failure to find the balance between the two, which is fundamental to experiential education. The gap, therefore, exists between theories-in-use and theories-in-action (Breunig, 2005, p. 110). When it comes to study abroad programs, this gap is represented by the great many that fail to put experiential education principles into practice, such as those that "simply transfer academic credits from one traditional discipline-based institution to another without intentionally utilizing the international experience as the basis for learning" (Lutterman-Aguilar & Gingerich, 2002, p. 3).

The Theory behind Experiential Education

Claiming that study abroad programs are not experiential makes complete sense once we understand the fundamentals of experiential education as a theory of learning. The theory operates under the assumption that although all experiences can be educational, experience alone is not educational in and of itself (Dewey, 1938). Dewey used the term "mis-educative" to refer to any experience that works to prevent or distort the growth of future experiences. He concluded that the potential to learn from experience depends on the quality of that experience, a quality divided into two aspects. The first aspect is the agreeableness or disagreeableness of the experience. The second, and equally important, aspect is the influence of that experience upon later experiences. Experiences can therefore be situated on an experiential continuum that distinguishes between those experiences which are worthwhile educationally and those that are not.

Kolb's (1984) model of experiential learning states that in order to turn experience into knowledge, one must first reflect on his/her own concrete experiences, comprehend the experience as a more abstract concept, and then actively engage in experimenting with this concept. Davies (2008) sees this cyclical model as an oversimplification, since it fails to include what he believes to be crucial elements, namely, the relevance of emotion, the importance of memory, and the nature of the learner. His more complex model of experiential learning deals with the nature of the experience and includes a number of possible interactions between the various elements of any given experience. Although Kolb's model, in comparison, does seem lacking, its focus on reflection and analysis as key components of experiential education is not challenged. Following this, Lutterman-Aguilar and Gingerich (2002) assert that "any educational endeavor, including study abroad, that does not structure reflection and critical analysis of the international experience itself into the curriculum is not engaging in experiential education" (p. 45). This critical analysis that they refer to is most often associated with the work of Paulo Freire (1974) and his experiential theory of education concerned with developing critical thinking skills through collective reflection and analysis of experience. These skills are often cited as both desired aims and resulting outcomes of study abroad programs, which leads Lutterman-Aguilar and Gingerich to argue that study abroad and experiential education are natural partners. They cite their common goals of empowering students and preparing them to become responsible global citizens. Furthermore, the notion of education for social transformation is generally embraced by both the field of study abroad and the field of experiential education. Basing study abroad program design on experiential education theory, Lutterman-Aguilar and Gingerich identify ten interconnected principles that can guide experiential pedagogy in study abroad.

Making Study Abroad Experiential

In experiential pedagogy, a connected learning is the best kind of learning. Learning should be integrated into one's own life, and outward experiences should be connected inwards. Study abroad programs, therefore, should include ways to let experience be used as a means to developing the self in their design. This includes providing opportunities for students to be challenged, to set their own learning objectives, and to share in the assessment of their learning. Problem-based content is a second important principle for experiential study abroad programs. This means that curriculum content should relate to real-life problems and, when possible, begin with themes generated by the students themselves. Lutterman-Aguilar and Gingerich (2002) add, however, that "if one of the goals of study abroad is to foment global citizenship, then it must broaden students' horizons by helping them to identify the problems and concerns of others within the global community" (p. 54) and not end with the students' interests alone. If Cameron's definition of "thick" global citizenship (see Cameron, chapter 2 in this volume) is used, study abroad programs must go one step further and help students identify their complicity as citizens of countries in the Global North at the root of these problems and concerns. In response to both Kolb and Freire's claims, critical analysis and reflection are also required to ensure experiences are educational. Reflection works best when it is engaged in with others, and within study abroad programs, this reflection should include analysis of societal aspects. The following chapter details how this reflection can happen through narratives, but also suggests the types of privilege, assumptions, and histories that should be questioned. For more on privilege, see MacDonald (chapter 11 in this volume). True critical analysis and reflection are thought to be the result of collaboration and dialogue, two further principles Lutterman-Aguilar and Gingerich suggest be present in any study abroad program. With collaboration and dialogue established as essential to experiential education, "it follows naturally that community is also an essential element of international experiential education" (Lutterman-Aguilar & Gingerich, 2002, p. 60). This translates into the need to immerse in the local host community as well as reflect upon one's connection to the wider global community. Intercultural communication flows from this immersion and is Lutterman-Aguilar and Gingerich's sixth element of experiential study abroad. Action, in the form of research, volunteer opportunities, or internships, is another central element. At times, however, it is not appropriate to take part in direct action during the time abroad. When this is the case, Lutterman-Aguilar and Gingerich suggest "study abroad faculty and staff help students engage in ongoing reflection upon their vocations and the type of action they may take in the future" (p. 69). Finally, experiential study abroad programs should be based on mutuality and reciprocity with the host community, be guided by skilled facilitators trained in experiential and intercultural education, and incorporate continuous evaluation and assessment methods.

Short-Term Study Abroad Programs: Do They Count?

As study abroad programs and opportunities increase in popularity, there is a growing variety in their length, aims, size, destinations, and ultimately their effectiveness when measured by their impact on the participants' learning and lives. In chapter 1, Tiessen and Huish outline some of these different models and participant groups. Cited among these, and perhaps the most obvious division amongst study abroad programs, is the one between short and long term. Critics of short-term study abroad programs or study trips argue that the amount of time spent abroad is a deciding factor in the degree of influential change experienced by study abroad participants. However, Donnelly-Smith (2009) argues that the way institutions frame their short-term study abroad programs will help counter the stereotype of them being simply vacations. The design of these programs and the experiences they produce are key to providing quality experiential education abroad over a short time period that impacts in the same way as longer-term programs. Chieffo and Griffiths (2009) believe properly designed short-term programs can actually benefit participants more than poorly designed long-terms programs. They write:

> A 4-week program with homestay lodging, courses in the host language, structured interaction with host-country students, and academic

assignments requiring journaling, community-based interviews, contributes more to students' cross cultural competence than a semester-long program in which students are housed together in apartments and have self-contained classes and tours, with most host culture interaction left to . serendipity. (p. 368)

In order to better understand what this design might entail, I carried out a study of a short-term study trip with participants at a Montreal college. Specifically, I sought answers to the following questions: what experiences are most effective in bringing about any real learning and transformation? What do study abroad participants value the most? What benefits do they perceive from the various exercises, activities, visits, and moments experienced throughout their time abroad? With a focus on the program design of a short- term study abroad experience, as opposed to the impact, which the bulk of study abroad literature deals with, key elements of this experience are examined from the perspectives of its student participants. By examining the way in which study abroad participants view the particular design and curriculum of their chosen program and how they feel these aspects enhance their overall learning experience, specific activities, features, and characteristics that students find most and least beneficial to their overall learning experience emerge.

How to Benefit from a Limited Time Abroad

The Study Trip was organized by a Montreal C.E.G.E.P (post-secondary college) and was part of a larger two-year project aimed at raising awareness and inspiring involvement among the immediate C.E.G.E.P community and surrounding local area on the issue of universal primary education in the developing world, with an emphasis on inaccessibility for girls. The experiences and characteristics of the trip that its seven participants valued and learnt the most from correlate with many of Lutterman-Aguilar and Gingerich's (2002) ten critical elements. Namely, participants valued being immersed and able to interact with the host community and each other; being able to see or make meaning out of what they were experiencing; and having their time abroad fall between well-organized pre- and post-trip activities.

Immersion and participatory involvement were the principles that provided the most memorable and educational experiences for the Study Trip participants. Students valued the opportunity to stay in a local village, despite the very different living conditions. They appreciated being able to see what they assumed was daily reality and routine for these people, who had graciously invited them into their community. They had new and exciting experiences alongside intense and emotional ones, all of which they felt were made possible by the type of interaction this program provided. Not only did they live in a local village but they also spent their days observing at local schools, interviewing people for their various projects, and were given enough space and free time to bond with their hosts. With thought and preparation, immersing participants in the host culture and maximizing their opportunities to interact with the people of that culture are two simple guidelines that meet Lutterman-Aguilar and Gingerich's (2002) call for incorporating community, collaboration and dialogue, diversity and intercultural communication, and mutuality and reciprocity into an experiential study abroad program.

There is an important inward element to the valued interaction that goes beyond connecting with the host community, however. Group dynamics play an essential role in determining which experiences are educational and valued. A diverse group of students whose interests and backgrounds differ will provide new perspectives and lead others to uncover new areas of interest. Although there were minor issues and disagreements, the participants formed strong bonds with each other. The majority of them grew close, and the community that they formed enhanced the entire experience. Not only did they have people who had shared and lived similar situations, moments, and feelings to talk to and reflect with but they also relied on one another to help them through their individual issues and achieve their personal goals.

Immersion and participatory involvement provided the opportunities for experiential learning, but what turned these opportunities for learning into actual learning was the ability to attach meaning and/or purpose to their experiences in context: a good illustration of connected learning. Meaning was created through the personalization of experience and through emotion. Giving the students space to pursue their own interests, having them set personal goals, and helping them embrace and explore both positive and negative emotions leads to meaningful or connected learning experiences. Attention paid to these elements ensures that a study abroad program includes the type of personal integration and development central to experiential education.

Critical analysis and reflection are what make an experience educational. Participants need to question the reality they are studying and rethink past assumptions. This is much more successful when it is engaged in with others. Reflective journals, like the ones encouraged in this Study Trip, are generally a private exercise and therefore do not fulfill this last requisite. In addition, reflection is not always part of journaling. Although journals can be useful reflective tools, participants need time, direction, and practice to make the most of reflective journaling. It was not uncommon for Study Trip participants to use their journals to keep a chronological record of their daily meals, activities, and routines. Rarely did their entries capture their thoughts and questions regarding their experience or changes to their thinking. Entries also became less frequent as time elapsed. Post-trip interviews with participants revealed that several began to resent writing in their journals, as there were often other things they would have rather been doing. There was no evidence suggesting students disliked reflection and critical thought, just that they would have preferred time devoted solely to this and that they may have needed more guidance in this process (an example of what this guidance might look like is highlighted in chapter 11, as the author recounts her experience with facilitating reflective seminars). However, through their constant interaction, participants did discuss and question what they were seeing and why they were feeling the way they were. The level of comfort the students felt with one another was crucial in ensuring they engaged in this informal reflection and critical discussion on their own.

What Lutterman-Aguilar and Gingerich (2002) do not count in their ten suggested elements for experiential study abroad, but which is important for its participants and creates the framework for the implementation of all other elements, is the overall structure of these programs. In other words, study abroad programs require at least three interrelated phases of learning. The first phase, preparation, is extremely important; there must be a preparation phase aimed at addressing expectations and assumptions. As noted by Drolet in the preceding chapter, this phase generally begins four to six months prior to participants travelling abroad. Participants should know what to expect from the trip, the host community, themselves, and each other, as well as what is expected of them and what assumptions their hosts may have of them, their trip, and their intentions. Pre-trip activities should also be spaces where participants are encouraged to deconstruct their motivations for going abroad and begin the process of addressing their privilege. Participants must also learn to get along and work together as a group, as it is the group's cohesion and perceived security that will dictate the depth and success of reflection. Chapter 9 provides a detailed discussion of these and other types of pre-departure considerations.

While abroad, participants should be immersed as much as possible in the host community and provided with ample opportunities to interact with both this community and their peers, to the extent that this is desired from the host community. They should have both personal and program goals to meet within a flexible yet meaningful structure. Throughout the duration of their trip, they should be encouraged to reflect, analyse, and feel; although there are personal levels to each of these, the group should work as a whole to explore their thoughts, concerns, and feelings. Value conflicts and other ethical dilemmas (detailed in chapter 9) need to be addressed while abroad so as to ensure they act as catalysts to learning and not as roadblocks.

The end of the time in the host country signals the beginning of a post-trip or post-experience phase. Without this structured time to reflect, the meaning of the time abroad loses its value (Epprecht, 2004, p. 16). Students appreciate this phase as it helps them readjust, gives meaning to their time abroad, and helps maintain the closeness of the group. In many cases, there is an ethical obligation to help make the public aware of the reality that was explored, which might include rethinking the practices and beliefs in the North. Post-trip activities to engage the public help fulfill that obligation while inspiring participants to take further action and maintain their dedication to the program and its goals. For the Study Trip participants, these activities included presentations to peers, but also to local high school students and other community audiences. These sorts of public engagement activities aimed at increasing awareness also help to cement the learning abroad. Post-trip activities should support long-term change as students work towards deconstructing inequality and their roles in perpetuating this inequality (Tiessen, 2012).

Conclusion

I have argued that, not surprisingly given their abundance and diversity, not all study abroad programs can be classified as examples of international experiential education. Second, I have argued that length of time abroad does not need to limit the learning or benefits associated with these programs. If the time spent abroad is well designed and falls between equally well-designed pre- and post-trip phases, short-term programs can still allow participants to reap the many associated benefits of studying or volunteering abroad, and lead to a lasting relationship with the host community. I have reviewed the key elements of

experiential education and suggested, based on the views of participants in a short-term study trip (with lengthy pre- and post-trip phases),
how these elements can be incorporated into the pedagogical design
of these programs. The findings illustrate the important learning moments and formal and informal situations that can be created as a result
of the study abroad experience. Knowing when and how these occur
helps to better plan the educational impact of similar programs. The
lessons drawn from this case study and analysed here can be used by
study abroad stakeholders to increase the number of successful study
abroad experiences. These stakeholders include not only the institutions, administrators, and coordinators, who can draw on this case
study to better plan and design meaningful curriculum, but also the
study abroad participants, who can use this chapter to start thinking
about how to better prepare themselves for their own experiences and
maximize not only their learning abroad but also their learning upon
their return.

The Challenge

Despite a possible way forward in terms of designing study abroad
programs so that they are meaningful to participants, it is still important to question if studying or volunteering abroad is always the best
path to take. Questioning the motivations underlying decisions to go
abroad will remain fundamental. The challenge for organizers and participants alike, especially for short-term programs, is to find ways for
local hosts and their communities to reap equal benefits from these programs. Meaningful partnerships and thoughtful planning will be key to
meeting this challenge. The future value of study abroad as an educational endeavour lies in a more balanced and reciprocal relationship
between host country citizens and visiting participants. Let's embrace
the diverse critiques presented in this collection and work towards an
alternative vision and a more ethical and reciprocal study/volunteer
abroad experience.

REFERENCES

Breunig, M. (2005). Turning experiential education and critical pedagogy
    theory into praxis. *Journal of Experiential Education*, *28*(2), 106–122.
    doi:10.1177/105382590502800205

Chieffo, L., & Griffiths, L. (2009). Here to stay: Increasing acceptance of short-term study abroad programs. In R. Lewin (Ed.), *The handbook of practice and research in study abroad: Higher education and the quest for global citizenship* (pp. 365–380). New York: Routledge.

Davies, L. (2008). *Informal learning: A new model for making sense of experience.* London: Gower Publishing.

Dewey, J. (1938). *Experience and education.* London: Collier Macmillan Publishers.

Donnelly-Smith, L. (2009). Global learning through short-term study abroad. *Peer Review, 11*(4). Retrieved from http://www.aacu.org/about/index.cfm.

Epprecht, M. (2004). Work-study abroad courses in international development studies: Some ethical and pedagogical issues. *Canadian Journal of Development Studies, 25*(4), 687–706. doi:10.1080/02255189.2004.9669009

Freire, P. (1974). *Education for critical consciousness.* New York: Continuum Publishing Company.

Jarvis, P. (1994). Learning practical knowledge. *Journal of Further and Higher Education, 18*(1), 31–43.

Kauffmann, N.L., Martin, J.N., & Weaver, H.D. (1992). *Students abroad: Strangers at home.* Yarmouth, ME: Intercultural Press.

Kolb, D. (1984). *Experiential learning as the source of learning and development.* Englewood Cliffs, NJ: Prentice Hall.

Lutterman-Aguilar, A., & Gingerich, O. (2002). Experiential pedagogy for study abroad: Educating for global citizenship. *Frontiers: The Interdisciplinary Journal of Study Abroad, 8*(Winter), 41–82.

Tiessen, R. (2012). Motivations for learn/volunteer abroad programs: Research with Canadian youth. *Journal of Global Citizenship & Equity Education, 2*(1), 107–127.

Tiessen, R., & Heron, B. (2012). Volunteering in the developing world: The perceived impacts of Canadian youth. *Development in Practice, 22*(1), 44–56. doi:10.1080/09614524.2012.630982

11 (De)colonizing Pedagogies: An Exploration of Learning with Students Volunteering Abroad

KATIE MacDONALD

I think there is cause to worry about international experiential learning programs. My borrowing of the parenthetical gesture around the "de" of (de)colonizing from Celia Haig-Brown indicates this. Haig-Brown suggests in a course outline that the "parenthetical 'de' gestures towards the (im)possibility of non-indigenous people and people in a university setting doing this work in light of the histories of research and universities' ongoing contributions to shoring up Western epistemologies." I use the parentheses here to signal the difficulty and impossibility of conceptualizing a pedagogy that would decolonize. I use the "ing" to signal this pedagogy as a process that is not, and perhaps cannot be, completed while working with privileged students in a system that remains colonial. To travel is, in part, possible because of colonial and capitalist histories (and presents), and these parentheses indicate that there are ways in which volunteering abroad for young people is an enactment of privilege that has parallels to colonization (cf. Heron, 2007; Simpson, 2004, 2005; Baaz, 2005; White, 2002; and Goudge, 2003). In this chapter I do not suggest a way to escape these histories that make international experiential learning programs possible, nor do I suggest a way to ameliorate them. Through a close reading of my experience in Nicaragua in the summer of 2009, I suggest that a questioning of the ground on which we (teachers and students) stand is a possible way forward in volunteer abroad, and a way to reflect back to the lives of both student and teacher to think not only about international inequity but also about ongoing settler-Canadian[1] relations. This pedagogy moves towards making international experiences less about the student's learning through an experience with marginalized others and engages a pedagogy that does not guarantee a kind of learning, or a kind of citizen but rather resists answers and embraces questions.

Intercordia Canada

In the summer of 2009 I spent three months in Esteli, the third-largest city in Nicaragua. Throughout this time I worked with five Canadian students who were participating in a program called Intercordia, a student volunteer abroad program. As a mentor[2] for Intercordia, my role was to help students adjust, attempt to solve difficulties that may arise, help students through struggles, and facilitate four seminars. Each of these seminars was based around one question developed and assigned by Intercordia.[3] These questions were created to elicit stories and help students engage with their experiences and learning in an ongoing way. These stories were also explicitly about the experiences of students, to challenge them to think about and process their *own* actions, rather than the lives of others. The focus on telling stories was central to each question designed by Intercordia, and a component that I felt was crucial to student experiences abroad because of their difficulty sharing their experiences once they return home (see Roddick, chapter 13 in this volume).

I was initially drawn to working with Intercordia because I understand their work to be significantly different from mainstream volunteer abroad programs, which tend not to adopt critical practice (see Travers, chapter 10 in this volume). Intercordia partners with universities in Canada to facilitate volunteer abroad programs to undergraduate students. Participants in the program are required to complete a university course through their institution designed by a professor at their university prior to departure (see Drolet, chapter 9 in this volume, for an explication of pre-departure). In addition, through the Intercordia program, students engage in reflections throughout their time abroad, are encouraged to *be with* rather than *do for* those with whom they work and live while abroad, and attend a re-integration seminar when they are back in Canada. I see this in-depth preparatory work as crucial to thoughtful volunteer abroad programs and as an integral component for helping students orient towards self-reflection in their time abroad (see Heron, 2005, for an excellent explication of reflecting on social location versus subjectivity and the importance of the latter).

Intercordia was conceived by Jean Vanier, son of the nineteenth Governor-General of Canada and founder of L'Arche Canada – an organization that creates communities where people with intellectual disabilities and those without live in community with one another in the spirit of being with one another and recognizing vulnerability. Intercordia shares many founding principles of L'Arche, including the challenge to students to live in vulnerability as others in the world are often forced to do. Primarily, Intercordia works from the understanding that through experiencing vulnerability and a reliance on others, students will learn to relate in ways they would not have otherwise, and that this experience will challenge them to stand *with* people. The traditional, tenuous framework of *need* in communities in the Global South and *ability* of those in the Global North is highlighted in the Intercordia program. Students are encouraged to question their ability to volunteer, and these questions are posed to students throughout their preparation before leaving. Students are often asked to consider that, rather than being helpful to their host families and organizations, they may actually cost both time and resources. Within the seminars facilitated by Intercordia staff, we work to *destabilize* the way students may imagine themselves as travelling saviours, helpers, and workers. This challenges the assumed right to travel under the auspices of helping and volunteering.

Intercordia aims to create global citizens through their focus on creating *relationships* across difference. This work with students prior to their departure situates and readies them for engagement with their experiences throughout their time abroad.

The strength of Intercordia for me, compared to other volunteer abroad programs, is in the amount of *work* that students are asked to put into considering their experiences – the academic course, seminars, and reflections while volunteering, and their re-integration seminar upon returning home. Students are asked to think about the tensions presented to them, that emerge for them through their experiences, and to begin to think about how practices of solidarity and *being with* may be different than charity and *doing for*. Intercordia, like many programs, is framed as an experience that cultivates global citizenship.

My desire to create a (de)colonizing pedagogy is to be able to begin to *situate* for students where their learning is taking place and under what conditions. This pedagogy offers significant challenges not only to the formatting of international experiential learning programs but also their existence. Understanding that the curriculum often has a hidden agenda, and that in a classroom educators and students are participating in *and* resisting colonial discourses, the attempt to develop a (de)colonizing pedagogy is a move to unearthing these assumptions, discourses, and ideas – to see and examine them together. This (de)colonizing is not just Freire's (1970) *conscientization* or a metaphor for learning, but also has implications for land and considering the ways in which we live (Tuck and Wayne Yang, 2012). The privileges of global citizenship and volunteering become moments to explore and deconstruct in a (de)colonizing classroom. In the next section I explore the assumptions of volunteer programs that aim to cultivate global citizenship through international experiences.

Global Citizenship Education and Learning about Development

A global citizenship education approach suggests that *through* education, students will become global citizens. In current literature, global citizenship is posited as both desirable and attainable, and yet often remains vague in definition (Cameron in chapter 2 of this volume; Young and Cassidy, 2004; Noddings, 2005; Davies, 2006). While there is much literature about how global citizenship education may be taken up in a critical lens, it seems that programs are often adopted in institutions which constrain this possibility (Andreotti & de Souza, 2012). Global citizens are assumed to be cultivated through an experience with someone other than them, particularly those in the Global South. Often, particular skills such as cross-cultural communication and compassion are framed as essential to global citizenship and facilitated through global citizenship education.

Global citizens are not found outside of states, but within – usually in a classroom, and created through an international learning experience. These global citizens have countries from which their passports originate. Global citizenship in the thin sense (see Cameron, chapter 2 in this volume) generally neglects the *actual* citizenship of students. The states that are home to these global citizens are states that are usually wealthy, privileged, and dominant; states that are able to adopt global citizenship education and discourse, and that can send their students abroad to learn about and cultivate global citizenship. The language of "citizenship" indicates rights and responsibilities which, in global citizenship, there is no one to govern (Pashby, 2012; Jefferess, 2012; Zemach-Bersin, 2012; Tarc, 2012). This erasure is true for both the thick and thin varieties of global citizenship by Cameron (chapter 2). The ability to travel to learn is often predicated on an enactment of privilege and an ability to move across borders.

International experiential learning programs adopted as facilitators of global citizenship are rarely exchanges. Through the privileged act of travelling, global citizenship is enacted, attained, and exercised: "[t]he global citizen assumes the right to travel unhindered, to penetrate cultures without the hassle of boundaries, to extend his or her rights of citizenship transnationally, and to unabashedly profit from this imperialist global arrangement" (Zemach-Bersin, 2007, p. 22). This is particularly true in the case of global citizenship facilitated through travel abroad experiences. Canadian students can easily travel to Nicaragua – paying the cost of a tourist visa only at the border. However, Nicaraguans are often denied visas to Canada after paying significant application fees. The formulation of global citizenship as developed through international experiential learning programs denies the possibility accrued to many Canadians to those without privileges. In this frame, global citizenship is only attainable to the Western privileged subject. As these subjects are made into global citizens, their privileges and perspectives are normalized as those of the global citizen, and those Third World Others from whose lives they learn remain rooted in their particularity. Yet as Jefferess (2012) argues, often "the intercultural encounter, particularly with the framework of international development, reaffirms one's own cultural identity rather than unsettles it" (p. 42). The Canadian student is oriented to attain the status of global citizen while those with whom they live are rendered immobile.

Global citizenship education often focuses on international development theories or thinking about being with others across difference. Even if this curriculum does not embrace or teach international development, it is a pervasive and ambiguous concept within the global citizenship approach. Although learning about international development may not be a part of the global citizenship curriculum, students come with an understanding of development – whether informed through peacekeeping, World Vision charity programs, or Craig Kielburger's column in the *Toronto Star*.[4] Development is not simply an action or set of actions, but is also a way of seeing, understanding, and being in the world. This means that "to speak of development, one must adhere to certain rules of statement that go back to the basic system of categories and relation" (Escobar, 1995, p. 17). Thus, when we talk about the world in terms of development (countries as "developed" and "developing"), we invoke narratives that people have, both in relation to theories but also in the context of popular understandings of the world. Development discourse is pervasive enough that it can appear as a justification for buying a new pair of TOMS shoes, or bottled water that donates a portion of its profits to supplying developing communities with access to clean water.

Commonly and broadly, development is thought of as a process facilitated by Western countries, people, or non-governmental organizations to help people in the developing world. Even the basic terms, which we employ to describe the world in terms of development, point to a privileging of the West – the develop*ed* world and the developi*ng* world. Dividing the world into two categories based on their "development," with tenses that indicate either completion of the task of development or a current engagement with it, juxtaposes peoples in specific relation to one another, and the West as the end of a line of progress the rest of the world is journeying towards. This framing is related to colonial understandings of "progress" and "modernity." It is in the space created between the "developed" and "developing" world where students and teachers are able to imagine the entrance of international learning. It is this frame that enables a helping model in global citizenship education which is, as Jefferess (2012) points out, significantly different from "redress" or "compensation" (p. 38).

International development studies is not the only place where these discourses are found (and is one of the places where thoughtful critiques of international development emerge). These narratives are also in everyday Canadian understandings of the world that provide framing or understanding of our continued presence in Afghanistan, our eventual rejection of Kyoto, and our claim to a multicultural nation (S. Razack, 2008; Bannerji, 2000). The shift of rhetoric in volunteer abroad programs, from helping models for those in the South to programs for student personal growth and development, runs alongside critiques of imperialism in international development (the assumed ability to know what is best for others) and shifts to community development (living in communities and learning from them) in international development literature. Yet this shift does not question the persistence of volunteer abroad, or the circumstances that make it possible.

This examination of development enables us to look at what happens under the auspice of development and its ability to construct the world in specific ways, which then work to regulate the relationships we form and the possibilities for relation across difference. Ferguson (1994) says, then, that "in the 'development' version of things, 'less developed' means historically retarded, and poverty appears as a result of not yet having been introduced to the modern world" (p. 56). To bring these questions of terms such as "developed" and "developing" or of international development and the discursive implications to global citizenship education, especially programs that rely on volunteer abroad, is to question the foundations on which these programs stand. It is to work to politically contextualize international experiential learning programs. Global citizenship programs assume international development as a tool to educate privileged students without the critiques articulated by international development scholars. As critiques of development grow, global citizenship disguises how international experiential learning programs maintain the privilege of Canadian students not only through their ability to become global citizens but also through the uninhibited right to travel and maintain a presence internationally. Although global citizenship education realizes the critique of development through a *denial* of development language (Simpson, 2004), it purports to address inequality through education and travel opportunities for those in the Global North. Although programs such as Intercordia are committed to witnessing and being with rather than doing for, the very *possibility* of these programs relies on these divisions. Yet there is a potency to a program built on models of solidarity, witnessing, and vulnerability that lends itself to a (de)colonizing pedagogy.

Colonizing Education

Although much has been done to illuminate the harmful effects of development and, especially, "First World" intervention on behalf of others, development remains a constant presence in our way of understanding the world and often has simply resulted in the creation of new terms, such as "community" or "participatory," which are then added to development. Critiques of development discourse, however, are not often strongly connected to colonial education. Considering these histories of education is crucial to a practice of (de)colonizing pedagogy and to an engagement with the constitution of our ideas. Tracing how people talk about "seeing India" or knowing of particular places of importance to see in India, Willinsky (1999) connects these strands to modern travel, so that the colonial impulse to know and experience the other still plays its part in our everyday lives (p. 81). Colonial images of being close to the other are brought to life not so subtly through movies like *Out of Africa, Blood Diamond, Avatar*, and *Dances With Wolves* that feature heroic white characters (all helping those others while learning about themselves), and perhaps more subtly through travel brochures and "adventure" travel.

A colonial way of understanding the world permeates how we, as students and educators who aim to be global citizens, position ourselves in relation to others. The colonial impetus to know and encounter difference is a reoccurring theme through international experiential learning – it is the experience of the other that propels learning. This process is not always one which makes us feel powerful or reinforces power relations, but, as Tiessen (2008) argues, international experience can "lead to an emotional and academic paralysis: without the proper tools and space for analyzing the experience abroad, some students are unable to make sense of their experience and feel they cannot continue with their academic studies" (p. 77). Many students I have worked with related to this sense of paralysis upon returning home, particularly because of a confrontation with their own privilege and the desire to "do" something. Confrontation with privilege can be a moment when students begin to reflect on their own space and actions within the world, but it can also enable a quick jump to action. Although there are problematic underpinnings to volunteer abroad and global citizenship, as I have outlined, it is these moments when students confront privilege and are faced with its complexities that I am interested in focusing on and asking students to sit in, rather than to jump to action or paralysis. It is in this reflection back that is the (de)colonial move. This pedagogy moves to consider what is colonial and how it shapes who we are, while remaining a pedagogy without guarantees.

(De)Colonizing Pedagogy

In the article "Toward a Decolonizing Pedagogy: Social Justice Reconsidered," Tejada, Espinoza, and Gutierrez (2004) argue that decolonizing pedagogy

> encompasses both an anticolonial and decolonizing notion of pedagogy and an anticolonial and decolonizing praxis. It is an anticolonial and decolonizing theory and praxis that insists that colonial domination and its ideological frameworks operate and are reproduced in and through the curricular content and design, the instructional practices, the social organization and learning, and the forms of evaluation that inexorably sort and label students into enduring categories of success and failure of

schooling … [they can] become sites for development of a critical decolonizing consciousness. (p. 6)

Thus, this pedagogy is a rethinking not only of content but rather of education as a whole. In my view, an anticolonial and (de)colonizing pedagogy will work to not only challenge the ways students *already* understand the world in colonial terms (primitive, modern, civilized, developed, and developing all being terms I would consider colonial or terms with colonial origins), but also to *create* a framework that enables students to begin to develop an anticolonial practice. Following Tuck and Wayne Yang's (2012) criticism of the motivation of "decolonizing" as a metaphor for learning, I suggest that this pedagogy has implications for the ways we move through the world and see the actual ground below us. My understanding of the difference between anticolonialism and (de)colonizing is that to (de)colonize is to focus on current frameworks that need to be *de*prioritized and *de*stabilized, and move towards a new way of seeing and understanding that may be considered anticolonial. This practice also recognizes that all pedagogical choices are political (Mohanty, 2003). The aim of this practice is an awareness of colonial legacies, recognition of the effects of colonization in the world we find ourselves moving in, and a gesture to create a world which disassembles (neo)colonial relations. This is to learn not only about colonial pasts but also how those pasts are carried with us, embodied, altered, and continued today.

I am concerned in these programs about the quick move to action – to help; to fundraise; to do. In a (de)colonizing pedagogy, these moves, this desire for development (Heron, 2007), are questioned. As Ahmed (2006) argues, "[c]olonialism makes the world 'white,' which is of course a world 'ready' for certain kinds of bodies, as a world that puts certain objects within their reach. Bodies remember such histories *even when we forget them*" (pp. 153–4, emphasis added). We must ask after which objects are in our reach and how we are able to reach them – how is it that young students, for example, can reach for development tools or funds that those whom they work with cannot?

While international experiential learning programs often involve discussions of privilege or colonization, this is not enough – the *pedagogy* of the classroom must itself make a (de)colonizing gesture. This would include, for example, a move away from the banking model of education (Freire, 1970), an inclusion of the experiences of not only students but also teachers (hooks, 1994), and a questioning of the university in which those programs are embedded (Cameron, chapter 2 in this volume). Experience in this pedagogy is not as true thing (Scott, 1991), but becomes a moment for inquiry. This could include expanding the texts of a course to include plays and poems, to having students choose their own readings, or to focus on how to learn in community.

This (de)colonizing international experiential learning pedagogy seeks to cultivate citizens who, rather than simply claiming their globality, recognize their rootedness and citizenship and the legacies they inherit. Developing a pedagogy that attempts to consider a project of (de)colonization is a signal to the possible harmful effects of a colonial pedagogy that privileges the ability to know and the position of Canadian students, and that re-instates hierarchies and differences. This work deconstructs the ability of some to claim a global identity, while others remain rooted in their particularity.

In the following section I want to consider how students spoke of Nicaragua in our seminars and in their reflections, and ask after xnarratives students motivate to make sense of their experiences of Nicaragua. In particular I am interested in the quick movements that students (and teachers) will often make from observation to narratives that claim knowledge or expertise and how this is a, perhaps academic, kind of doing.

Mastering Place through Narratives[5]

The narratives that students tell about the places they are in interest me. This interest is not only because of the difficulties of narration and the attempt at being able to know a place but also because once volunteers return home, they are often greeted with questions about how their experiences were, and will be expected to have such stories (see Roddick, chapter 14 in this volume). I call this "mastering place" because narratives of place often work to define and claim expertise of a place. This mastering often negates nuances and complexities while figuring the narrator as "knower." This is typical not only of the Intercordia participants but also of people who have international experiences generally. I consider this mastering in relation to our seminars and the stories students shared about Nicaragua, as well as my own use of Nicaraguan experiences in the seminars, as a way to illuminate this tension created in international experiential learning programs.

In the first seminar we sat around a table together, sipping on strong coffee loaded with sugar, pens in hand. We talked briefly about the first question. The first reflection question for students asks them to tell a story of arrival and to talk about their vivid impressions. After spending some time considering how students may conceptualize these questions, I thought it might be best to focus on their arrival through *senses*, as a way of drawing them back to these vivid experiences.[6] As the students had only been in Nicaragua for a few weeks, it seemed hard for them to think about saying something concise and to articulate their experiences so far. As a way to prompt discussion, I asked students to focus on their senses on their arrival.

I asked the students to take some time to write about their first impressions of their time so far in Nicaragua. Borrowing inkshedding from Russ Hunt (1999),[7] I asked them to write their impressions without thought to grammar, spelling, or sense – that their biggest priority would be to keep writing for the full ten minutes, ideally without their pen leaving the paper. Using inkshedding was a move I made to encourage learning and community and, borrowing from Russ, to think about the possibilities in written dialogue that are not possible in a move immediately to discussion. I also asked students to focus specifically on their senses, thinking that this would be a way to bring them back to the particularity of their experiences. I also told them that they would be sharing this writing with the other students. Having students write in a new and vulnerable way where they share that writing is not only a way of reconsidering their relationship with writing and texts but also a way of asking them to trust one another. Using the inkshed method, I was also hoping to be able to elicit some questions that students had not yet been able to articulate and to create textual community.

After the ten minutes, I asked them to pass their writing around to share with one another, commenting and circling or underlining where they wanted – not on grammar or spelling, but on ideas or thoughts that caught their attention either because of agreement, or disagreement. This marking is about resonances and dissonances between reflections. I assert that this conversation, which happens textually, silently, and with much time around it, allows students to move to discussion with more comfort. They each received their reflection back with notes, pictures drawn, circling, and so on to see what sort of response the others had. The discussion from this reflection took some teasing out. The students seemed to struggle to articulate their arrival in *stories* (as the question asked them to) and most of the conversation was *agreement* with one another, rather than highlighting differences.

Part of this may have been my focus on senses – descriptor words about sense perhaps do not lend themselves well to stories that question the basis of knowing but rather move towards what senses "know." In the stories they shared, I heard what they imagined in these first few days what Nicaragua was – the roads bumpy, the climate hot, the housing substandard – and about what life was like for them – fun, exhilarating, challenging, humid. These stories and initial impressions of Nicaragua were told as statements, not as questions, and seemed definitive. Rather than being based in our experiences, they felt like an attempt to define Nicaragua – a claim about the nature of the country. This desire to be knowledgeable about a place that is not our own, and the imagined ability to know and define place, is connected to Willinsky's (1999) discussion of colonial education and processes of ordering. These stories are difficult to pull apart as they are narrated as experiences and told as truth about the places they are in and people they are with. Opening this naming and ordering is crucial to undermining the ability to know and questioning the desire to manage difference.

From my reflections on the first seminar and the difficulty in opening the stories for room for other perspectives, I wanted to consider ways to open up a plurality of narratives towards Nicaragua. My initial vision for the next seminar was to bring in other stories of Nicaragua – Nicaraguan stories of revolution, family life, and so on – to include narratives that may encourage students to reflect on their ideas of Nicaragua and reconsider their place there. In an attempt to (de)colonize the class, I wanted to rely on other narratives of Nicaragua as a way of displacing our position as *knower*. Narda Razack (2009) suggests this is useful because "varied experiences of culture and histories in the classroom allow us to shape and shift our identities as we come to challenge what we know and how we come to know what we know" (p. 15). In this framing, differences are used as sites for learning. I am concerned, however, about this reliance on "others" to complicate our sense of self. Surely there are ways we can complicate our ways of knowing without demanding more from people who have historically been and continue to be marginalized. Sherene Razack (2008) writes of this experience, and says she can "recall clumsily trying to explain to a colleague that *we* (people of colour) are always being asked to tell our stories for *your* (white people's) edification, which you cannot *hear* because of the benefit you derive from them" (p. 48). While inclusion of the stories of others is important for thinking about our ideas and impressions, as people travelling because of privilege we need to be aware of our inability to hear these stories because of, as Sherene Razack (2008) points out, the benefit we derive from them. This move to questioning where learning takes place asks crucial questions of global citizenship facilitated through international experiential learning – trying to engage students to ask about their experiences as a place to learn and the position of others. It is a question of where learning takes place and the ways students are put into relation with others.

In spite of my reservations about their inclusion, I attempted to mobilize the experiences of others as evidence in a seminar where I included a reading about a Canadian-owned mine in Nicaragua. A student had been approached by a member of one of the host families who then told them about Canadian mining in Nicaragua, and students wanted to learn more. My desire in including these readings was to introduce these narratives as a way of undermining our refrain of "Canadians-as-helpers-abroad," and to enable students to think about possibilities for solidarity. This move is an important looking back to Canadian citizenship – as Tiessen (2008) recommends learning about foreign policy or Cameron (chapter 2 in this volume) suggests about the university's divestment interests.

I was surprised by student reactions in the seminar, for example, wanting to see the mine because it did not feel real to them, and wondering if there would be a difference if the mine was publicly owned rather than by a Canadian corporation. I wonder about the nature of these desires and questions. Where are these questions rooted and pointed? Who is this question asking about? What might this moment look like if I were to ask students to turn towards Canada and question our role(s)? How does a reading about the experiences of others enable this sort of questioning after the choices of other, or of the very *possibility* of Canada's implications, rather than about the ability to hear or read these stories? What material orients students towards thinking about the self and the position of our actual citizenship?

I walked away from this seminar very frustrated with the response of the students and my own inability to facilitate a deeper dialogue. Asking students why unethical mining practices by Canadian companies didn't feel "real" may have opened up a space to talk about how we imagine the presence of Canadians abroad and our reluctance to displace the positive and ethical identity of Canada with responsibility for environmental destruction. It may have also opened up questions of implications – how are we, as Canadians, responsible not only for the current situation of the communities but also for trying to understand the complexities that have occurred because of this (such as dependence on the mining industry, outside companies, and subsidies, and an increase in sex work)?[8] This move to connect our experience to Canadian citizenship is a rejection of global citizenship material and a claim to globality – this move is a recognition of our place in the world *as Canadians*. This also complicates for students the possibility of claiming to be global citizens, as their countries become positioned as causes of problems in the Global South. The specificity of our countries of origin is significant here.

In the final seminar, I asked students to return to their first reflections about their arrival and asked them how their impressions had changed since then. I did this hoping to elicit questions about "mastering" and a realization of the contingency of knowing, and the inability to articulate *what* a place is after so little time. In this seminar, I heard students talk about what they had discovered Nicaragua *really* was – that after their three months, they had discovered many of their initial impressions were wrong, but that through their time there they had found out what Nicaragua was really like. Again, these stories were statements about what Nicaragua was "like," rather than allowing questions of "what we did not know," or how the three months had complicated their understandings and questions. Although discussion pointed to the difficulties in their first reflections about Nicaragua, this questioning did not extend to their new attempts to talk about what Nicaragua is. The desire to know and order remains intact.

My desire in these two seminars was to disrupt stories that attempt to "master" Nicaragua, stories that attempt to exert a definitional force from student experiences onto the country (and the people who live there). I was concerned with their adoption of narratives, descriptions, and ideas that do not allow participants to pay attention to tensions, complexities, and nuances in the lives of Nicaraguans, and that in developing these narratives they would not be able to maintain nuances they had recognized as they returned home. A way to pull apart the quick move students make to similarities between their reflections, and therefore to a common definition of place or people, would be to look for differences between their responses, and to highlight tensions. This highlighting of differences works to complicate not only their assertions of similarities between responses but also the possibilities of knowing and mastering place. Following Simon's (2005) exploration of listening to Sayisi Dene's testimonials of forced relocation, I am not arguing that students are unable to learn about Nicaragua's history, or that there is an impossibility of connections, but that we should encourage ourselves to "pose questions to ourselves, questions about our questions, interrogating why the information and explanations we seek are important and necessary to us" (p. 98). These questions resist the impetus to know, and instead ask after that impetus itself.

A (de)colonizing pedagogy would refuse to rely on bodies already marked as different to complicate our understandings, asking instead about the ethical implications of learning about our privilege through the lives of others. In (de)colonizing my practice as a facilitator, I would have been able to lead our discussion into wondering about the nature of questions about Nicaraguan implication in mining, rather than addressing the questions they asked. These questions about mining demanded answers and accountability from others, rather than asking on what grounds this situation became possible, and on what grounds these *questions* became possible. This pedagogy would also encourage a discussion where these questions would become unintelligible. A (de)colonizing pedagogy would consider the historical implications of demanding of others, learning from, off of, and through the bodies of people who have been othered and colonized, and to seek alternatives. A pedagogy whose aim was to pull apart the ways we think of and imagine the world would also ask students to question their own implication in the lives of others and as Canadians. Rather than embracing the desire to see the mine because it was unimaginable to us, instead we might begin to think about how this unimaginability was constituted. Here the pedagogy would point not only to the histories of those with whom we are living, but to how our histories are entwined, and what this learning might mean for our subjectivity as Canadian citizens. Each student is necessarily different and will see things in a different light – how might these differences push them to consider not only the ways they see and experience differently among themselves, but how limited these attempts to narrate are? A (de)colonizing pedagogy would also aim to encourage students to pay attention to these difficulties in their everyday lives, particularly in relation to Canada as a settler state.

My interest in breaking apart these mastering narratives of places and peoples is rooted in a concern for the violence it does to people's lives. Talking about the strength and centrality of families in Nicaragua, for example, does not allow for conversations of people who died in the revolution and the impact on families today, or the reliance on family members who had to leave Nicaragua to support their family, or for conversations about domestic violence. Talking about machismo can silence discussions about change and challenge to patriarchy *within* Nicaragua, and to patriarchy at home. Stories students tell of Nicaragua and how they share their experiences may talk over and silence differ-ence, or smooth out bumps to create stories that are more understand-able, digestible, and simple. This, too, can happen as students return home and begin to share their experiences: their narratives become more concise and less nuanced. As they return home the people they share stories with may not have the same frame of reference for under-standing as they do, and so they may be read through many lenses (see Clost, chapter 12 in this volume). I do not mean to imply that students are *unable* to see these folded and textured stories, nor that the stories they tell are not true, but that to consider them, relay them, and hold tensions is difficult, and that most international experiential learning programs are not designed to allow space for this questioning.

Students' stories of their time abroad often work to knead out these striations, and aim to make sense within frameworks they already have. It is often difficult to maintain tensions, as frameworks – such as helping and doing, international development, modernity, and prog-ress – often work to erase them. The (de)colonizing move here is to question our own perspectives and frameworks and what they mean, not only for learning abroad but also for our place as Canadians; to consider the impulse not only to define and order, nor the desire to know ourselves through the other, but also to consider the very grounds upon which international service learning programs stand. This is a recognition of our desire to help *not* as a natural impulse but as a his-torically constituted and directed one. The (de)colonizing move is to question the very basis of international experiential learning.

Conclusion

Using stories and experiences to learn can be not only a move to incor-porating "real life" experiences into the classroom but also a push against certain ways of knowing. This inclusion of experience should not be seen as an inclusion of truth, but rather as a starting point for reflections (hooks, 1994). Opening up sites of knowledge to include our stories and our lives can be a tool to radically rethink not only pedago-gy but also how we understand the world and our place in it. Asking students to turn back and ask questions of their own practices of hear-ing, listening, and learning is to ask after the very grounds on which those practices have been built. Although in the seminars I asked stu-dents to share stories, I do not think I highlighted the importance of this project enough – to not only think about telling our stories about our time in Nicaragua, but also about how we are able to *hear* other people's stories and what hearing them does to our own stories. Sherene Razack (2008) warns us that storytelling's potential "as a tool for social change is remarkable, provided we pay attention to the interpretive structures that underpin how we hear and how we take up stories of oppressed groups" (p. 37). Storytelling as a political practice involves questioning and reflection that was often difficult for us to reach in our seminars.

A (de)colonizing pedagogy is fraught for settler-Canadians, and for Canadians enacting privilege in moving to other parts of the world. The outcome of a course like this would not be to (de)colonize students but to destabilize their ideas of privilege and power, and to provoke questions about how we are constituted in and through this privilege. Framing seminars that would allow students to think about their changed readings of their international experiences would be a way to point to how we cannot really "know" a place, and to point to the inconsistencies inherent in narratives that work to master a place. Increasing focus on what it feels like to be read as privileged, and yet to feel as though we are not privileged (often because of student status), and then to confront what it means to be able to live elsewhere for a summer would also have the potential to lead students to thinking about their identity as Canadians and how their privilege is also en-acted in Canada. Asking them to talk about how they came to be in their program could also be a window into thinking about how they came to be in Canada (whether through settler or immigrant histories):[9] to question histories of relations here; and to think about persisting internal colonial relations in Canada and imperial relations outside Canada. These questions would not only push pedagogy to the horizon of (de)colonization, but maybe also to question the lenses through which we see how we are able to live in the world. This pedagogy, how-ever, remains a pedagogy without guarantees, as it is not prescriptive but rather creative, responsive, and imaginative.

NOTES

1 I use "settler-Canadian" here to indicate the histories of particular bodies
  in Canada that arrived as settlers and colonizers and continue to
  experience privilege in a state that has not undergone a successful decolonizing and anticolonial movement and whose government still represents
  settler-Canadians.

2 This designation as a mentor prior to meeting the students is problematic in that mentors are chosen, not assigned.

3 These questions were as follows, although they have since changed:

  1. What are your most vivid first impressions of your new community? (think of settings [institutional and physical], people and roles, actions and positive and/or negative feelings you are having) Write a short story from your experiences (approx. 250 words) to communicate these first impressions.

  2. How do you think your presence in the community impacts the person(s) with whom you work, or with whom you live? (i.e. work placement or host family) Write a short story (250 words) from your experiences to communicate these impacts you are having.

  3. What impact has your presence in the local community had on you? Write a short story (250 words) from your experiences to communicate the impact that your work, or your host family, or another aspect of life there has had upon you.

  4. Having been abroad now for several months, how have your initial impressions of your placement been altered? How have your perspectives or feelings changed (or not) since you first entered the Intercordia program in Canada? Write a short story (250 words) about your experiences to communicate these changes.

4 This column, "Global Voices," discusses "global issues" and invites junior journalists, including Craig and Marc Kielburger, to write for the column.

5 My experiences of the seminars and what I asked students to do is (re)constructed through journals, emails, notes, student reflections, and my memory.

6 Throughout the seminars I did some reworking of the questions designed with Intercordia Canada, facilitated discussions around the wording, and tried to pull apart the questions to make them more approachable for the students to consider.

7 Inkshedding is a method of writing developed by Russ Hunt and James Reither similar to free writing but as a written dialogue. I learned it in my undergraduate degree in a program called Truth in Society, taught by Russ Hunt, Thom Parkhill, and John McKendy. Inkshedding begins with a free write, and then marginal responses (substantive responses, rather than comments on form) are encouraged. Normally readers are asked simply to mark passages they find striking (true, not true, needing qualification or expansion). Possible next stages include:

  • reading frequently marked passages aloud (discussion or a further round of writing can ensue);

- choosing a marked passage to respond to with a further inkshed; writers can begin by transcribing the passage, and then responding. This writing can then be read and annotated in the same way;
- transcribing, photocopying, and distributing to the class the most frequently marked passages; this task can be done by an editorial committee chosen from the class (Hunt, 1999).

8 Using the term "sex work" here, I hope to point to common assumptions around "prostitution" and to encourage us to consider what assumptions are displaced when we consider this stigmatized activity as *work*. Understanding, of course, that the lives of sex workers vary considerably, I think it would be useful to develop separate terms for different circumstances within sex work; however, for now, I retain the term "sex work."

9 The lack of Aboriginal people in this formulation is not to suggest that a (de)colonizing pedagogy is not possible or necessary with Aboriginal people. Certainly the (de)colonizing move is not only about the student, but also about the classroom, the learning experience, and the frameworks we bring with us. I refrain from including Aboriginal people in this frame because it deserves more attention than simply adding into the classroom or seminars.

REFERENCES

Ahmed, S. (2006). A phenomenology of whiteness. *Feminist Theory, (8)*2, 149–168.

Andreotti, V., & DeSouza, L. (2012). Introduction: (Towards) global citizenship "otherwise." In V. Andreotti and L. DeSouza (Eds.), *Postcolonial perspectives on global citizenship education* (pp. 1–8). New York: Routledge.

Baaz, M.E. (2005). *The paternalism of partnership: A postcolonial reading of identity in development aid*. New York: Zed Books.

Bannerji, H. (2000). *Dark side of the nation: Essays on multiculturalism, nationalism and racism*. Toronto: Canadian Scholars' Press.

Davies, L. (2006). Global citizenship: Abstraction or framework for action? *Educational Review, 58*(1), 5–25. doi:10.1080/00131910500352523

Escobar, A. (1995). *Encountering development: The making and unmaking of the Third World*. New York: Princeton University Press.

Ferguson, J. (1994). *The anti-politics machine: "Development," depoliticization, and bureaucratic power in Lesotho*. Minneapolis: University of Minnesota Press.

Freire, P. (1970). *Pedagogy of the oppressed*. London: Burns and Oates.

Goudge, P. (2003). *The whiteness of power: Racism in Third World development and aid*. London: Lawrence and Wishart.

Heron, B. (2005). Self‑reflection in critical social work practice: Subjectivity and the possibilities of resistance. *Reflective Practice: International and Multidisciplinary Perspectives*, 6(3), 341–351. doi:10.1080/14623940500220095

Heron, B. (2007). *Desire for development: Whiteness, gender, and the helping imperative.* Waterloo, ON: Wilfrid Laurier University Press.

hooks, b. (1994) *Teaching to transgress.* New York: Routledge.

Hunt, R. (1999). "What is 'inkshedding'?" Paper presented at Inkshed Working Conference 16, Mont Gabriel, Quebec, May 6–9. Eric Microfiche Card ED 454 515.

Jefferess, D. (2012). Unsettling Cosmopolitanism: Global Citizenship and the Cultural Politics of Benevolence. In V. Andreotti & L. DeSouza (Eds.), *Postcolonial Perspectives on Global Citizenship Education* (pp. 27–46). New York: Routledge.

Mohanty, C.T. (2003). *Feminism without borders: Decolonizing theory, practicing solidarity.* Durham: Duke University Press.

Noddings, N. (2005). Global Citizenship: Promises and Problems. In N. Noddings (Ed.), *Educating citizens for global awareness* (pp. 1–21). New York: Teachers College Press.

Pashby, K. (2012). Questions for global citizenship education in the context of the "new imperialism": For whom? By whom? In V. Andreotti & L. DeSouza (Eds.), *Postcolonial perspectives on global citizenship education* (pp. 9–26). New York: Routledge.

Razack, N. (2009). Decolonizing the pedagogy and practice of international social work. *International Journal of Social Work*, 52(1), 9–21. doi:10.1177/0020872808097748

Razack, S. (2008). *Looking white people in the eye.* Toronto, ON: University of Toronto Press.

Scott, J.W. (1991). The evidence of experience. *Critical Inquiry*, 17(4), 773–797.

Simpson, K. (2004). "Doing development": The gap year, volunteer-tourists and a popular practice of development. *Journal of International Development*, 16(5), 681–692.   doi:10.1002/jid.1120

Simpson, K. (2005). Dropping out or signing up? The professionalisation of youth travel. *Antipode*, 37(3), 447–469. doi:10.1111/j.0066-4812.2005.00506.x

Tarc, P. (2012). How does "global citizenship education" construct its present? The crisis of international education. In V. Andreotti & L. DeSouza (Eds.), *Postcolonial perspectives on global citizenship education* (pp. 105–123). New York: Routledge.

Tejada, C., Espinoza, M., & Gutierrez, K. (2004). Toward a decolonizing pedagogy: Social justice reconsidered. In P. Trifonas (Ed.), *Pedagogy of Difference* (pp. 9–38). New York: Routledge.

Tiessen, R. (2008). Educating global citizens? Canadian foreign policy and youth study/volunteer abroad programs. *Canadian Foreign Policy, 14*(1), 77–84. doi:10.1080/11926422.2007.9673453

Tuck, E., & Wayne Wang, K. (2012). Decolonization is not a metaphor. *Decolonization: Indigineity, Education & Society, 1*(1), 1–40.

White, S. (2002). Thinking race, thinking development. *Third World Quarterly, 23*(3), 407–419. doi:10.1080/01436590220138358

Willinsky, J. (1999). *Learning to divide the world: Education at empire's end.* Minneapolis: University of Minnesota Press.

Young, M., & Cassidy, W. (2004). The impact of a global education course on students' citizenship attitudes and behaviour. *Canadian and International Education, 33*(2), 57–87.

Zemach-Bersin, T. (2007). Global citizenship and study abroad: It's all about US. *Critical Literacy Journal, 2*(1), 16–28.

Zemach-Bersin, T. (2012). Entitled to the world: The rhetoric of U.S. global citizenship and study abroad. In V. Andreotti &L. DeSouza (Eds.), *Post-colonial perspectives on global citizenship education* (pp. 87–104). New York: Routledge.

12 Visual Representation and Canadian Government-Funded Volunteer Abroad Programs: Picturing the Canadian Global Citizen

ELLYN CLOST

Introduction

The authors in this book grapple with the ethical issues of Canadians teaching and "doing" global citizenship and experiential learning. This chapter examines the inherent ethical challenges and obligations of promoting and "picturing" global citizenship through photographs used by Canadian volunteer abroad programs. Volunteering abroad is marketed to Canadians as a means to achieve global perspective and as an agent of development through carefully selected photographs that highlight the positive, constructive role of Canadians in the so-called developing world. In this chapter, volunteer abroad photographs are considered primarily as a source of visual information for the prospective volunteer, but also as aesthetic incentives to participate in a volunteer abroad program, with their own visual language and history.

I begin by connecting photography to lived experience following Mary Louise Pratt's (2008) concept of the "contact zone": a space wherein those previously separated by geography and history now intersect, and where power relations are imbalanced. I use Pratt's idea to introduce the kind of complex behavioural and ethical challenges faced by those volunteering or studying abroad. I suggest that as Northerners/ Westerners working in the Global South, our paths are always linked with the colonial past but are seldom discussed – the implications of which are the subject of the rest of this chapter.

I follow with a brief history of colonial-era image-making and some theoretical perspectives on the viewing of photographs – particularly those of European colonial subjects in the nineteenth century – as the foundation for present-day ways of seeing in the West. I link present-day imagery with colonial examples through a visual discourse analysis[1] of a selection of online promotional photographs for five CIDA-funded volunteer abroad organizations.

The importance of Canadian national identity in the promotion of volunteer abroad programs is evident in the substantial funding provided to these organizations through the Canadian International Development Agency (CIDA).[2] Over several weeks in 2010, I collected all available online still photographs used by the following CIDA-funded organizations to promote short- and long-term volunteer abroad programs: CUSO International (formerly CUSO-VSO, and before that Canadian University Service Overseas), World University Service Canada and Centre de l'Education et de Coopération International (WUSC-CECI [Uniterra]),[3] Canadian Executive Service Organization (CESO), Canadian Crossroads International (CCI), and Canada World Youth (CWY): 270 photographs in total. The above-mentioned organizations have different mandates, different geographical areas of focus, and work towards different development targets (for a brief summary, see CIDA's "Project Browser," 2012). Despite their differences, each organization uses remarkably similar modes of representation, creating a library of stock photographs which I term the "visual economy of volunteering abroad."[4] I focus on volunteering abroad as a common vehicle for young Canadians to engage with the quest for global citizenship, and as a case study for what could be called "global citizenship marketing."

I discuss three categories of images in terms of their ethical challenges and sociocultural implications for potential and returned volunteers: the first relates to the power of the camera and the notion of photographer as "owner"; the second explores the imbalanced contribution of white and non-white bodies in photographic space; and the third focuses on the specialized role of female Canadian volunteers as child caregivers. Each represents a key concept in the visual economy of volunteering abroad: a visual construct that creates and sells stereotypes of "development" and presents them as instances of "global citizenship."

This chapter draws on my master's research (2010–11), newer (2012) photographs from the same online sources, and my personal experiences during my short time as an intern in northern Ghana in 2008.[5] I add to that the thoughts of several volunteers – whom I interviewed as part of my master's thesis in 2011 – to show that as aspiring global citizens, we need to understand that how we visualize and recreate our realities through photography affects our lives and the lives of others.[6]

National identity plays a key role in how we make sense of our experiences volunteering abroad. I close with a discussion of the Canadian government's version of global citizenship as presented in both volunteering abroad promotion and multiculturalism discourse. Our attempts at global citizenship are inextricably linked to our understandings of our own citizenship – a concept which, in Canada, is highly contested. Studies of Canadian nationalism have suggested that despite multiculturalism legislation, and despite the remarkably diverse makeup of the Canadian population, the Canadian "cultural centre" is perceived to be white and English-speaking (Mackey, 1999; Bannerji, 2000). In fact, the majority of all pictured volunteers – understood to be "Canadians" – appear to be white. I argue that such photographs promote a version of global citizenship that suggests access only for white Canadians.

Kamboureli (1998) has argued that multicultural legislation is constructive of ethnicity in Canada (p. 210). I add to that argument that the "global citizenship marketing" performed by the above-mentioned volunteer abroad programs, and by extension CIDA, supports the idea that cultural difference and ethnicity rest (literally and figuratively) outside of "Canadianness." To illustrate the manufacture of visible "Canadianness," I refer to the "imagined community" of the nation (Anderson, 2006) and the "imagined multicultural community" (Stratton & Ang, 1998). My examination of CIDA-funded volunteer abroad promotional photographs suggests that neither the volunteer abroad organizations nor the Canadian government agencies concerned are prepared to reconcile Canada's colonial past with its current foreign and domestic cultural policies, including global citizenship initiatives.

As more young Canadians participate in volunteering abroad and other forms of development work, adequate preparation and the formation of a "politics of accountability" (Heron, 2007, p. 144) are essential. Interviews and testimony with returned volunteers have shown that the experiences they have while volunteering abroad can spark critical and reflective thought about Canada's foreign and development policy, as well as the meaning(s) of privilege and cultural difference (Clost, 2011; Tiessen, 2011; Heron, 2007; Kelly & Case, 2007; Simpson, 2006; Universalia, E.T. Jackson & Associates, & Salassan, 2005). This is encouraging. However, the number of Canadians exposed to volunteer abroad promotion who do *not* volunteer is greater than those who do. The creation and perpetuation of unchallenged stereotypes of development and global citizenship through photographs must be considered. If Canadians are not questioning the versions of reality proffered by volunteer abroad promotional photographs – and by returned volunteers (see Roddick, chapter 13 in this volume) – then we are literally buying into a system of representation that is semiologically charged by colonialism, thereby perpetuating its use and standing as a legitimate way to represent the developing world. Can effective partnerships and anti-oppressive experiential learning be achieved on this basis? Developing an understanding of the contribution of images to Canadians' perceptions of development work, volunteerism, and the representation of culture may contribute to a more refined understanding of the meaning of "thick" global citizenship (Cameron, chapter 2 in this volume).

Lessons from the Contact Zone: How Photography Impacts Lived Experience

A photograph – no matter what kind – represents several different interactions. There are interactions between photograph and subject; between the subject and his or her surroundings; and between the viewers and the subject. This chapter considers all of these interactions in relation to Mary Louise Pratt's (2008) concept of the "contact zone": an idea that re-introduces historical, social, geographical, and political context to situations where they are most often denied.

"Contact zones" are places where "subjects previously separated by geography and history are co-present, the point[s] at which their trajectories now intersect" (Pratt, 2008, p. 8). Pratt's idea explains relationships between groups in three-dimensional spaces of colonialism, but I believe it also identifies the processes at play when viewing images of volunteer abroad destinations and their peoples for educational or informational purposes. She emphasizes the importance of the term "contact," and how it "treats the relations among ... travelers and 'travelees,' not in terms of separateness, but in terms of co-presence, interactions, interlocking understandings and practices, and often within radically asymmetrical relations of power" (Pratt, 2008, p. 8). "Co-presence" begins through photographs prior to entering the destination country: on an imaginary plane, volunteers are co-present with the host countries' cultures and peoples from the perspective of their home country (Clost, 2011). All formal volunteers[7] undergo some kind of orientation prior to departure or before placement begins in the host country. Volunteers also often undertake independent research to learn more about the region in which they will be living. Through such training, volunteers are given power in the form of authoritative knowledge.

Those living in the host country may not have equal access to information about the volunteers coming into their communities. Asymmetrical power relations begin in the planning stages of volunteering abroad and can carry forward into volunteers' lived (and photographed) experiences.

While on placement in the destination country, volunteers compound the knowledge gained during the planning stages of volunteering abroad with knowledge acquired through "experience" (see Roddick, chapter 13 in this volume). Kate Simpson (2006) describes the link between the gaze of modern volunteers and that of their colonialist forebears. She cites the importance of the natural sciences in the nineteenth century to the acquisition of knowledge: the concept that "seeing is believing" but also "seeing is knowing" (discussed in the following section). Those "back home" confer authoritative status on those who have travelled. However, Simpson argues that the "holiday" side to volunteering abroad invites participants to see their host country with an "innocent gaze": one that denies his or her own (colonialist) history for a better holiday experience (p. 29). The end result is a generation of young people "claim[ing] powerful knowledges without having to take responsibility" (p. 29). Photographs invite others (including non-volunteers) to take part in this simultaneously authoritative and innocent dichotomy through widespread online dissemination and advertising (Clost, 2011). Based on photographs and second-hand knowledge alone, an uncritical volunteer (at both the pre-departure and placement stages) runs the risk of producing and sharing knowledges "that can only ever be, at best, ahistorical and, at worst, exploitative: knowledges inevitably based on superficial appearances" (Simpson, 2006, p. 29). To address this possibility, we must understand not only our power as travellers but also the roots of photography's strength as an authoritative medium.

Seeing and Knowing: The Formation of Power-Knowledge

Photography was once considered an authoritative, objective, and scientific medium, underscoring the Western "common sense" notion that "seeing is believing" (Wang, 2000): that the popular media provides access to "real" information about a place, time, or event. However, the popular media is not constructed for critical subjects (Fuery & Fuery, 2003), nor are individuals prepared to view images in photographs, television, film, magazines, newspapers, and the Internet critically

(Weintraub, 2009). We live in a time when images are taking over the work of language as tools of communication (Weintraub, 2009). We must therefore understand the historical, social, and political-economic influences that shape our ways of seeing. I argue that when discussing international development, volunteering abroad, international experiential learning, and the global citizenship initiatives that drive them, participants must face their links with the colonial past and work to understand the connections. Roland Barthes (1984) says that societies are able to "read" photographs and connect them, "more or less consciously, to a traditional stock of signs" (p. 19). This section briefly considers the Western "traditional stock of signs" formed through the classification and aestheticization of colonized bodies in the nineteenth century (Clost, 2011). By denying or ignoring the links between colonial patterns of intervention and travel and those of volunteering abroad, participants run a very real risk of replicating colonial relationships instead of breaking them down. The paragraphs that follow demonstrate some of the visual links to our colonial past and describe their effects on both the viewers and the viewed.

A. Classification and Aestheticization

David Spurr (1993) defines classification as "a rhetorical procedure by which Western writing generates an ideologically charged meaning from its perceptions of non-Western cultures" (p. 62), which allows for the naming and ordering of races and nations. In mid-nineteenth-century Europe, a new discipline, natural sciences, was becoming the single most respected form of scientific thought. Charles Darwin – famous for his controversial theory of evolution and his scientific travel missions – adapted natural history and natural science from their original purpose (classifying animal and plant species) to apply to humans. It was common at the height of Western colonialism for scientific treatises, philosophy, travel writing, and journalism to be combined in the same written work, allowing for ideological norms to reinforce what was presented to the public as scientific fact (Pratt, 2008; Spurr, 1993). Darwin's opinions were widely accepted, then, when he introduced indigenous Tierra del Fuegians to Europe as the "lowest grade of man" (Darwin, 1988, p. 267).

The positive-negative photographic process was invented around the same time Darwin rose to fame, and solidified positivistic scientific methods as the most legitimate form of inquiry (see Pieterse, 1992, pp. 19–35; Wang, 2000, pp. 155–71). As Weintraub (2009) states, photography "support[s] [its] authoritative claim of truth through the notion of realism," allowing for the assertion that "the camera never lies" (p. 204). However, the combination of Western empiricism with the subjective process of viewing an object or image creates a viewer whose "observation is ordered in advance; a misrecognition that allows interpretation to pass for objective truth" (Spurr, 1993, p. 71). To presume objectivity is to deny the subject position and the social, cultural, and political contexts of both the viewer and the viewed. Divorced from their context, people within an image can be assigned any number of traits based on Western "rules."

Western rules of classification are supported by Western rules of aestheticization: the deliberate beautification of an object, subject, or scene to serve a particular purpose. Aestheticization of colonized bodies in the nineteenth century was governed by either the concealment or promotion of cultural difference. Concealment served to neutralize any perceived threat posed by colonized peoples within their home country.[8] In the early years of tourism in Jamaica, a postcard entitled "Cane Cutters" was distributed throughout the British Empire. It depicted a group of nine Jamaican workers half hidden among stalks of sugar cane (Thompson, 2006). The title of the image is ambiguous: it could refer to the individual workers in the image, or to the machetes they hold in their hands. Images like "Cane Cutters" were the initiators of co-presence for the "domestic audience of imperialism" (Pratt, 2008, p. 62): sold to potential tourists to convince them that Jamaica was lush, tropical, and, most importantly, harmless.

As opposed to concealment, promotion of cultural difference sought to inscribe skin colour as a marker of concrete (often negative) difference (see Pollock, 1992). Paul Gauguin, the French Post-Impressionist, spent the last years of his life living and working in Tahiti, the result of which was a series of world-famous paintings of nude Tahitian women. These paintings were sent back to Paris and read by viewers as an informative text on the differences between races, cultures, and classes in France and Tahiti (Clost, 2011). As the painter, Gauguin controlled how the women were represented, but French societal mores and norms dictated how their images were read. As mentioned earlier, the classification of races and nations under the guise of "science" was well underway in Europe before the turn of the twentieth century, and such developments would inform French audiences' opinions on Tahitian life. The moment the women's images left Tahiti, so did their control over their own bodies (see Fanon, 2008).[9] From then on, their images became objects to be used as means to an end: at the time, to sell gallery tickets. Both promotion and concealment allowed for the perception of total control over colonized bodies and spaces. Photographic image-making united the principles of aestheticization and classification and quickly became the central mode of representation for modern institutions.

B. Photography as Power-Knowledge

The nineteenth century ushered in an institutional boom in Europe; prisons, hospitals, and schools of all kinds became the dominant form of social order in the West (Clost, 2011). John Tagg (1988) (following Michel Foucault's work on the rise of the institution) conveys the primacy of photography in ordering and classifying those considered deviant from societal norms: bodies are "isolated in a shallow, contained space; turned full face and subjected to an unreturnable gaze; illuminated, focused, measured, numbered and named ... Each device is a trace of a wordless power, replicated in countless images, whenever the photographer prepares an exposure" (p. 62). Tagg describes the photographer as master over the scene as its composer. The photographer has technological superiority through the possession of a camera and the knowledge of how to use it. In Tagg's description, the photographer uses images of deviant bodies and spaces to invoke understanding of desirable, healthy spaces and orderly, disciplined subjects (p. 63). Photographs such as Tagg describes invite intervention without opposition from the viewed.

With this in mind, consider what I have termed "the visual economy of volunteering abroad." Unhealthy, impoverished, tropical spaces are presented to potential volunteers as appealing destinations: not only because of the perceived need for intervention due to a difference in status (classification) but also because of the attractive, touristic manner in which the photographs are constructed (aestheticization).[10] Local people are presented with little voice and little context for the viewer to understand the reasons for their perceived need.[11] Without contextual information surrounding the perceived "need," it is difficult to formulate a truly appropriate and beneficial response. The opportunity to analyse the correct course of action is blocked by powerful images wherein "help" has already arrived and viewers can see "good" being done by Canadian volunteers. The following section outlines three categories in the visual economy of volunteering abroad that describe this power.

The Visual Economy of Volunteering Abroad

Photography constructs social realities (Weintraub, 2009; Urry, 1990). Visual discourse analysis reveals the ways in which photographs can be decontextualized and *recontextualized* to meet various ends. In the case of volunteer sending, images are shaped to create a visual "language of purpose" (Simpson, 2006, p. 55), which will secure future business for the industry as well as justify the continued presence of volunteer abroad organizations in the Global South. I highlight three categories that clearly depict the power imbalances inherent to both photography and volunteering abroad. Each of these categories draws on colonial visual history – Barthes's (1984) "traditional stock of signs" (p. 19) – which favours white, Western volunteers in positions of authority over locals.

A. Photography and the Camera

Most volunteers and tourists who have spent time in developing countries will recall the local people – particularly children – being interested in their digital cameras. This is a recognized experience within volunteering abroad based not only on volunteers' personal photographs, but also in volunteer-sending organizations' readiness to use these images to promote their programs. CESO invites people to "Become a Volunteer" on their website with an image of a white woman standing in the centre of a group of five black men and women in what appears to be a village setting. Each person in this image is smiling, and all but the white woman in the centre is looking at her digital camera's screen display (CESO-SACO, "Get Involved," 2012, August 21). Focus on the camera as an object invests it with power: the power to capture attention as well as the power to capture an image. The woman as the holder of this camera is by extension powerful. Imbalanced composition (which I discuss shortly) draws attention to the smile, camera, and body of the white woman.

The camera is a powerful tool and cultural symbol; it represents a long history of Western cultures' shared appreciation for the simultaneously scientific and artistic nature of photography. As mentioned earlier, the scientific discourse surrounding photography contributes to its power; its early use as an object for the documentation and verification of travel to exotic destinations is a part of how the tourist camera functions today. The camera is also a marker of social status. It indicates a certain benchmark of material wealth; digital cameras are relatively affordable in Canada, but still represent a purchase outside of basic needs. Cameras are markers of identity: as Urry (1990) says, someone standing with a camera around his or her neck is undeniably a "tourist" (p. 139). Perhaps the distinction between tourist photography and volunteer photography is the willingness of the volunteer to share his or her photograph with local people, as described above; the photograph represents an interaction, not just a memento. However, it is important to remember that as long as the camera is in the volunteer's hands, so is the control.

Despite the fact that I used a disposable camera in Ghana, I was still invited by local people to "snap" them. In a previous draft of this paper, I included an image of two men in Tamale Central Market that I had taken in October 2008. I did not know the men in this photograph, but they requested I take the picture. My possession of this image supposedly gives me control over its distribution and, to an extent, its interpretation. Consent to record this image was implied when the men asked me to take it, but how far does that consent extend? Have they granted me permission to reuse this image in any way? No. As the assumed "owner" of this photograph, I believed that I could reuse this image, not only to illustrate a thought but as a convenient way to avoid copyright infringement. As photographers, viewers, and travellers, we confer ownership status to the person who captured the image, rather than those whose images are represented. Volunteers do not in most cases have permission to reproduce and reuse personal photographs, and yet these images are used time and again, by individuals and organizations, to illustrate a variety of experiences and geographies. To reproduce a photograph without the consent of those pictured is an unethical practice. So, how does it happen?

One of the challenges of volunteering abroad is separating it from tourist practice – the act of travelling for pleasure. The camera has been an integral part of mass tourism since its invention, and the deliberate act of capture through a camera lens has been theorized as an important way for tourists to make sense of space (Sontag, 1977). None of the organizations in this chapter admits any explicit relationship with tourism or "voluntourism"; some deny it vehemently (CESO, personal communication, 10 August 2012). Photography is an integral part of their promotion, public engagement, and in some cases their programming,[12] yet none acknowledge the touristic elements inherent in picture-taking abroad.

Volunteers, on the other hand, shared openly with me that most of them decided to volunteer abroad because of their love of travel. Volunteers took pictures of everything – the landscape, their coworkers, local children, animals – and these images were shared upon their return to Canada with family and friends, in presentations and fundraising initiatives (Clost, 2011; see Roddick, chapter 13 in this volume). However (as with my own photographs), the people and places within volunteer photographs are often framed only to exist in relation to a volunteer, rather than as independent individuals.[13] The volunteer, and subsequently the sending organization, assume freedom to use this image, because there are no repercussions – because there are no standards beyond personal ethics – for improper or unfair use of a personal photograph. This is not to say that volunteers do not value the individuality of local people, or that they are not genuinely engaging in global citizenship initiatives. Perhaps the connection between travel and picture-taking (the idea of a tourist preserving an image for personal use) is so ingrained that we do not consider the reuse of pictures taken while working or volunteering abroad as out of bounds. In Canada, any person or organization which reuses a person's image without their permission runs the risk of violating both privacy and copyright laws. As it stands now, the onus is not put on volunteers to understand the power that is exercised in the simple act of picture-taking.

B. An Issue of Balance

When considering the promotion of volunteering abroad, it makes sense that the majority of images focus on the actions of volunteers; they are, in the eyes of the organization, the ones who need to be convinced by the photograph that volunteering abroad has value. However, in prioritizing the position of volunteers, these photographs give the impression that the presence of locals is incidental. Visually, this amounts to the white volunteer as the central figure, with a large group of non-white locals on the periphery.

I describe two key photographs to illustrate this configuration. The first photograph is the cover of a book about volunteer tourism (Lyons

& Wearing, 2008). A white woman in trousers and a T-shirt has the attention of eight Asian men in golden-yellow robes. All sit at desks in a classroom setting. The men have arranged their desks to focus on the woman: she is central to the composition and anchors the viewer's eye to her image. The second photograph is a volunteer's personal photograph, submitted to CESO's website.[14] An older white man in a T-shirt and trousers stands in a massive crowd of women in African-style clothing. The white man stands in the centre of the frame with a black man in front of a whiteboard in a grove of trees. The caption reads: "CESO Advisor Michel Duval speaks with women of a microfinance institution on the importance of savings and loans reimbursement. Photo provided by CESO Advisor Michel Duval" ("Where We Work"). There is potential for partnership here – the black man is presenting to the group as well, on the same visual level as the white man – but the caption removes this potential by naming only Michel Duval, the CESO volunteer. The photo-caption combination denies any contribution by Michel's counterpart, making this event Michel and CESO's achievement alone.

The imbalanced treatment of these photographs appears deliberate; the eye is drawn to the odd one out – the volunteer – through the use of colour and the arrangement of figures (Clost, 2011). Photographs in which the compositional balance centres attention on a white volunteer do a few things. First, subsuming the individuality of the local people into a large group transforms the people in the host country into "them," a convention that Said (1977) argues obliterates the humanity of a group. In contrast to "them," there is "me" or "us": an invitation for the viewer to identify with the solitary Western volunteer, who is usually white. Second, photographs such as the ones described above suggest a level of expertise or mastery in the volunteer-sending context; the attention of many local people is directed to a single outsider, someone who apparently possesses knowledge or skills they desire to gain. The volunteer is master at the compositional and conceptual levels.

This compositional structure echoes similar images that colonial missionaries sent back to Europe from Africa, the goal being to elevate missionary figures and subjugate African peoples. Historically, Christian iconography and painting positioned those who were closer to God on a higher register within the composition. In one case, Dutch missionaries created a photomontage entitled "White Father" (Pieterse, 1992, p. 72), which depicted an innumerable mass of half-naked, crouching black children and a single white erect missionary figure dressed in pure white on the left half of the frame. Through the explicit use of racial classification, and the compositional conceit of the missionary taking up half of the frame, the image sends a message of white spiritual and racial superiority.

The photographs described above illustrate an imbalance in power through an imbalance in number with overtones of racial classification. The impression given is that the power-knowledge possessed by the white volunteer-as-instructor (and, in the colonial example, the missionary-as-saviour) is equal to the power-knowledge possessed by a large number of non-white locals who are presented as undereducated (denoted by classroom-like surroundings).

The power of whiteness in the context of volunteering abroad was often discussed during my time as an intern in Ghana, and in my conversations with past volunteers. The majority of images collected for this analysis – gathered strictly from Canadian websites – showed only white volunteers. Those I interviewed admitted that in the host country and in photographs, whiteness is the primary identifier of volunteers. Interestingly, the concept of "whiteness" is not confined to white people. One volunteer noted that she was "considered white" in her destination country (which implies that, in Canada, she is not) (Clost, 2011, p. 112). A Canadian volunteer I worked with in Ghana self-identified as black and Muslim (which defined the majority of the population where we lived), yet was called *salaminga*, meaning "white," everywhere she went.[15] One volunteer remembered an image of a "Japanese-Canadian girl with a bunch of local people" and knew immediately she was the volunteer because "she looked physically different" (Clost, 2011).

"Foreignness" is equated with "whiteness" in both the photographic and lived spaces of volunteering abroad. Such labels are about perception and power, rather than real distinctions between groups. Perceived whiteness elicits a certain form of treatment in the spaces of volunteering abroad – sometimes positive, sometimes negative, but never actually dependent on the colour of the skin. The privileges of mobility and of comparative wealth and power are associated with the historical roles of white travellers (colonizers), and that same association transfers to foreigners of all origins. It is interesting that Canadian volunteer abroad organizations continue to promote their activities with images of almost entirely white volunteers when this does not reflect the reality of the Canadian population, nor the volunteer population abroad; this points to the possibility that Canadians more readily identify a white person than a non-white person as a "Canadian." I revisit the concept of non-white skin as outside of "Canadianness" shortly.

C. The Volunteer Madonna

The role of women as agents of development is a prominent feature in modern development programs. However, what appears to be emphasized in volunteering abroad is the role of white women as rescuers or caregivers in the developing world. Heron (2007) writes of white women's internalized onus to "do good" as "a way of performing appropriate bourgeois femininity" (p. 154). When transatlantic tourism became possible for Canadians in the late nineteenth century, women would travel to Britain to visit the slums, poorhouses, and particularly orphanages and state schools as part of their trips (Morgan, 2008, pp. 220–31). Volunteering abroad today continues to take place in a "children's geography" (Simpson, 2006, p. 55), again with an emphasis on orphanages and schools. The visual economy of volunteering abroad reinforces this belief by flooding the market with images of young, white women in a mothering role for non-white children in developing countries.

An excellent illustration of the availability of this image in public consciousness is a sketch that was included in an opinion piece for the *McGill Daily* at McGill University (Miatello, 2009). The author writes that development studies internships are misguided attempts to "make life better for all the starving babies of colour in remote (and distant) places" (Miatello, 2009).[16] The sketch shows a white woman, posed fully frontal, smiling. She is surrounded by five black children, in what appear to be school uniforms, in front of a collection of huts. Similar images surface on all of the organization websites I studied.[17] CECI illustrates "What We Do – Volunteer Programs" (25 August 2012) with an image of a young white woman – smiling – standing over four black boys. These images evoke an iconic Christian figure: the Madonna and Child (Virgin Mary and Baby Jesus).[18]

The Madonna, or Virgin, is a protective figure in Christian ideology, and is considered the most sacred of all women. By emulating the figure of the Madonna, female volunteers are invited to attain the highest level of Western "bourgeois femininity" (Heron, 2007, p. 154). They also recycle the powerful colonialist image of the Christian saviour and missionary discussed in the previous section.

The Volunteer Madonna is a well-used and well-known sign for volunteering abroad (just type "volunteer abroad" into Google Image search and see what comes up). Volunteers recognize this figure as a part of volunteer sending practice. One volunteer said, "I thought I was going to go in and be the mother for these orphan children, for sure. You can't walk away from that, that's definitely part of ... our social construction" (Volunteer East Africa, interview, 24 March 2011). Our "social construction" may invite you to read an image of me standing over two young Ghanaian girls in a similar light. However, there is a very important distinction between what is happening in a photograph and what is "read" by the viewer – denotation vs. connotation, as Barthes (1984) describes it. The denoted aspects of this image show me, a white woman, posing with two young black girls – a classic Volunteer Madonna configuration. The connotations of this image – how the viewer perceives the situation – are up to the viewer. My point is, it does not actually matter what is happening in this image, just what your "social construction" allows you to think is happening.

Many volunteers mentioned Madonna-and-child imagery without solicitation on the subject, some of them expressing disdain – a desire to roll their eyes (Volunteer South America-India, interview, 12 April 2011) – and anger. Volunteer El Salvador was puzzled, given that these volunteers "mostly don't know the kids' names, where they live, where their parents are. They just know that they're running around where we're working for whatever reason so why is that, as an image, so important" (interview, 29 April 2011)? CECI's image, mentioned above, shows a white woman with a group of black children to illustrate their volunteer programs, but CECI's list of projects have nothing explicit to do with schools, orphanages, or children (CECI, "What We Do – Volunteer Programs," 25 August 2012). Why did they choose this photograph?

A possible explanation lies in Urry's (1990) hermeneutic circle of tourism (p. 140).[19] He argues that tourists see an image of their chosen destination that appeals to them. Upon arrival in the destination country, the tourist finds and visits the location (or one similar) that was depicted in the image. The tourist then reproduces that image through their personal photography. Volunteers do the same. During an interview, one volunteer shared an image of herself, a white female, at the centre of the frame, kneeling in front of ten black children: an imbalanced composition that highlights her position of power as a white volunteer and as a Madonna figure. It was the same volunteer who stated earlier in this paper that she believed she was going to go to East Africa and "be a mother for these orphaned children." By replicating the Madonna trope in her photograph, she completed phase one of the hermeneutic circle. She completed the hermeneutic circle when she shared this image with other potential volunteers and donors in a fundraising newsletter back home in Canada. She knew it was an image to which her friends and family would respond. The widespread use and replication of images of the Volunteer Madonna indicates its power as a sign for "helping." In retrospect, she expressed concern over what her use of this image "meant." I turn now to discussion on volunteers' own ethical concerns.

Visual Literacy and Ethics

I have addressed some of the ethical challenges of volunteer abroad promotional photography concerning distribution and "ownership"; the power of "whiteness" and imbalanced compositions; and the very deliberate use of a salient ideological sign to encourage participation. As I stated earlier, photographs represent several relationships at once. If we return to the concept of the contact zone, and treat photographs as such, we can see that such spaces are aptly described as involving "conditions of coercion, radical inequality and intractable conflict" (Pratt, 2008, p. 8). The next pertinent question this chapter asks is: Are participants aware of these conditions within photographs, and their links to lived experience?

Some volunteers showed clear understanding of the relationships between image and experience, as well as the specific desires and emotions volunteer abroad promotional media try to evoke. Several acknowledged that volunteering abroad is currently marketed effectively, stating that promotional photographs are designed to be "inspirational" and convince people that they will change the world (Volunteer Ghana, interview, 31 March 2011) or are meant to "hook" potential participants (Volunteer El Salvador, interview, 29 April 2011). Volunteer El Salvador admitted that "from an advertising point of view, they're doing it right." She continued, "What I'm trying to figure out is ... whether it's wrong for them to be selling it in this kind of way" (interview, 29 April 2011).

"Accuracy" within photographs was a topic of much conversation. All volunteers described a disconnect between their expectations and their experiences while on placement. Some were annoyed with stock photographs that provided no "real" information or were frustrated that the promotional images did not accurately convey the experience.

Volunteer Uruguay-Ghana suggested that the photographs currently used are "realistic representation[s] of what could occur on a volunteer placement but ... I don't think someone should use those pictures and be like 'this is going to be my experience.' I think you need to take them with a grain of salt." I asked if other volunteers know how to take promotional photographs "with a grain of salt." She replied, "No, I would say not ... For someone's first time they're probably going to go 'this is going to be my experience' and if they don't get that experience they may be disappointed" (interview, 14 April 2011).

Fuery and Fuery (2003, p. 2), as well as Weintraub (2009, p. 198), argue that people are not prepared, nor are they encouraged, to view images critically. On the other hand, Urry (1990, pp. 100–2) suggests that "the postmodern tourist" has a certain degree of semiotic skill in interpreting tourist signs.[20] Five of the twelve volunteers I interviewed were able to discuss image construction and interpretation based on formal university education on the subject. Apart from being able to recognize and reproduce tropes like the Volunteer Madonna, other volunteers did not do this. This suggests that active and critical participation in international experiential learning as a practice, as well as in the interpretation and use of the visual economy of volunteering abroad, is well supported by formal education. However, as John Cameron (chapter 2 in this volume) has suggested, universities that promote the idea of global citizenship through experiential learning programs do not operate with a firm definition of the term, nor do they engage their students in the moral and ethical questions behind the performance of global citizenship. Doing good, as he says, should carry with it the responsibility not to cause harm: something that is seldom discussed in volunteer abroad or experiential learning literature. A proactive approach to the ethical dilemmas posed by international experiential learning – beginning with initial expectations and images – needs to be introduced to actively work towards "thick" global citizenship (Cameron, chapter 2).

The following section illustrates the importance of functional visual literacy in the Canadian multicultural context and its relationship with volunteering abroad. Discussions of global citizenship cannot exist within a vacuum and must be related to our ideas of Canadian citizenship first. As such, Canada's official policy of multiculturalism must be addressed (see Kamboureli, 1998, p. 210). I treat the Canadian Multiculturalism Act (1985, hereafter the act) as a regulatory discourse concerning the representation of "diversity" in Canada. Volunteer abroad websites actively tap into Canada's "discourse of diversity" (Bannerji, 2000, p. 35) to give international experiential learning programs, such as volunteering abroad, an impression of intrinsic value. The fact that the act and other state "metanarratives" have fallen into "disarray" through debates surrounding their colonial legacies (Kamboureli, 1998, p. 209) is encouraging, but such debate has not yet informed the creation and distribution of images produced by government-funded volunteer programs.

Volunteering Abroad, Global Citizenship Marketing, and Multiculturalism in Canada

International learning experiences rely on the effective and attractive representation of cultural difference to be successful. Canadian organizations can rely on the visual system already in place in Canada for representing difference: official multiculturalism policy visualized through the "discourse of diversity" (Bannerji, 2000, p. 35). The visual "discourse of diversity" and the visual economy of volunteering abroad both replicate "old polarities in the guise of benevolent hegemonies" (Kamboureli, 1998, p. 210) by regulating and managing the perception of cultural and ethnic difference through binary structures.

Since the passing of the Canadian Multiculturalism Act (Bill C-93) in 1988, the Government of Canada has presented itself as an institution deeply committed to the promotion of cultural inclusion and to the elimination of racial discrimination. Such an image is achieved through what Bannerji (2000) terms the "discourse of diversity": a collection of terms that acts as a "device for managing public and social relations and spaces ... [and] as a form of moral regulation and happy coexistence" (p. 47). Multiculturalism is similarly defined in a government publication:

> As fact, "multiculturalism" in Canada refers to the presence and persistence of diverse racial and ethnic minorities who define themselves as different and who wish to remain so. Ideologically, multiculturalism consists of a relatively coherent set of ideas and ideals pertaining to the celebration of Canada's cultural mosaic. Multiculturalism at the policy level is structured around the management of diversity through formal initiatives in the federal, provincial and municipal domains. Finally, multiculturalism is

the process by which racial and ethnic minorities compete with central authorities for achievement of certain goals and aspirations. (Lehman, 1999, para. 2)

By this definition, multiculturalism is a pervasive policy meant to simultaneously "celebrate" and "manage" "diversity" in Canada (represented here by "racial and ethnic minorities"). It identifies "minorities" as the bearers of "race": an inherently visible quality. The concept of the "visible minority" is a strange one; an emphasis on "visibility" denotes physical differences between whites and non-whites, and the use of "minority" suggests that those who bear "difference" are "politically minor players" (Bannerji, 2000, p. 30). The above definition does not include the "invisible majority" against which all diversity is positioned: white, European, English-speaking Canadians.[21]

The first characteristic of Benedict Anderson's (2006) imagined community of the nation is that it is "limited": that nations are not "coterminous with mankind" (p. 7). This means that nations are exclusive, and criteria must be in place to determine who is "in" and who is "out." The passing of the act transformed Canada (on paper) from a country that rejects and punishes immigrants to the benefit of white Anglo-Canadians (remember the Chinese Head Tax?) to one that welcomes (and depends on) immigration for economic growth. But the criteria that define who is "in" and who is "out" are just as active in this supposedly positive legislation. Official multiculturalism teaches the "invisible majority" (or "old Canadians") to see "difference" only in others ("new Canadians") by constituting "ethnic" identity in Canada only in relation to "white" identity.[22] It is that mentality that allows large groups of people of colour in volunteer photographs to be viewed as "visible minorities" and as representing "diversity" where, in actuality, the white volunteer (likely for the first time) is the visible minority. My earlier observation, that "foreignness" and "whiteness" are often equated in the spaces of international experiential learning, is reversed in Canada. Prior to departure, volunteers view promotional images *in Canada*, where official multiculturalism informs their perceptions as a "behavioural imperative" (Bannerji, 2000, p. 51) – one that extends beyond Canadian individuals to Canadian institutions.

Each federal government agency in Canada is obligated under the act to promote multiculturalism at home and abroad and assist private, public, and voluntary organizations in doing the same (Canadian Multiculturalism Act Consolidated, 1985, p. 5). Programs administered by

CUSO International, CWY, CCI, CESO, and CECI are all CIDA-funded and therefore subject to conditions of the act. These organizations actively recruit volunteers with an understanding of the discourse of diversity. When asking the question "Who can participate?" CWY replies, "Canada World Youth subscribes to diversity and equal opportunity in its recruitment efforts. It welcomes applications from indigenous peoples, visible and ethnic minorities, persons with disabilities, women, persons of a minority sexual orientation and gender identities, and others who may contribute to further diversification" (CWY-JCM, "Youth Leaders in Action," 2011, August 26). CESO conveys this sentiment simply as: "We respect others in all their diversity" (CESO-SACO, "Mission, Vision and Values," 2011, August 26). Like Urry's (1990) hermeneutic circle of tourist photographs, volunteer sending projects and their associated visual representation draw explicitly on – and contribute to – Canada's official discourse of diversity.

There are two important points to make here. First, in volunteering abroad, particularly when the programs are funded by CIDA – which works very closely with the Department for Foreign Affairs and International Trade (DFAIT),[23] as well as Citizenship and Immigration Canada (CIC) – participants become informal ambassadors or diplomats on the part of the Canadian government (Tiessen, 2011). This relationship may lead to a reinforcement of "Canadian identity" viewed from both the inside and the outside; a particular kind of Canadian citizen is positioned to view themselves as a "global citizen," and a particular kind of Canadian citizen is being recruited and marketed to the world. Following this thought, the second point is somewhat disturbing. Despite the difference in language between these two diversity statements, both maintain the location of difference as outside of a cultural, ethnic, sexual, and gender norm.[24] The images on these Canadian-government-funded websites suggest that the best way to represent the Canadian ideals of multiculturalism, inclusivity, social justice, and international cooperation is through young, white, privileged Canadians.

Multiculturalism discourse, in combination with the increasing presence of the visual economy of volunteering abroad in popular online media, has real effects on the expression and experience of racial, ethnic, and cultural difference in Canada (see Stratton & Ang, 1998, p. 157). It is my concern that the "invisible majority" (who, according to the above definition of multiculturalism and my analysis, constitute not only the government but also Canadian global citizens as well) allows citizens of the developing world to be depicted as inferior to "Canadians" because they embody "difference" or "diversity" alongside "poverty" and "need." Tying these concepts together is the thread of "develop-ment," the notion of progress and modernization as the driving forces of social, economic, and political stability: that those who embody di-versity do not possess those things and will be forever outside of "regu-lar society" (see Heron, 2007, p. 4; Stratton & Ang, 1998, p. 158). Most importantly, these visual and discursive constructs eliminate people living in the Global South and people of colour from the category of "global citizen."

Conclusion

The visual economy of volunteering abroad as a tool of global citizen-ship marketing, alongside the representation of Canadian multicultur-alism policy, encourages viewers to perceive non-white people in de-veloping countries as in "need" of "help." A unique aspect of this visual system is that the viewer is led to believe that he or she – a young, supposedly white Canadian who may or may not have experience with development issues – is able to provide that help. Because the visual economy of volunteering abroad is a structure based on binary opposi-tions, the corollary to the perceived power of volunteers is the per-ceived weakness of the local, non-white, non-Western population. The authority of photography as a medium – combined with the signs and symbols of global citizenship and the Canadian discourse of diversity – creates ideal conditions for vicarious experiential learning: seeing and therefore knowing that the power structures represented in volunteer sending's promotional media is "true." Such perceptions cannot go un-challenged. The encouragement of visual literacy and critical analysis in international experiential learning activities is vital to this task.

Fortunately, international experiential learning initiatives may offer the ideal opportunity to challenge the versions of reality presented by volunteer abroad promotional media. As Cameron (chapter 2 in this volume) notes, experiential learning activities such as volunteering abroad have in many cases sparked "thick" global citizenship in those who have returned with a critical and analytical viewpoint on their ex-perience. Over time, volunteers look back on their experiences and question their involvement in volunteer development projects, usually as a result of further education. Navigating the ethical complexities of volunteer sending is difficult and to succeed volunteers must actively politicize their decision to participate prior to departure. This means acknowledging the roots of their desire to volunteer and the routes by which they came to their privilege. Volunteers must understand that their physical presence in the developing world has meaning; "whiteness" or "foreignness," in many cases, embodies privilege, as does the English language and the simple fact of their mobility. Understanding these aspects of volunteering abroad can help "excavate colonial continuities" (Tiessen & Heron, 2011) and help Canadians tackle the concept of becoming effective global citizens.

NOTES

1 Like discourse analysis applied to text, visual discourse analysis considers visual representation as a tool for communicating power-knowledge and as a form of social power (Clost, 2011). By analyzing composition, subject matter, content (i.e., activities performed, geographical locations, etc.), and frequency of image use, I was able to outline a consistent pattern of representation for volunteering abroad, a partial analysis of which appears later in this chapter. For my original analysis, see *Voluntourism: The Visual Economy of International Volunteer Programs* (Clost, 2011).

2 At the time of writing, CIDA was funding the following organizations: Engineers without Borders, CUSO International, WUSC-CECI (Uniterra), CESO, CCI, CWY, SUCO, Oxfam-Québec, and Youth Challenge International (YCI). The present funding cycle runs from 2009 to 2014 and amounts to a maximum total of $179,410,405 ("Project Browser," 2012). The pending unification of CIDA and the Department of Foreign Affairs and International Trade may change this list significantly.

3 At the time of original data collection (2010), I used only the CECI website and disregarded WUSC. I had selected the above-mentioned organizations based on a report by Sean Kelly and Robert Case (2007), entitled *The Overseas Experience: A Passport to Improved Volunteerism: A Research Report*. The report listed Canada's top volunteer sending organizations (by number of volunteers sent since 1960), and I selected the top five for analysis; this did not include WUSC.

4 Originally, this was called the "visual economy of voluntourism." My use of the term "voluntourism" does not refer to the very short (one- or two-week) volunteer holidays offered by some private tourism companies. I use the term to make explicit the link between volunteering abroad and patterns of travel and marketing used in mass tourism. My original study draws heavily on the work of John Urry (1990; 1994, with Scott Lash; 1997,

with Chris Rojek) and Ning Wang (2000) who examine mass tourism as a sociological phenomenon. Urry particularly suggests that tourism patterns and "the tourist gaze" reflect what is going on in "normal society" (1990, p. 2). The original version of this study (Clost, 2011, chapter 2) dedicates a chapter to the demonstration of volunteering abroad as a niche market within mass tourism, because it satisfies Urry's nine requirements of tourist practice (1990, pp. 2–3). However, the term "voluntourism" has specific meaning in the context of international experiential learning and is therefore not appropriate for this collection.

5 An earlier draft of this paper included the online photographs I describe, but they have since been removed due to copyright issues. I encourage you to look at the images listed, and explore the rest of the websites on your own. My personal photographs have also been omitted, as permission to reuse the images could not be obtained from those pictured.

6 I interviewed twelve previous volunteer abroad participants between March and May 2011; all were female and all were either pursuing or had completed at least one university degree. Eight volunteers had degrees (at both graduate and undergraduate levels) in global development studies. While none of the volunteers were asked about their ethnic or racial background, such information was often volunteered because of the impact their racial identification had on their volunteer abroad experience. Volunteers are identified only by their destination country, and where personal details are included, their pseudonym is omitted. Inclusion of their responses here is within the guidelines of the ethics and confidentiality agreement signed at the time of interview. As a prerequisite for participation, all interviewees self-identified as "Canadian." Each of the organizations analysed in this chapter – with the single exception of CUSO International – require that participants hold Canadian citizenship or landed immigrant status (Clost, 2011). Volunteers' self-identification as "Canadian" and the organizational requirements for Canadian citizenship connect volunteering abroad with Canadian policy as part of both the "imagined community" of the nation (Anderson, 2006) and the geopolitical community of "Canada."

7 By "formal volunteers" I mean those whose experiences are coordinated by an organization, such the CIDA-funded organizations mentioned in this study.

8 For further discussion, see *Imperial Eyes: Travel Writing and Transculturation* (2008) by Mary Louise Pratt; *An Eye for the Tropics: Framing the Caribbean Picturesque* (2006) by Krista A. Thompson; and *Tourism and Visual Culture* (2003) edited by David Crouch and Nina Lübbren.

9 Speaking specifically of his experiences in Martinique, Frantz Fanon (2008) says "as long as the black man remains in his home territory … he will never have to experience his life as being for others" (p. 89). This means that, in Fanon's opinion, outside of the "black man's" home country, his existence is postulated only in relation to the "white man."

10 More specifically, "tropicalization" is the process of picturing tropical regions of the world for consumption through manipulation of the landscape and its inhabitants. See Krista A. Thompson's *An Eye for the Tropics: Tourism, Photography and Framing the Caribbean Picturesque* (2006) and David Arnold's "Illusory Riches: Representations of the Tropical World, 1840–1950" (2000) for a more in-depth analysis.

11 An important exception is Cuso International, which in many cases offers viewers the opportunity to "read the story behind this picture" as they move throughout the website (CUSO International).

12 For instance, Canadian Crossroads International requires their volunteers to "document [their] work and experiences with stories and photographs for consumption back home" ("While Overseas," 21 August 2012), and WUSC explicitly requires their International Seminar participants to be concerned with the "education of the public" (Roddick, chapter 13, in this volume).

13 This is similar to Fanon's (2008) concept of "being for others" (p. 89). Here, individuals from the destination country exist only in photographic space to meet the particular ends of an organization and/or a returned volunteer.

14 This photograph has since been removed from CESO's website, and the link is no longer active.

15 Benedict Anderson (2006) recounts a similar convention. He explains that in Indonesia, the word *londo* means "Dutch" but also "whites," strange given that the Javanese peasants of the colonial era likely met no whites who were not Dutch. He also notes that in French colonies the whiteness of *les blancs* was indistinguishable from their "Frenchness" (p. 153).

16 This article, while raising some important points, is a vitriolic assessment of the downside of development projects. Those who read this article should also take a look at reader responses (posted to the left of the article on the website) and get a taste of the debate surrounding volunteering and internships abroad at the university level.

17 CESO is the single exception. Because this organization caters to an older demographic (namely "experts" with ten or more years of experience in their chosen field [CESO-SACO]), it is possible that some female participants with CESO have already satisfied "appropriate bourgeois femininity" in their own lives as partners and/or mothers and do not need to project those desires into development and volunteer sending contexts.

18 Laura Briggs (2003) explains the figure of the "mother-with-child and the imploring waif" as traditional depictions of "hunger" and "need" in photojournalism surrounding crises in the developing world (p. 180). By decontextualizing the mother and child from the structural causes of poverty and hunger, Briggs argues that photojournalists create a "visual idiom of 'development'" (p. 195). The difference between the "development" Madonna and the Volunteer Madonna is that the latter is almost always smiling to make the image appealing to potential volunteers.

19 This is a common concept when discussing the relationship between sight and knowledge: see Said (1977, pp. 5–6) on how "The Orient" could be *made* "Oriental"; and Simpson (2006, p. 214) for a discussion of Paolo Freire's "circle of certainty," in which new experiences are used to reinforce pre-existing knowledge.

20 The postmodern tourist is aware that he or she is a tourist and enjoys that awareness (Urry, 1990, pp. 101–2).

21 The idea that Canada's cultural "centre" is white and English-speaking relies heavily on Canada's status as a British colony and Dominion, and the deeply held belief that Anglo-Canadians were members of the superior and civilized "British world." While changed, Canada still maintains strong ties to Great Britain and the monarchy; we cannot fully separate our current policy and cultural practice from British history (Clost, 2011, p. 8).

22 Stratton and Ang (1998), in their paper on Australian national identity and multiculturalism, note that "'Anglo-Celtic'" Australians are not viewed as an ethnic community. They suggest that this is because the government that creates and controls multiculturalism legislation is made up largely of Anglo-Celtic Australian men (p. 158). They suggest that official multiculturalism "suppresses the continued hegemony of Anglo-Celtic Australian culture by making it invisible" (p. 158). For a similar assertion in the Canadian context, see *The House of Difference: Cultural Politics and National Identity in Canada* (1999) by Eva Mackey.

23 In late 2013, CIDA and DFAIT were merged to form the Department of Foreign Affairs, Trade and Development (DFATD).

24 It is important to note that CWY and CUSO International (specifically) translate their diversity statements into their promotional media; there are pictured volunteers who are not white, and each of these organizations runs a South to North volunteer exchange. Overall, however, white volunteers are still most prominent in volunteer abroad visual representation.

REFERENCES

Anderson, B. (2006). *Imagined communities: Reflections on the origin and spread of nationalism* (Rev. ed.). London: Verso. Retrieved from http://hdl.handle .net.proxy.bib.uottawa.ca/2027/heb.01609.0001.001

Bannerji, H. (2000). *The dark side of the nation: Essays on multiculturalism, nationalism and gender.* Toronto, ON: Canadian Scholars' Press.

Barthes, R. (1984). *Image, music, text.* (S. Heath, Trans.) London: Flamingo.

Briggs, L. (2003). Mother, child, race, nation: The visual iconography of rescue and the politics of transnational and transracial adoption. *Gender & History, 15*(2), 179–200. doi:10.1111/1468-0424.00298

Canada World Youth–Jeunesse Canada Monde. (2010, Sep 10; 2012, Aug 10). Retrieved from http://canadaworldyouth.org/

Canadian Crossroads International–Carrefour canadien internationale. (2012, Aug 10). Retrieved from http://www.cintl.org/page.aspx?pid=1500

Canadian Multiculturalism Act (Consolidation), Revised Statutes of Canada (1985, c. 24). Retrieved from the Department of Justice Canada, http://laws-lois.justice.gc.ca/PDF/C-18.7.pdf

CECI: Centre for International Studies and Cooperation-Centre d'études et de coopération internationale. (2010, Sep 18; 2012, Aug 24). Retrieved from http://www.ceci.ca/en/

CESO-SACO: Canadian Executive Service Organization. (2010, Sep 16; 2012, Aug 24). Retrieved from http://www.ceso-saco.com/

Clost, E. (2011). *Voluntourism: The visual economy of international volunteer programs* (Unpublished master's thesis). Queen's University, Kingston, ON.

Crouch, D., & Lübbren, N. (Eds.). (2003). *Visual culture and tourism.* Oxford: Berg.

CUSO International. (2012, Jul 10). Retrieved from http://www .cusointernational.org.

CUSO-VSO: North America. (2010, Sep 26). Retrieved from http://www. cuso-vso.org/

Darwin, C. (1988). In R.D. Keynes (Ed.), *Charles Darwin's Beagle diary.* Cambridge: Cambridge University Press.

Fanon, F. (2008). *Black skin, white masks.* (R. Philcox, Trans.) New York: Grove Press.

Fuery, P., & Fuery, K. (2003). *Visual cultures and critical theory.* London: Arnold Publishers.

"Get Involved – Become a Volunteer." (2012, Aug 21). *CESO-SACO.* Retrieved from http://www.ceso-saco.com/Get-Involved/Become-a-Volunteer.aspx

Heron, B. (2007). *Desire for development: Whiteness, gender and the helping imperative*. Waterloo, ON: Wilfrid Laurier University Press.

Kamboureli, S. (1998). The technology of ethnicity: Canadian multiculturalism and the language of law. In D. Bennett (Ed.), *Multicultural states: Rethinking difference and identity* (pp. 208–222). London: Routledge.

Kelly, S., & Case, R. (2007). *The overseas experience: A passport to improved volunteerism: A research report*. Ottawa, ON: Imagine Canada.

Lash, S., & Urry, J. (1994). *Economies of signs and space*. London: Sage.

Lehman, M. (1999, Feb 15). Canadian multiculturalism. *Political and Social Affairs Division – Government of Canada*. Retrieved from http://publications. gc.ca/collections/Collection-.R/LoPBdP/CIR/936-e.htm# A.%20Bill%20C-93

Lyons, K.D., & Wearing, S. (2008). *Journeys of discovery in volunteer tourism: International case study perspectives*. Wallingford: CAB International.

Mackey, E. (1999). *The House of difference: Cultural politics and national identity in Canada*. London: Routledge.

Miatello, L. (2009, Oct 9). Something's fishy about IDS internships. *The McGill Daily*. Retrieved from http://www.mcgilldaily.com/2009/10/somethings_ fishy_about_ids_internships/

Mission, Vision and Values (2011, Aug 26). CESO-SACO: Canadian Executive Service Organization. (2010, September 16). Retrieved from http://www .ceso-saco.com/About/Vision-and-Mission.aspx

Morgan, C. (2008). *A happy holiday: English Canadians and transatlantic tourism, 1870–1930*. Toronto, ON: University of Toronto Press.

Pieterse, J.N. (1992). *White on black: Images of Africa and blacks in Western popular culture*. New Haven, CT: Yale University Press.

Pollock, G. (1992). *Avant-garde gambits, 1888–1893: Gender and the colour of art history*. London: Thames and Hudson.

Pratt, M.L. (2008). *Imperial eyes: Travel writing and transculturation* (2nd ed.). New York: Routledge.

Project Browser – Simple Search "Volunteer sending." (2012, Jul 3). *CIDA Project Browser*. Retrieved from http://les.acdi-cida.gc.ca/servlet/ JKMSearchController

Rojek, C., & Urry, J. (Eds.). (1997). *Touring cultures: Transformations of travel and theory*. London: Routledge. http://dx.doi.org/10.4324/9780203427736

Said, E. (1977). *Orientalism*. New York: Pantheon Books.

Simpson, K. (2006). *Broad horizons? Geographies and pedagogies of the gap year* (Unpublished doctoral dissertation). University of Newcastle-upon-Tyne, Newcastle-upon-Tyne, United Kingdom. Retrieved from http:// www.ethicalvolunteering.org/downloads/final.PDF

Sontag, S. (1977). *On photography*. New York: Ferrar, Straus & Geroux.

Spurr, D. (1993). *The rhetoric of empire: Colonial discourse in journalism, travel writing and imperial administration*. Durham, NC: Duke University Press.

Stratton, J., & Ang, I. (1998). Multicultural imagined communities: Cultural difference and national identity in the USA and Australia. In D. Bennett (Ed.), *Multicultural states: Rethinking difference and identity* (pp. 135–162). London: Routledge.

Tagg, J. (1988). *The burden of representation: Essays on photographies and histories*. Houndsmills: Macmillan Education.

Thompson, K.A. (2006). *An eye for the tropics: Tourism, photography and framing the Caribbean picturesque*. Durham, NC: Duke University Press.

Tiessen, R. (2011, May 14). Educating global Citizens? Canadian foreign policy and youth study/volunteer abroad programs. *Creating Global Citizens?* Retrieved from http://cdnglobalcitizenship.wordpress.com/2011/05/14/educating-global-citizenscanadian-foreign-policy-and-youth-studyvolunteer-abroad-programs/

Tiessen, R., & Heron, B. (2011, Jan 27). The problem with "culture shock": Canadian youth experiences and host community reflections. Studies in National and International Development (SNID) Seminar Series. Queen's University, Kingston, Ontario, .

Universalia, E.T. Jackson & Associates, & Salassan. (2005). *The power of volunteering: A review of the Canadian Volunteer Cooperation Program*. Universalia: Montreal.

Urry, J. (1990). *The tourist gaze: Leisure and travel in contemporary societies*. London: Sage.

Wang, N. (2000). *Tourism and modernity: A sociological analysis*. Amsterdam: Pergamon.

Weintraub, D. (2009). Everything you wanted to know but were powerless to ask. In K. Kenney (Ed.), *Visual communication research designs* (pp. 198–222). New York, NY: Routledge.

"What We Do – Volunteer Programs." (2012, Aug 25). In *CECI*. Retrieved from http://www.ceci.ca/en/what-we-do/volunteer-programs/

"While Overseas – What You Need to Know." (2012, Aug 21). In *Canadian Crossroads International*. Retrieved from http://www.cintl.org/page.aspx?pid=433

"Youth Leaders in Action: Who Can Participate?" (2011, Aug 26). *Canada World Youth-Jeunesse Canada Monde*. Retrieved from http://www.canadaworldyouth.org/apply/youth-leaders-in-action/

13 Youth Volunteer Stories about International Development: Challenges of Public Engagement Campaigns

MANDA ANN RODDICK

Introduction

Youth volunteers are often the "public faces of development" in Western nations (Smith & Yanacopulos, 2004). As Clost (chapter 12 in this volume) examines, a common image presented upon return from international experiential learning is that of a white female from the Global North surrounded by seemingly impoverished African children (Cameron & Haanstra, 2008; Clark, 2004). The relationship between youth volunteers and poor, black children depicts one of power and inequality. Youth volunteers from the Global North imagine themselves as the ones providing services, such as digging wells or constructing schools, for those "in need" in the Global South. The "helping" narrative that youth portray in their public presentations implies that there is another group integral to this power relationship: the ones in need of help. This simplistic dichotomy between helper and helped reinforces preconceived ideas of what it means to volunteer abroad and how international experiential learning unfolds. In this chapter, I focus on youth volunteers from Canada who return home after time abroad and are met with the expectation of participating in public engagement activities for the purpose of educating the Canadian public about development-related issues in the Global South. As one of the most prevalent "faces" of development, youth volunteers can have far-reaching impacts on how Canadians understand their relationships with those in the developing world. In the examination that follows, I conduct an in-depth analysis, primarily using interview data, to improve our understanding of why public engagement, and the strengthening of positive relationships between people of the Global North and South, is fraught with challenges for Canadian youth who have recently returned home after volunteering abroad.

In this chapter I draw on data from my own empirical research with a program coordinated by the World University Service of Canada (WUSC) to explore participants' thoughts on, and experiences with, public engagement after returning to Canada. The analytical core of this paper examines the challenges faced by returned volunteers when taking part in public engagement activities. I begin by reviewing the methods used for my data collection and move on to discuss international development education in a Canadian context. Then, I examine the challenges participants faced in their own public engagement efforts, and I specifically address how returned volunteers discuss: (1) their inability to find time to fully articulate their experiences abroad with others; (2) feeling as though time spent abroad was not real (or a "time-out" from life); and (3) discovering that their international experience was not enough to solidify "expert" status on international development. I build on the challenges of knowledge acquisition (gaining "expertise") and translation by examining some of the problems associated with public engagement campaigns. I conclude by introducing the work of social justice scholar Boaventura de Sousa Santos to highlight a possible opportunity to address some of the complexities of public engagement and development education while also identifying ways to transform, rather than perpetuate, social relations characterized by extreme inequalities of wealth and power.

Research Methods and Case Study

Through a case-study analysis of WUSC's International Seminar program,[1] I examined Canadian post-secondary students' understanding of global citizenship and explored the multiplicity of factors affecting their public engagement activities upon their return to Canada. WUSC is one of Canada's largest NGOs, and the International Seminar has been part of WUSC's programming for over sixty years (WUSC, 2012). The seminar was selected because of its stability as an annual program that has maintained a long-standing funding relationship with the Canadian International Development Agency (CIDA) since the early 1970s (WUSC, 1997, p. 85).

The study I conducted relied primarily on longitudinal interview data collected with a sample of three participants over a period of five months, and a specific point-in-time interview phase conducted with sixteen participants while in Ghana. Recruitment for the longitudinal phase was done through email and was facilitated by a WUSC program coordinator. I did not personally contact participants until they responded to the recruitment email. The longitudinal data was collected at three points in time during 2007 with three seminar participants, and each interview phase had a separate, semi-structured interview guide. The participants interviewed were all female undergraduate students.

The first round of longitudinal interviews began in June 2007, while students were preparing to travel abroad. The interview guide in this phase focused on understanding participants' current feelings and knowledge of international development and global issues while also identifying the goals and outcomes that participants expected before they went abroad. The second round of interviews was conducted in late August and focused on re-entry experiences, plans for public engagement, and how participants felt about their time in West Africa right after they returned home. Final interviews were conducted in late October, after students had been back in Canada for two and a half months.[2] The final interviews gave participants another chance to reflect on their experiences both abroad and back in Canada, as well as providing an opportunity to discuss their public engagement activities up to that point in the fall. The final interview guide also asked explicit questions about global citizenship.[3]

Before delving into the thematic analysis, it is important to clarify what is considered "public engagement." In this study, public engagement is considered to be any type of information sharing between participants of the seminar and the public at large. This includes, but is not limited to, family and friends of the participants. "Information" is used in the broadest sense of the term[4] and can be shared in a variety of manners, including storytelling, public presentations, conversations, and visual displays. In this paper, I focus on three broad categories of public engagement experiences expressed by youth in my study. The challenges I examine do not constitute an exhaustive list of experiences, nor do they intend to imply that all experiences with public engagement have been negative. However, I believe they merit further examination because of what these experiences suggest about expectations of public engagement for returned volunteers.

Volunteering Abroad: An Introduction to the Rationale for Public Engagement

Non-governmental organizations (NGOs) around the world offer opportunities for youth to volunteer abroad each year (Tiessen, 2012).

Many Canadian NGOs, including WUSC, receive some of the funding for volunteer programs from CIDA, and together, CIDA and various NGOs coordinate initiatives that send Canadian youth abroad (Tiessen, 2010, p. 144). In addition to boosting Canada's image abroad through personal interactions with communities in the Global South, many programs require youth volunteers to return to Canada and share stories and information on the country they lived in and the projects they worked on, as well as more general information on international development and poverty. It is this component of youth abroad programs that I now turn to in my analysis, specifically the complex challenges that arise for youth when they are expected to participate in public engagement and education activities with the Canadian public when they return from volunteering abroad.

Sharing stories and information with friends, family, and larger communities upon return from international experiential learning programs is more than a voluntary activity. Public engagement is often a core component of the volunteer-sending organization's mandate. For example, one of the selection criteria for the six-week International Seminar program in 2011 was that participants must show "interest in matters related to international development and *education of the public*."[5] In 2007, seminar participants were also expected to participate in public engagement activities, and many of my interview questions were focused on engagement.

Public education about development and countries in the Global South is not the only benefit that Canadians reap from volunteer programs abroad. Although there is criticism that short-term volunteer placements with youth largely benefit young people from the Global North while doing little to enhance the lives of those in the Global South, these programs continue to flourish (Simpson, 2004). One of the most common reasons that programs with limited impact "on the ground" persist is because of the emphasis on the "life-changing" experience youth have while away.[6] The participants in my study often did suggest the seminar changed their life in some way, but not necessarily in a way that increased their ability to provide international development knowledge to their friends, family, and the Canadian public. Moreover, the students' perceptions and perspectives of West Africa appeared to be increasingly reaffirmed rather than changed after the experience and did not necessarily position them in a place of expert knowledge, although they may have been viewed that way by some Canadians with whom they interacted upon their return.

Breaking down stereotypes is another positive outcome often cited in support of volunteer placements and youth internships abroad. As Tiessen (2010) writes, stereotypes can be broken through learning/volunteering abroad programs, but these same stereotypes can also be affirmed while abroad. Youth from the Global North may learn that there are Peruvians in the Amazon who possess a wealth of knowledge and skills on software development, and Peruvians may think differently about affluence in Canada if working with heavily indebted students, as Tiessen found in her 2010 research (p. 149). However, there is also the risk that stereotypes become reaffirmed during volunteer experiences, particularly in short-term placements. For example, Sarah, a short-term volunteer from the United Kingdom working in Peru, believed she possessed an authoritative knowledge on Peruvian people after only a month of residing in the country; because her time in the country was so brief, there was limited opportunity for engagement and discussion with local people. In Kate Simpson's (2004) analysis, this allowed students like Sarah (a pseudonym assigned by Simpson) to "confirm, rather than challenge, that which they already know" (p. 688). In all likelihood, the duration for which youth volunteer abroad does affect their ability to rethink and reflect on their preconceived notions of a place and peoples (Lonely Planet, 2010), but for our purposes here, I highlight this tension to illuminate an area in need of further investigation – that is, whether presentations and discussions carried out by youth who have recently returned from short stints abroad are a primarily positive way of increasing knowledge of global issues within the Canadian public.

In addition to potential cross-cultural learning experiences and contributions to local communities abroad, young Canadians also benefit immensely from the skills and social capital they acquire. In an examination of youth activists in Canada, Jacqueline Kennelly (2009) finds that "those with middle class aspirations and experience learn early how to play the game of the good citizen in order to make themselves and their resumes more marketable in the new global economy" (p. 140). Kennelly compares and contrasts the experiences of "good citizens," such as the famous young Canadian Craig Kielburger, and activists seen as defiant of the state (2009, p. 131). Similarly, Simpson claims that the increasing popularity of gap-year programs in the United Kingdom has brought young people "into contact with neoliberal understandings of education and citizenship, where emphasis is placed on young people's acquisition of global knowledge as governable subjects with market potential" (2005, p. 447). Again, understanding the tensions youth face when trying to address urgent social issues, such as poverty, highlights the challenges of deciding where to volunteer, when to be a good citizen (or, for some, a good global citizen), and when to address the same issues those volunteering abroad may hope to work on by staying in Canada and acting outside the norms of "good citizen behaviour" (Kennelly, 2009). Often, young people participating in well-known, federally funded programs are provided many more opportunities to speak to a broad public audience than activists in the streets are. The struggles youth face when deciding how, and when, to act within or against institutions in the name of social justice deserves further research in the future.

Challenges of Informed Public Engagement and Development Education

To say that the term "international development" encompasses a vast array of material and conceptual baggage is a considerable understatement. According to Philip McMichael (2008), the four contentious questions about development concern (1) the goals of development given a finite planet; (2) the core values of development (and who decides them); (3) questioning why development is realized through inequality; and (4) determining the appropriate scale of development (p. 20). From a material perspective, on the global institutional agenda, there are the Millennium Development Goals (MDGs) ambitiously set to be reached by 2015 (UNDP, 2013).

The participants in the study described in this chapter were all post-secondary students. When participants were questioned about public engagement upon their return to Canada, their concerns related to their knowledge level on international development, but much of that emanated from feeling uncertain about the experience as a whole and how it may or may not have contributed to their overall understanding of development and the role that people from the Global North can play in the lives of those in the Global South. In the pages that follow, I introduce the three participants and then examine three challenges they faced upon their return to Canada. I provide analysis on how their perspectives, ideas, and the structure of their everyday Canadian lives may have influenced their public engagement efforts.

The Participants: Jess, Jill, and Sue

The three women in the longitudinal interviews held different perspectives and ideas about public engagement and development knowledge before departing for West Africa. Sue exhibited the most excitement of the three participants regarding public engagement. Jess declared herself a non-activist before leaving for the seminar. She explained that it is important to her to speak up when something is "wrong," but otherwise her primary forms of engagement were reading the newspaper and learning about injustice in her university classes. Jess and Sue both expressed concern about the superficial nature of their personal interactions with other Canadians, and neither participant had conducted a presentation by their final interview, nor did they have any scheduled in the foreseeable future.

Like Sue and Jess, Jill identified plans to conduct presentations when she returned to Canada. Jill planned her academic program around her desire to participate in engagement campaigns, and she was the most successful in engaging others by the time of her third interview in late October. Not only had Jill conducted a formal presentation, but she had confirmed plans for a second one. In addition, although she self-identified as having experienced challenges when speaking with people on a one-to-one basis about her trip, she found ways to manoeuvre and introduce complexity into these situations and have meaningful conversations about her experience.

Challenge One: There's Not Enough Time!

The seminar concluded just before the participants needed to return to school in the fall. Thus, when the participants' experiences were still fresh in their minds, it was a busy time for their schoolmates. Both Jess and Jill noted that people often asked in passing, "How was Africa?" but the question was often felt to be posed out of obligation rather than real interest in hearing their stories. By the time things had calmed down at school, the seminar was something that had already been discussed in a superficial way and thus was rarely revisited. Sue and Jess both explained that by the end of October, they were rarely receiving any more questions about their time in West Africa, and only Jill appeared to take advantage of the relative calm that came after students were readjusted to school. Jill aptly explained:

> Before, I felt like when someone asked me how it was I had to say a quick little summary, but now I find I am having longer conversations about it because I have school. The beginning of the year everyone was seeing each other for the first time so it's not like you wanted to hear the long drawn-out version. So I find I am having deeper conversations and yeah, that

with people, still people are asking me [now]. It comes out in conversations and stuff.

Jill's experience highlights not only the hectic nature of her own life, but also the time-constrained lives of those around her, while at the same time emphasizing her ability to insert more aspects of her experience and knowledge into conversations as the semester progressed.

When NGOs claim to foster youth who are able to engage in public discussions about international development, there is little attention dedicated to how to reach out to a public that is constrained by time. The people that youth are intended to engage with on their return often have their own busy lives and do not have time to listen to the intricacies and complexities of the experiences participants had overseas. In order to meet the time constraints of those around them, participants focused on a few short stories or brief descriptions of their experiences. At her re-entry interview in August, Jill explained:

> So, I find myself just saying the same thing over and over again and realizing that there are so many other aspects of it that I could explain but you don't have the time talking to somebody if you don't know them that well, you are just talking to them for a short time, it's not, you know, you don't want to give them the full-winded version. So you start limiting yourself to saying that one aspect of your experience over and over again and that kind of in a short time and that can make it seem like that was the only part of it.

Likewise, Jess noted the tight timelines of those around her when explaining that she "never had the chance to sort of sit down and really look at photographs and explain things in different roles like I had envisioned and hoped." Jess attributed this loss of opportunity largely to time, noting that

> I think that is partly due just [to] time constraints – like my parents don't live near me and when I got home I was trying to get photos developed and moving and you know just life kind of got in the way. And it's not that I think people aren't interested, it just hasn't been convenient for me or them to sit down and have those talks.

Here the inability to discuss her experiences extended beyond her own time limitations to the temporal constraints of those around her. Jess hoped for time to explain pictures as she showed them to family and friends, but all of the time constraints made having photos ready for viewing a challenge, and she was fearful that her own experience was getting lost. Jess's situation also speaks to the point made by Clost (chapter 12 in this volume) that all Canadians are exposed to the propaganda and marketing materials for international experiential learning. Therefore, the stereotypes and expectations held by those Canadians who have not travelled to the Global South but are learning about it through the stories told by Canadian youth are deeply influenced by the often problematic images and discourse all around us.

Jess explained that it is important to have the time to engage with others so that the experience is remembered more accurately. She cautioned that when time is limited, there is generally only one version or sound bite of the experience, and then the whole seminar can be reduced to that. She notes that "memories fade quickly. But when you are thinking or feeling something and you voice it then it almost makes it more real or more relevant." Reducing one's experience to a few sentences has consequences not only for the participant but also for the people with whom they interact. The one version, or "single story" (Adichie, 2009), of their "African experience" can pose a danger to increasing knowledge transfer between participants and other Canadians. One negative impact that volunteers can have when talking to Canadians about their time abroad is contributing to the single story of Africa, the continent most often used synonymously with the "developing world" or the "Third World." To many people in the Global North, Africa is a land of catastrophe, where the negative descriptors far outweigh the positive, and the people living there are seen as so different from us that it becomes unthinkable for Canadians to imagine having any deep similarities with them (Adichie, 2009). To elaborate, the stories that people want to hear through development education reduce the people living in Africa to helpless and in need, in the same way that images do (Clost, chapter 12). Those of us returning from abroad can accidentally or purposefully recreate these tropes or images with the pictures we choose to share and the stories we relate. We are caught in a limiting environment where no matter what we say, what is heard is one particular message that reinforces rather than challenges stereotypes.

In addition to the danger of a single story, there is another challenge inherent in sharing stories. Often the stories people want to hear, or the stories that allow participants to "join the club" of experienced travellers, are the "war stories" of intestinal diseases and skin infections that create bonds between fellow volunteers. These types of stories provide a legitimate way to gain credibility in a group and help travellers "present themselves to other people" (Desforges, 2000, p. 932). The ability to share common experiences with peer groups in university provides an opportunity for participants to "acquire both identity and capital" (Simpson, 2005, p. 451) from the experience of travelling abroad. In fact, in the United Kingdom, Simpson argues that "a person risks cultural impoverishment if going to university (and into other arenas) without the capital of Third World travel" (2005, p. 451).

The six-week design of the seminar had inherent temporal constraints that affected youth participants wishing to work with local NGOs in West Africa. Six weeks is a brief time to be abroad, and a short time in a country may do more harm than good in terms of building cultural understanding and shattering stereotypes. Simpson (2005) notes that the common "default setting" of organizations sending students abroad is one that assumes contact between people of different nations will, in itself, create greater understanding (p. 462). However, "to assume that a short period of contact with the stereotyped other will automatically contradict, and hence unseat, such stereotypes is, at best, naïve" (Simpson, 2005, p. 462). It is likely that the brief time students spend abroad serves more to reaffirm pre-existing notions about West Africans and international development than to change them. In addition, because Canadian participants return home to people that may not have time to discuss the seminar with them in depth, participants are left repeatedly reciting the simplified version of their experience or distributing pictures haphazardly, leaving friends and family to interpret the images on their own. The combination of a short time in the field and a fast-paced Canadian society works to create simplistic and often slanted forms of engagement, if engagement happens at all.

Challenge Two: Was It a Dream?

In addition to feeling like the duration of the trip affected their ability to learn, participate, and understand issues, two of the women felt as though they had never had the experience in the first place. During Jess's second interview, one of her first remarks was,

> I was just thinking today how it feels like I never even went anywhere …
> I thought I would be really surprised or really appreciative and just really
> conscious of you know, "wow I have running water this is so amazing"

– "running water is incredible," you know all the things, like refrigerators, you know – all these things I thought they would take a bit of time to get used to again, and no. It is hard to believe a week ago, well now it has been eight days, but I could say that two weeks ago I was in Africa.

It could be argued that this comment is simply reflective of the fact that Jess was experiencing reverse culture shock when returning to life in Canada. But two and a half months later, after completing half a semester back at university, Jess was still relatively disengaged from her experience. At the end of her final interview Jess explained,

Yeah, I guess it is still perplexing to me or maybe it's frightening that I can just, there is potential to experience all of this and then to completely ignore it. Like it was just something I did, like a holiday I went on. I think there is very much a danger of that happening for anybody that's involved and yeah, it's frightening.

With only six weeks abroad, and several of those days dedicated to pre- and post-departure training, there is very little time for meaningful connections to be made between the seminar participants and the communities in which they live and work. Not alone in her sentiments, Jill also found the experience almost dream-like. In her return interview, Jill explained that

I think I was just … realizing that it doesn't feel like it really happened. It feels like I have just been kind of like, like that's part of my memory but I never actually went there. I think it's just because we were plunked into this situation for a short period of time and expected to do a lot of different things that, I don't know, that I think that maybe there are some things that I probably missed about the entire experience that I guess that you notice in retrospect. And I don't know what those things are, but I think that I feel like maybe my whole experience wasn't fully complete or maybe that's the reason I am feeling like it wasn't really real.

For Jill, not only was the experience incomplete, but she explicitly linked this feeling to the constraints of time itself.

Another significant challenge to overcoming the feeling of a dream-like experience is conceptualizing the seminar as a "time-out" from life (Elsrud, 1998, p. 315). When discussing her re-entry to the country, Sue explains that when one returns home the desire is to "get your life back." Viewing her overseas experience as separate from life at home allowed a disconnect to occur between actions at home and connections to host communities abroad. Barbara Adam (2003) notes that in a time of reflexive modernization "our actions lose the character of personal involvement; we no longer accompany them and their effects to their destination. Lines of responsibility are severed. Irresponsibility becomes structurally located" (pp. 64–5). The structural location of responsibility warrants further discussion, particularly because neoliberal discourse emphasizes the responsibilities of citizenship over rights (Kennelly, 2009, p. 133).

Without lingering commitments to work with the communities encountered, or connections to host families or organization staff, it is not surprising that people see their experience abroad as a dream. The snapshot, or dream-like, experience reinforces the very challenges of these programs in terms of achieving the key goals of cross-cultural connection. These reflections on dream-like experiences reinforce the value placed on the individual's personal growth (although momentary and fleeting) rather than the impact of the placements on the host communities. A shift in reflection is needed for participants to understand their time abroad as more meaningful than a "time-out" from their everyday life in Canada.

At the beginning of Philip McMichael's book *Development and Social Change* (2008), he highlights how difficult it is to teach post-secondary students about development. McMichael believes that until students move beyond thinking that "development" is a linear (or "evolutionary") process – a game of catch-up that we in the Global North can help those in the Global South win – students have "difficulty valuing other cultures that do not potentially mirror their own" (p. xvi). When students go beyond this evolutionary and linear perspective of development, they are better able to evaluate their own culture and to think reflexively about social change, development, and global inequalities (p. xvi). In order to provide the best education to the Canadian public, volunteers must also be able to push away preconceived notions of development to reflect more on their place in the global picture of poverty and social inequality.

Ideally, that shift in understanding will help volunteers understand that conceptualizing their time abroad as a "time-out" from their everyday life in Canada is highly problematic. Volunteers need to understand that we are all continually connected, historically speaking, because of colonialism and other processes that create enduring structures and maintain systems of inequality (Escobar, 1995; McMichael, 2008). Moreover, we are all connected in the present by neoliberal ideology (Farmer, 2005) and "The Lifestyle Connection," premised upon Northerners consuming products and experiences produced by people living in the Global South (McMichael, 2008, p. 13). This relationship of production and consumption embodies lived inequalities and is mediated by various organizations and corporations in the global marketplace. As Western consumers, we often place the responsibility of fair trading practices and safe working conditions in the hands of intergovernmental organizations and corporations beyond our daily gaze. And, because products are made from components produced all around the world, we do not always think about how the chocolate bar we are about to eat today could have been made from the cocoa farmed by a Ghanaian community visited during a volunteer placement last summer. When meeting Ghanaian people for six weeks is described as a "time-out" from life, it highlights one of the greatest challenges that must be overcome in public engagement campaigns: understanding and conveying that we are never on a "time-out" from people we have only briefly met or places that we have never been. We are all connected through interdependent relations of various kinds, and the disconnected feelings we experience with faraway places is something we must aim to eliminate. Such a conceptualization is a disservice to everyone, as it reduces opportunities to see the often vastly unequal relationships between people across the world. Furthermore, when meaningful and lasting cross-cultural connections are not made through travel abroad for international experiential learning, it is even more difficult to imagine how public engagement and awareness-raising will occur.

Challenge Three: Am I an Expert Now?

Europe and North America have dominated many aspects of the global world order. When the countries in these regions rose to power centuries ago, Western and Northern assumptions and knowledge about development dominated their relationships with the Global South (Parpart, 1995, p. 223). In the field of development, the possessor of technical knowledge continues to be the Northern "expert," even though critiques of such a model exist. Barbara Heron (2007) cites work conducted by the African Research, Education and Development Association (AFREDA) that doubts the use of Northern expertise. Heron points out that much of AFREDA's critique appears to be aimed at students doing field placements and other short-term programs abroad (p. 13). Some literature would suggest that students have little expertise in any field to offer to Southern communities, despite a plethora of options for young people to volunteer abroad (Simpson, 2005; Tiessen, 2012). In addition, in programs such as the International Seminar, short-term placements do not provide enough time for volunteers to become experts on international development or the region they are visiting. And yet, when they return to Canada, that is often what is expected of them – presentations that convey some level of mastery on international development and the region in which they volunteered.

Interestingly, despite the intention of international youth programs to reduce stereotyping others and expand young people's knowledge of global issues, in my data collection the case was the opposite. In such a short period of time, it seemed that participants were able to solidify pre-existing notions of the Global South, and their views on global issues were, to some extent, reinforced. In June, for example, Sue indicated that despite her classmates' disgust at her opinions, she was a supporter of the World Bank and International Monetary Fund. Although she said she was open to a change of opinion while overseas, she returned with renewed enthusiasm for these institutions so often the sites of activist attack. Sue believed Ghana had appalling levels of corruption, and the only way to rectify the situation was to increase outside intervention in the activities of the country. Sue's interpretation of the Ghanaian political climate served to reaffirm her ideas about development, adding credibility to her long-standing personal perspective. Sue could back up her perspective after the seminar because, as she explains, "you have to see it to believe it in a situation like that. And to even understand concepts like poverty and development ... you really have to see it because it is hard to explain and people here [in Canada], they just don't get it." Such a view highlights how essential the experiential component of the seminar was for participants in increasing their expertise as "knowers" of Africa. In contrast, it demonstrates one way we continually prevent people in the Global South from developing "expertise"; if programs are primarily designed for Northern youth to travel abroad, but rarely for youth from the South to travel, then our reliance on "first-hand knowledge" continues to be more advantageous for Northern youth.

Unlike Sue, Jess felt that she gained a curiosity in the field of international development, but she was still not a credible resource on the topic. Her feelings of inadequacy on the topic of international development seemed to affect her ability to engage her home community. She explained, "I never really knew what I was doing and I still don't." When discussing the possibility of conducting presentations with the Canadian public, Jess expressed concern that people in the audience may ask her difficult questions that she would be unprepared to answer.

The substantial knowledge acquisition that is assumed to occur, even after short stints abroad, was not evident in my study. This provides yet another example of how challenging it was for these youth to acquire enough knowledge to take part in complex and reflective presentations despite participating in a program that set informed public engagement activities as a goal for returned participants. The actual level of knowledge gained is hard to determine for a variety of reasons, and yet, participants are led to believe they have a much deeper understanding about countries, people, and international development than they probably do because of the value we place on experiential learning (Simpson, 2004) and on the assumption that students from the Global North always have some kind of expertise to offer NGOs in the Global South. The knowledge gap created between what participants are expected to know before, during, and after the seminar and what they actually feel they know creates another challenge for well-prepared public engagement activities.

Another challenge when transferring knowledge to the public is determining the style of engagement. A common introduction to a conversation on international development is to read off a litany of depressing statistics on the state of the world. Naming a list of issues, such as poverty, ecological destruction, and gender violence, is another common tactic for talking about development-related and experiential learning opportunities.

A third mode of knowledge transfer is through the recounting of personal and professional stories about time spent abroad. Stories themselves are not inherently harmful; however, storytelling from returned volunteers is of great concern because their stories carry a particular kind of credibility that we often associate with "first-hand experience." When stories are combined with statistics, the picture can become even more precarious. One of the dangers of describing the Global South, and sub-Saharan Africa in particular, as a place characterized by economic and social hardship is that, even though there is considerable hardship for the majority of people on the continent, "the description of these conditions via ahistorical statistical information has the effect of obscuring how the situations being depicted are rooted in colonial processes of wealth extraction and are perpetuated though political-economic arrangements that many African development theorists, along with critical writers from the North, have named as 'neo-colonial'" (Heron, 2007, pp. 16–17). The partial picture of the Global South portrayed by participants in international experiential learning programs reinforces a specific image of the Global South as a poor world full of needs that only "development" can conquer.

Ahistorical accounts of volunteering and international development are also deeply problematic stories. When Sue described the "corrupt government" in Ghana, there was no mention of colonization in her interview. If a similar story of a corrupt Ghanaian government is shared with friends and family, what impact could her story have if she does not note that colonization affected the current social organization of Ghana?[7] Several authors suggest that stories hinging on limited knowledge of history, politics, or reasons for global inequality present the Western – often white – volunteer as the sole agent of change in developing nations (Cameron & Haanstra, 2008; Heron, 2007; McMichael, 2008). Furthermore, the story of why volunteering is deemed necessary, and prevalent, is often ignored. We fail to discuss why so many young, and often middle-class, Westerners volunteer abroad and why communities in the Global South may wish to continue with these programs. In addition, stories from short-term volunteers sometimes lack reflection and discussion of the ongoing role people living in the Global North have in perpetuating poverty in the Global South.

If historical and political explanations are not brought to light in presentations during public engagement activities, power relations may be overlooked as well. It is important for audiences to question who is sharing stories, whose voices are heard, and what subjectivities are being constructed by whom (Escobar, 1995). By teaching fellow Canadians about development through the lens of a Westerner describing an African "Other," public engagement activities may continue to "make the Third World" (Escobar, 1995) and perpetuate unequal social relations. Presenting their experiences in this way may also suggest to audiences that participating in development projects is less contentious than it seems.

Presenting detailed stories and discussing complex global issues can be daunting for someone at any age and experience level, let alone someone young and having returned from only a short, first-time experience abroad in West Africa. Even the most reflective volunteers may inadvertently build on the single story of Africa (Adichie, 2009). With

this in mind, how do we avoid or overcome the challenges that returning volunteers discussed in this case study experienced? Portuguese
scholar Boaventura de Sousa Santos (2006) articulates a strategy that
may minimize the dangers of knowledge translation elaborated on
above. From de Sousa Santos's perspective, in order to have global social justice,[8] we need global cognitive justice – that is, justice that recognizes many epistemologies and the work that is required of all of us
around the world to translate epistemological positions between people, places, and time. De Sousa Santos recognizes this is not an easy feat
and will require sustained energy, emotion, and spaces for translation
to occur. In this theoretical articulation, he identifies the spaces for
translation as "Cosmopolitan Contact Zones" (p. 143) and he discusses
the Popular University of Social Movements proposed at the World Social Forum in 2003 (p. 150). Coming from such a framework may help
us avoid perpetuating stereotypes or partial information when returning from abroad. Learning about other cultures, organizations, and social movements striving for greater equality and justice by building
trust and respecting alternative ways of knowing may be part of the
solution to building diverse stories of the Global South and relationships between people across the world.

Conclusion

One of the most interesting findings in this study is that the experience
of the International Seminar was not significantly "life-changing" for
participants in the sense that the international experiential learning
program disrupted preconceived ideas of the Global South. Rather, it
served to reaffirm previously held beliefs and ideas. Six weeks in West
Africa served as a temporary "time-out" from life in Canada. Narratives on poverty, development, and the Global South were offered by
seminar participants before travelling abroad, and for the most part,
similar perspectives were reinforced upon return to Canada (Roddick,
2008).

When we move beyond the individual challenges that youth in this
study had with public engagement activities, what remains as a pressing area for further examination is what images and narratives are
relayed to the Canadian public by returned volunteers. For many Canadians without personal international experience, one of the only sources they may have on international development in the Global South[9] is
stories from those who have volunteered abroad. Public engagement

activities can be central to helping Canadians develop a deeper understanding of the Global South. For example, rather than viewing Africa as primarily a place of brutal genocide, wars, and famine, Canadians can also learn from volunteers about the wonderful things African people do, both individually and collectively, in their daily lives. This is not to suggest that storytelling should gloss over the tragedies and struggles for Africans, but highlighting the complexity of people's lives and dispelling the myth of an African continent filled with mainly negative and hopeless adjectives needs to be a vital goal for public engagement activities.

Even better, returned volunteers could learn additional skills to portray complex, and unequal, global social relations and explain how these relations reinforce poverty, not only in the present, but also in the past. Complex storytelling would also challenge the single story of the global marketplace that is presented to all of us as the universal route for advancement in all areas of our lives (McMichael, 2008). When stories told by participants work to break down the single story of the Global South as poor countries working to "develop," the focus shifts from beneficent Northern volunteers that possess "the wisdom and agency needed to help Southern 'others'" (Cameron & Haanstra, 2008, p. 1486) to an examination of the structural issues that sustain global poverty. As Devereux (2008) suggests in his examination of long-term volunteering, "if we want meaningful change in North-South relationships and structures required for enabling equitable development ... [then] international volunteers who return home may in fact be a crucial complementary element" (p. 368) in this endeavour.

In order to provide the best education to the Canadian public, volunteers must also be able to push away preconceived notions of development to reflect more on their place in the global picture of poverty and social inequality. This can often be a tall order for youth that have returned from a short-term placement as my interview data suggests. As one of the most accessible public faces of development, youth volunteers therefore need ample time to reflect on their role in international development and have opportunities to work through the complexities encountered abroad before widespread engagement occurs in Canada. When participants in a program such as the seminar return from a six-week program, often physically weakened, time constrained, and feeling as though they may possess authoritative knowledge on an entire continent, misrepresentation is likely to occur. Further academic research is needed to examine both why public expenditure on young

Canadians volunteering abroad continues with the justification that it will improve public knowledge on global issues at home, and, more pertinently, how participants are taught and encouraged to share their experiences with other Canadians. With further research and attention focused on the content of public engagement campaigns, more Western volunteers may find ways to not only avoid a single story of the Global South but also learn better tools for reflection that allow them to increase the complexity of their own personal stories involving international development and their ongoing role in helping to reduce global poverty. We therefore need to complicate the images of less developed countries, and to do so, we must share diverse images beyond "white saviours" and black children in need of assistance.

NOTES

1 Additional information on the International Seminar can also be found online at http://www.wusc.ca/en/volunteer-overseas or http://www.uniterra.ca/become-an-international-volunteer/international-seminar/

2 Further details on the methods of this study, conducted for my master's thesis, can be accessed at https://dspace.library.uvic.ca:8443/dspace/handle/1828/1160

3 The second part of this study was a one-time interview with sixteen of the twenty seminar participants on global citizenship. These interviews took place in Ghana at the end of the six-week seminar while all participants were together for their final days of debriefing at the University of Ghana.

4 "Information" comes from a variety of sources and could include first-hand experience overseas, opinions on development policy, or, as WUSC suggests, information on the Millennium Development Goals.

5 My emphasis added. Citation can be found at http://www.uniterra.ca/become-an-international-volunteer/international-seminar

6 Study participants anticipated that their seminar experience would be "life-changing" before leaving for Ghana and Burkina Faso. WUSC's website also notes that this six week experience will "change their [the participants'] lives" (WUSC, 2008). Heron (2007) notes that volunteering abroad is "touted as a 'life-changing' experience for *us* [Western volunteers], and its constitutive effect on Canadian and other Northern development workers' identities is considered indisputably laudable" (p. 2). In 2011, the "life-changing" aspect of the seminar is still

promoted on the program's website (http://www.uniterra.ca/
become-an-international-volunteer/international-seminar/).3

7 Examples from participants are not intended to suggest personal shortcom-
ings of individuals, but rather serve as demonstrations of how larger, structural facets of public engagement strategies play out in individual stories.

8 I assume here that global social justice holds goals similar to those of
international development on many fronts (such as eliminating poverty
and reducing gendered violence).

9 Mainstream media commentary is most likely the primary source of
"information" on the Global South with which Canadians are inundated.
Cameron and Haanstra (2008) review recent campaigns to "Make Development Sexy," and several authors mention the prevalence of fundraising
campaigns and news stories that focus on images of poor, suffering people
living in dire poverty as persistent representations of people in the South
(Heron, 2007, p. 2).

REFERENCES

Adam, B. (2003). Reflexive modernization temporalized. *Theory, Culture &*
Society, 20(2), 59–78. doi:10.1177/0263276403020002004

Adichie, C. (2009, Jul). The danger of a single story [Video file]. Retrieved
from http://www.ted.com/talks/chimamanda_adichie_the_danger_of_a_
single_story.html

Cameron, J., & Haanstra, A. (2008). Development made sexy: How it
happened and what it means. *Third World Quarterly, 29*(8), 1475–1489.
doi:10.1080/01436590802528564

Clark, D.J. (2004). The production of a contemporary famine image: The image
economy, Indigenous photographers and the case of Mekanic Philipos.
Journal of International Development, 16(5), 693–704. doi:10.1002/jid.1121

Desforges, L. (2000). Traveling the world: Identity and travel biography. *Annals*
of Tourism Research, 27(4), 926–945. doi:10.1016/S0160-7383(99)00125-5

de Sousa Santos, B. (2006). *The rise of the global left: The World Social Forum and*
beyond. London: Zed Books.

Devereux, P. (2008). International volunteering for development and sustainability: Outdated paternalism or a radical response to globalisation?
Development in Practice, 18(3), 357–370. doi:10.1080/09614520802030409

Elsrud, T. (1998). Time creation in travelling: The taking and making of
time among women backpackers. *Time & Society, 7*(2-3), 309–334.
doi:10.1177/0961463X98007002008

Escobar, A. (1995). *Encountering development*. Princeton, NJ: Princeton University Press.

Farmer, P. (2005). *Pathologies of power: Health, human rights, and the new war on the poor*. Berkeley, CA: University of California Press.

Heron, B. (2007). *Desire for development: Whiteness, gender, and the helping imperative*. Waterloo, ON: Wilfrid Laurier University Press.

Kennelly, J. (2009). Good citizen/bad activist: The cultural role of the state in youth activism. *Review of Education, Pedagogy & Cultural Studies, 31*(2), 127–149. doi:10.1080/10714410902827135

Lonely Planet. (2010). *Volunteer: A traveller's guide to making a difference around the world*. Footscray, Australia: Lonely Planet Publications.

McMichael, P. (2008). *Development and social Change: A global perspective* (4th ed.). Thousand Oaks, CA: Pine Forge Press.

Parpart, J.L. (1995). Deconstructing the development "expert": Gender, development and the "vulnerable groups." In M.H. Marchand & J.L. Parpart (Eds.), *Feminism/postmodernism/development* (pp. 221–243). London: Routledge.

Roddick, M.A. (2008). *Forming engaged global citizens: A case study of the WUSC International Seminar*. (Unpublished master's thesis). Retrieved from https://dspace.library.uvic.ca:8443//handle/1828/1160

Simpson, K. (2004). "Doing development": The gap year, volunteer-tourists and a popular practice of development. *Journal of International Development, 16*(5), 681–692. doi:10.1002/jid.1120

Simpson, K. (2005). Dropping out or signing up? The professionalisation of youth travel. *Antipode, 37*(3), 447–469. doi:10.1111/j.0066-4812.2005.00506.x

Smith, M., & Yanacopulos, H. (2004). The public faces of development: An introduction. *Journal of International Development, 16*(5), 657–664. doi:10.1002/jid.1118

Tiessen, R. (2010). Youth ambassadors abroad: Canadian foreign policy and public diplomacy in the developing world. In J. Marshall Beier & L. Wylie (Eds.), *Canadian foreign policy in critical perspective* (pp. 141–154). Toronto, ON: Oxford University Press.

Tiessen, R. (2012). Motivations for learn/volunteer abroad programs: Research with Canadian youth. *Journal of Global Citizenship and Equity Education, 2*(1), 1–21.

United Nations Development Programme. (2013). The millennium development goals: Eight goals for 2015. Retrieved from http://www.undp.org/content/undp/en/home/mdgoverview/

World University Service of Canada (WUSC). (1997). *Fifty years of seminars*. Ottawa, ON: World University Service of Canada.

World University Service of Canada (WUSC). (2012). About us. Retrieved from http://www.wusc.ca/en/about-us-page-1
World University Service of Canada (WUSC). (2008). Volunteer with WUSC: International seminar. Retrieved from http://www.wusc.ca/en/volunteer-overseas

14 Afterword
There Should Be Nothing *Experimental* about *Experiential* Learning: From Globetrotting to Global Citizenship

ROBERT HUISH AND REBECCA TIESSEN

The contributors to this edited volume demonstrate two clear trends within experiential learning programs. The first is that an overwhelming interest exists to create experiential curriculum across numerous disciplines. The second is that no agreed structure exists on how to develop, manage, and implement such programs. The growing enthusiasm coupled with the lack of agreed-upon normative ethics in experiential learning is a precarious combination. University administrators, ever hungry to attract greater numbers of students, may be quick to celebrate study abroad opportunities as an ideal means of experiential learning. Their departments are consistently under pressure to maintain high enrollment numbers and to offer innovative programs to attract students from across departments. In some cases the goal is to draw in students from other universities. The rush to meet increasing demand may bring in numbers and tuition revenue, but as every contributor in this volume has made clear, such vehemence can position students, faculty members, and partner communities in difficult ethical conundrums.

Negotiating these challenges requires careful attention. How can study abroad students critically reflect on broader socio-economic processes of globalization? Can science and medical students reflect on issues of dependency and social theory? Is it possible for students on volunteer placements to identify tensions of civic engagement against processes of growing inequity from neoliberal economic doctrine? Is it possible to move from a mindset of globetrotting to global citizenship? Beyond reflective pedagogy, study abroad and experiential learning programs can tacitly contribute to processes of dependency, neocolonialism, and shallow reflection on the structural differences between resource-flush and resource-poor communities. At the heart of these tensions is a similar theme. Many experiential learning programs create, and often reinforce, ethical challenges by employing vulnerable communities as extensions of the privileged classroom, for "photo ops" and travel opportunities. In doing so, experiential learning grounds itself in individualistic self-reflection of behavioural ethics, rather than an enabling process to ease socio-economic divisions. The difficulty is that there can be little engagement with the normative ethics of institutions and economic processes. Is it possible to develop curricula that go beyond thin global citizenship? Is there a greater place for advocacy and student activism in experiential curriculum that addresses structural inequity? Without further dialogue on these ethical challenges, and discussions about the role of curriculum in worsening or easing tensions, it is likely that quick responses to pressing demands for experiential learning will continue unabated, and solidarity with partner communities to address structural deficiencies will remain elusive.

Three areas of discussion are needed in order to facilitate a new era of experiential learning. The first comes with handling the growing demand for experiential learning opportunities, notably those through travel abroad programs. Even at the local level there is increasing pressure for universities to facilitate volunteerism opportunities within local communities as a means of bolstering town-gown relations. The pressure comes in a combination. First, it comes from students yearning to have top-level résumés upon graduation by demonstrating "real-world" experience. Second, university administrations create opportunities for students to include volunteerism within their academic record, even by developing co-curricular transcripts that place service activities alongside final grades. The danger here is that the pursuit to meet this demand comes without careful consideration of the community partners, the vulnerability of the students, or the long-term impacts in the community.

Many private, for-profit international volunteer programs, such as Projects Abroad, require very little in the way of background checks, ethics training, or pre-departure readiness for volunteers. Al Jazeera broke a story in 2012 that showed Canadian and European volunteers working without qualification or training as teachers in disparate orphanages in Cambodia.[1] Domestic volunteer placements tend to require a more rigorous application process for volunteerism. While this may help to alleviate some of the behavioural ethics concerns, the question of how to bring greater attention to the structural tensions of the place of the volunteer within society remains. More specifically, is there room for volunteers to critically engage in discussions of how governments, the private sector, and civil society are putting an ever-increasing amount of social responsibility upon underqualified volunteers? In Canada this is quite noticeable with regard to refugee services, seniors' home care, and literacy programs. For educational institutions to seek out and create more community-based volunteer programs at home or abroad is, in a sense, failing to engage the socio-economic processes that download social services onto volunteers. Is there room to celebrate experiential learning programs while holding a critical gaze upon broader policies that see the replacement of public or private service with volunteerism?

This comes down to ways in which programs structure the reflective component of experiential learning. If the reflection stage of the program only addresses personal reflection and critique, it may well pass the broader normative ethics of the shifting responsibility of public services and social security on to volunteers. While the personal reflection process is an important step in deconstructing a student's role in broader socio-economic processes, it may not be enough by itself to address the roots of power structures and social marginalization between communities. Without a pedagogy that brings such reflection into the classroom, there runs a risk of purely celebrating experiential learning, and in doing so remaining complacent to such power structures.

The second area of discussion that is needed comes down to the nature of ethics focused on in programs. At some level all contributors to this volume are calling attention to the need for a greater focus on ethics in experiential learning. While this call is warranted, engagement with deep understanding of ethics is much needed. It is too simple a process to consider the term ethics as merely "doing good." Rather, attention is needed to positioning pedagogy towards behavioural ethics, moral ethics, normative ethics, or all three. The closer programs get to an exploration of normative ethics of volunteerism, the better chances they have of engaging in the "thick global citizenship" approach that Cameron outlines in chapter 2. A focus on behavioural ethics is certainly important in equipping students for acceptable conduct in the field, but that itself does little to foster long-term community engagement. Moral ethics elicited from personal self-reflection may do little to further collaborative relationships between the student and the community. It may bring out rich thought and moral values for the student, but how does such pedagogy work towards the creation of cross-cultural solidarity? Experiential learning programs, by design, require partnership with often marginalized or resource-poor communities. The challenge ahead is how these partnerships can move from tendencies of neocolonialism and dependency towards progressive action. Langdon and Agyeyomah's chapter suggests that educators have a responsibility to explore advocacy aimed at normative change of such issues. We would like to think that such approaches are possible and worthwhile. Embracing them as a regular practice within experiential learning programs could be an important step forward. Otherwise, experiential learning programs will continue to see the world as a classroom, and globetrotting as a means to understand it.

This touches on the third area of discussion, which is the role of students, faculty, and program coordinators in facilitating advocacy through these experiences. The place of advocacy within volunteerism is a difficult one to begin with, especially in a Canadian context. Charitable non-governmental organizations may only contribute 10 per cent of their operating budget towards "political activities." Going beyond that amount may cause the organization to lose charitable status. As a result, many organizations that rely on individual donations limit their involvement in direct political action and advocacy. Volunteers for such organizations are often given strict instructions not to engage in political issues with clients, or tie any political campaigning to the project site. Even off duty, volunteers with certain organizations are asked to refrain from political advocacy.

If there is a moral value in pursuing advocacy to challenge structural inequalities, are volunteer placements fitting opportunities to do so? Can experiential learning facilitate advocacy alongside the tenants and regulations of volunteerism? Or is this an area in which to pursue partnerships through advocacy with marginalized communities? Can experiential learning move beyond the service learning or travel abroad models to build apertures of activism for solidarity, collaboration, and engagement? How can educators design curriculum that engages marginalized communities and yet champion advocacy for social justice, equity, and rights? Would such a paradigm bring about desired ethical challenges and move experiential learning into a realm of exploring normative ethics? And, most importantly, where is it possible to see such pedagogy in practice?

To say that students are apathetic to advocacy and progressive social change is a gross misassumption. Even though there has been a historic marked decline in youth voter turnout in Canada, students have demonstrated impressive capacity to mobilize, organize, and even become members of Parliament. The 2012 student strikes in Quebec assisted in the downfall of the Charest government in that province. Students concerned with fossil fuel consumption have launched the Power Shift movement, which aims to press government for progressive climate change action. The Idle No More movement was largely organized by First Nations university students. Internationally, the NGO Partners in Health is encouraging more students to stay on campus and set up advocacy groups to focus on issues of structural violence, human rights, and deep poverty in the Global South, rather than travel abroad to volunteer in a work site. These and dozens of other cases demonstrate that students, as a powerful demographic in society, have enormous potential for advocacy and political engagement.

Through the methods of experiential learning, which combines learning and practice, reflection, discussion, and critique, is it possible to embrace ever-increasing youth advocacy and activism? Do educators have a place in designing curriculum that can coalesce action with study in a way that mentors advocacy? It has been done in the past. In the 1950s James Lawson led peaceful non-violent resistance seminars at Fisk University. Student campus unions, along with professors, led organization and mobilization seminars to resist war and corporatization and advance equity issues. Some argue that this sort of campus action is constrained today. Could experiential learning have a role in securing a place for activism on campus? This conversation goes beyond the scope of this collection, but it invites discussion of the future of experiential learning into realms that can still combine experience with theory, but also conjoin progressive change, partnership, and solidarity. Would university administrators praise or scorn such initiatives? Testing the waters is the only way to find out for sure.

This concluding chapter is meant to draw out more questions rather than to reinforce any conclusions about experiential learning. What can be discerned, however, from this collection and this discussion is that there is no fixed place for experiential learning. It may have a role in numerous disciplines and levels of education. But without grounded and ethical understanding of the terms of engagement, the *experimental* approach to *experiential* learning may do little to advance solidarity, partnerships, and notions of thick global citizenship. Educators can use the experiences in this volume to assist in the design of curriculum. But more importantly, these cases should be taken as an invitation for greater dialogue and collaboration on what exactly is experiential learning and how it can be best placed into a world that encourages action as much as it demands progressive engagement.

Students involved in experiential learning have profound opportunities for reflection before they go, while they are engaged abroad, and upon their return. The challenge is to find the appropriate amount of time, a suitable setting for this reflection to take place, and a depth of analysis that is both critical and constructive in orientation. Langdon and Agyeyomah (chapter 3) refer to this process as scaffolding. For some, the reflection may result in a decision to not take part in international experiential learning or to find alternative ways of engaging globally. Others can use the opportunity to reflect on their motivations, particularly before going abroad. However, for those who have already travelled abroad in some volunteering or voluntourism capacity, the current moment is one of reflection on how differences become entrenched in how we think about ourselves in relation to the people we encounter in the world, among other ethical dilemmas to be addressed.

Ethical questions can guide this process and can include (but are not limited to) questions pertaining to the potential to do no, or less, harm. As the introduction to this book makes clear, the international experiential learning program must be viewed as a mutual learning process, and the world as a classroom for that learning to take place. The experience should not be primarily motivated by experimental or testing opportunities in which communities in the Global South become laboratories for young, privileged youth from the Global North to test a career choice or an academic background – or worse, to engage in experimental techniques that would be deemed unethical in the Global North. In addition, the motivation for global citizenship needs to be revisited and examined in light of Cameron's analysis of thick global citizenship versus superficial travel opportunities.

Other important ethical questions that need to be asked have surfaced throughout this book and include the broader framework in which international experiential learning programs are justified as valuable and to whom; how the "international" or Global South is depicted in the literature promoting volunteer abroad programs; and the messages that are reified upon return when presenting to the public with specific stories of one-directional knowledge transfer or charitable activities represented as development work.

Students can use the reflection time before going abroad to decide if there are more appropriate contexts in which they can travel and at the same time be effective and contributing members of communities and organizations. Throughout the reflection process (before, during, and after international experiential learning programs), students can benefit from a deep analysis of the discourse used, the problematique of discussions of "reverse racism," and/or ways in which those in the Global North talk about and experience privilege and inequality.

However, is reflection itself the panacea for the ethical conundrums of experiential learning? The questions of standards, ethics, and normative values within programs must be made as universal as the enthusiasm for the programs themselves. Without being too prescriptive, perhaps it is worth entertaining some of the standardization concerns Huish raises in chapter 8 with regard to international health electives. If there is room to recognize the need for ethical consistency, we offer three first steps as a call to action by practitioners, administrators, and students themselves.

First, deeper program reviews are needed to identify how higher education institutions are approaching experiential learning. The approach should be inclusive rather than accusative. By establishing a central network of programs in experiential learning, first steps towards dialogue on successes and challenges can be established. This sort of inter-institutional collaboration occurs frequently within medical education. It is not meant to be a competitive space, but a collaborative one that ensures that basic standards are met, regardless of the institution.

Second, upon organizing a network of programs, dialogue can emerge to identify pressing challenges, specific ethical concerns, and universal standards. Here program directors and facilitators have the opportunity to establish best practices criteria, curriculum guides, and even peer-review processes for new programs.

Third, annual meetings among program directors are encouraged. With such enthusiasm for experiential learning in a wide range of disciplines, a core meeting would be well worth it to invite new participants to the table and to strategize means by which to employ the best practices possible.

These steps have been taken in many professional fields, ranging from medicine to planning. It may well be time for program directors and faculty members in wider fields of expertise to discuss the merits of some form of regulation of experiential learning. Regulation need not be equated with prohibitive behaviour or cumbersome bureaucracy. It has the potential to establish ethical norms of practice, and to do so in a way that moves the opportunistic desire of globetrotting to a more dynamic and ethically attuned experience of global citizenship.

Many important questions, resources, and ethical dilemmas are provided in this book. We do not hope to solve them all, or even believe that steps towards standard practices could accomplish this in the short term. The challenge is for students and course instructors, study abroad coordinators, experiential learning facilitators, and so on to ensure time and opportunity for reflection at all stages of the experiential learning process (before, during, and after). Such reflection should be deep enough that normative ethics are brought to the conversation. There are many ethical challenges involved in international experiential learning, and with this in mind we must consider them carefully. However, to suggest that the international experiential learning programs should be eliminated because of the many problems that have arisen over the years would not suffice. We seek improvement without amputation. The "business" of international experiential learning is growing and it will continue to be available to those who have access to the means to take part in them, regardless of whether higher education institutions choose to walk away from it. The challenge is to improve programs so that we achieve the goals of thick global citizenship (see Cameron, chapter 2), of doing no harm (see Desrosiers and Thomson, chapter 7), and ultimately of creating globally engaged citizens who are able to act on their knowledge in ways that close the gap of inequality in the world, promote solidarity, and contribute to global justice (or what Thomas and Chandrasekera, chapter 5, call the formation of authentic allies) – to employ the age-old expression "Tell me and I will forget, show me and I may remember, but involve me and I become a part of it." The desire to be involved in the difficult challenges of solidarity and social justice can bring out the best in all of us, and it should be our desire to ensure that our institutions can bring about the best of experiential learning.

NOTE

1 "Cambodia's Orphan Business" (2012, Jun 27), ALJAZEERA, retrieved from http://www.aljazeera.com/programmes/peopleandpower/2012/05/201252243030438171.html

Index